# Before the Arts Council

# Before the Arts Council:

## Campaigns for State Funding of the Arts in Britain 1934–44

Howard Webber

BLOOMSBURY ACADEMIC
LONDON • NEW YORK • OXFORD • NEW DELHI • SYDNEY

BLOOMSBURY ACADEMIC
Bloomsbury Publishing Plc
50 Bedford Square, London, WC1B 3DP, UK
1385 Broadway, New York, NY 10018, USA
29 Earlsfort Terrace, Dublin 2, Ireland

BLOOMSBURY, BLOOMSBURY ACADEMIC and the Diana logo are trademarks of Bloomsbury Publishing Plc

First published in Great Britain 2021
This paperback edition published in 2022



Cover design: Terry Woodley
Cover image: The Old Vic theatre in Waterloo, London Chronicle / Alamy Stock Photo



A catalogue record for this book is available from the British Library.

Library of Congress Cataloging-in-Publication Data

Names: Webber, Howard, author.
Title: Before the Arts Council : campaigns for state funding of the arts in Britain 1934–44 / Howard Webber.
Description: London ; New York : Bloomsbury Academic, 2021. | Includes bibliographical references and index.
Identifiers: LCCN 2020037988 (print) | LCCN 2020037989 (ebook) | ISBN 9781350167933 (hardback) | ISBN 9781350169715 (paperback) | ISBN 9781350167940 (ebook) | ISBN 9781350167957 (epub)
Subjects: LCSH: Government aid to the arts—Great Britain—History—20th century. | Arts Council of Great Britain—History.
Classification: LCC NX750.G7 W43 2021 (print) | LCC NX750.G7 (ebook)
DDC 353.7/709410904—dc23
LC record available at https://lccn.loc.gov/2020037988
LC ebook record available at https://lccn.loc.gov/2020037989

ISBN: HB: 978-1-3501-6793-3
PB: 978-1-3501-6971-5
ePDF: 978-1-3501-6794-0
eBook: 978-13501-6795-7

Typeset by RefineCatch Limited, Bungay, Suffolk

To find out more about our authors and books visit www.bloomsbury.com and sign up for our newsletters.

*To Sandra, Gabriel, Manuella and the next generation*

# Contents

Acknowledgements

These acknowledgements are brief and selective. Any attempt to include everyone who in one way or another helped with this book would inevitably fail. But the book certainly would not have happened without the contributions of everyone listed below. I am very grateful to them all.

It begins with my MA at the Institute/Centre for Contemporary British History. The ICBH was part of the School of Advanced Study of London University when I began the MA, was for some reason moved to King's College, London, before I finished, and, sadly, is now no more. But it did me proud. Doctor Michael Kandiah and Professor Pat Thane performed miracles in turning the holder of a poor History A-level several decades ago into a credible student of history.

Pat then acted as an exemplary supervisor for my PhD. She, and my external examiners Professors Sally Alexander and Jean Seaton, were highly encouraging about the possibility of my developing the thesis into a book, and Pat's wise advice has been invaluable as I have done so.

The bibliography lists the archives visited in the course of the research. I am grateful to all of them for permission to quote from the papers in their care, and to Arts Council England for permission to consult the files of the Council for the Encouragement of Music and the Arts. One archivist above all others contributed greatly to this work: the eternally helpful Julia Aries at Glyndebourne. I was fortunate indeed that the Glyndebourne Archive, where much of the research was based, had Julia in charge.

At Bloomsbury, I was delighted that Emily Drewe chose to commission the book. She and Abigail Lane have been truly supportive and encouraging throughout; Juliet Gardner has been an exemplary copy editor and Merv Honeywood of RefineCatch has been a patient and helpful guide through the publishing process.

And then there is my family. Not only did my wife Sandra and son Gabriel put up for years with my rambling on about subjects of at best limited interest to them; they also provided vital and more specific help – Sandra as a proof-reader with a fierce eye for detail, Gabriel with unrivalled IT support. My love and thanks to both of you.

# 1

# The Creation Myth of the Arts Council

## Introduction

In 1930s Britain, the relationship between the state and the arts was a subject of intense debate and substantial press and public interest. There were active campaigns to gain government subsidy for live music and theatre, attracting support from those with otherwise deeply opposed political views. Conferences were held at which some of the best-known figures in the arts first debated issues which were to preoccupy the Arts Council of Great Britain for decades. Ministers, despite objections from their civil servants, gave tax breaks for live performances. And the debate continued in wartime: for years after 1940, when CEMA – the Council for the Encouragement of Music and the Arts – was set up, it was widely seen as an improvised short-term expedient, rather than as the basis of a permanent peacetime funder of the arts.

None of this is apparent from what has been written about the origins of government arts subsidy in Britain. Instead there has been largely unbroken consensus on four points:

- The British government in the 1930s provided no financial support for live music and theatre, and had no interest in doing so.
- In the 1930s there was little demand for subsidy. In various forms this view is almost universal in work published on the subject. Some writers choose, without explanation, not to look back before the founding of CEMA. Others regard it as so settled that government arts subsidy in Britain was not a live issue in the 1930s that they report it as a fact, cite no evidence and move on. Others again argue that on the relatively rare occasions before the war when state subsidy was discussed, it was generally opposed: the examples of Nazi Germany, Fascist Italy and Soviet Russia caused government funding of music and theatre to be seen as a route to state control of these arts.

- The coming of war changed all this. CEMA, initially a private charitable initiative, received from the start government help in kind. After a few months, Treasury funds, channelled via the Board of Education, made the government a co-funder. The general view is that this was due wholly to the war.
- The creation of the Arts Council of Great Britain in 1945 was the natural, almost inevitable, development of CEMA's wartime work.

This book considers the evidence behind each element of this consensus. It concludes that none of them withstands scrutiny.

Debunking an established myth becomes particularly worthwhile when it reveals more interesting truths behind the myth. That is the case with government funding of theatre and music in Britain. Three stories from the 1930s and wartime have been forgotten or untold: those of Alfred Wareing's League of Audiences, John Christie's 'Council of Power'/National Council of Music and Geoffrey Whitworth's Stage and Allied Arts Defence League. The names are redolent of their period; their history, individually and collectively, casts an unexpected light on the cultural politics of the time and on the personalities of those, famous and less famous, in the arts, politics and the church, who supported or opposed them.

## The Creation Myth and Its Persistence

John Maynard Keynes made probably the earliest, and certainly the most influential, statement of the Arts Council's 'creation myth'. Keynes, its founding Chairman, had also chaired CEMA. In July 1945 he gave a radio talk setting out his aims for the new organization and describing the origins of CEMA and the Arts Council:

> ... in the early days of the war, when all sources of comfort were at a low ebb, there came into existence ... a body officially styled the 'Council for the Encouragement of Music and the Arts' .... one of the last acts of the Coalition Government was to decide that C.E.M.A., with a new name and wider opportunities, should be continued in time of peace.[1]

Keynes presented CEMA as arising, without pre-war roots, from the early wartime landscape, and implied that the Arts Council was CEMA's almost inevitable successor. On both points he has been followed by almost all later commentators.

The most succinct – indeed, elliptical – statement of this view came fifty years later, in Andrew Sinclair's 1995 history of the Arts Council. It was a seven-word slogan: 'War was the foundation of the arts.'[2] Sinclair's 500-page account of the Council's first fifty years, *Arts and Cultures*, was commissioned by the Arts Council itself. His opening twenty-four pages are a prologue ambitiously covering the period from Gilgamesh and Nebuchadnezzar to 1939. The prologue's penultimate page lists a number of 'bodies interested in adult education and the arts in the nineteen-thirties'.[3] Despite casting his net so widely as to include the Women's Institutes and Townswomen's Guilds, Sinclair mentioned no 1930s campaigns for arts subsidy. Indeed he made two assertions which suggested that there was none of any significance. The first is the quotation above. The second is that 'the rise of Fascism and Communism' meant that the 1930s 'was no climate for the patronage of threatened cultures'.[4] In the context of a chapter on what preceded CEMA, the meaning is clear: the cause of public funding of the arts was neglected or actively unpopular in the 1930s and it took the war to change this. Having disposed of the pre-war period, Sinclair began Chapter 1 with an account of the December 1939 conference which led to CEMA's establishment. This, Sinclair suggested, resulted from the insight that 'There would be no victory without uplift as well as entertainment'.[5]

It is not only those associated with the Arts Council who have followed Keynes' lead in this respect; it is difficult to find anywhere a modern commentator expressing a contrary view. A few examples illustrate this.

The subtitle of Robert Hewison's *Culture and Consensus* (1995)[6] is *England, art and politics since 1940*. Hewison explained in his introduction why he chose this starting date: 'To understand how the present status and condition of the arts were arrived at in the British – or more specifically English – context, it is necessary to go back to the point when a British government first took on a formal and general responsibility for the arts in January 1940.'[7] It seems that no purpose would have been served by going back before 1940.

John S Harris' *Government Patronage of the Arts in Great Britain* (1970)[8] contains a chapter about public subsidy up to 1945. It begins by discussing British government support for museums and galleries from the eighteenth century. The following section, headed 'World War II and the Emergence of Government Support', places government subsidy in this context: 'When Britain declared war on Germany in 1939, few observers of the contemporary scene could have predicted that the six years of bitter conflict and privation would induce the nation to undertake a new and significant activity – public patronage of the arts.'[9] Harris' view was, clearly, that this public patronage was a consequence of the war.

Clive Gray, in *The Politics of the Arts* (2000),[10] was clearer still: 'This change from [state] avoidance to direct intervention originated with the establishment of the Council for the Encouragement of Music and the Arts (CEMA) in 1940 by the Pilgrim Trust.'[11]

Janet Minihan's *The Nationalization of Culture* (1977)[12] considered arts subsidy in the United Kingdom from 1800 to the 1970s. She argued that the Labour Party, and the Labour governments of 1923–4 and 1929–31, 'wanted to secure a more honourable place for the arts than either the Conservative or Liberal Parties'.[13] Her reasoning was slightly different from that of other commentators – she did not assume that arts subsidy was in principle a dead issue in the 1930s – but her conclusions were equally downbeat. She mentioned no 1930s campaigns for arts subsidy, and in her view there was no realistic hope of subsidy during the decade: 'If the Depression had not occurred, the story of Great Britain's official arts policy might have been accelerated by twenty years, but the economic catastrophe effectively destroyed all chances for significant support for the arts between the wars.'[14]

Fred Leventhal began his otherwise helpful brief survey of CEMA's history, 'The Best for the Most' (1990),[15] with this assertion: 'Until 1939, public expenditure to subsidize the performing arts in Great Britain was widely regarded as objectionable, and efforts by the Soviet Union and later by Nazi Germany to "nationalize" culture only reinforced the long-standing bias against state intervention.'[16] He then examined the history of CEMA without reference to events preceding it.

These views have been widespread and largely unchallenged. A writer who exemplifies this in extreme form is Jörn Weingärtner. His book *The Arts as a Weapon of War* (2006)[17] is the most detailed study so far published of CEMA and the founding of the Arts Council. More than a quarter of its length is taken up with an attempt to establish that CEMA represented a break with the past rather than continuity with it.[18] Weingärtner began his analysis of UK government cultural policy before and during World War II by setting out 'Four hypotheses [which] form the analytical frame of this study'.[19] The first was that 'Active, programmatic and institutionalised arts sponsorship through the state in Britain began only in the winter of 1939/40 with the setting up of the Committee/Council for the Encouragement of Music and the Arts during the "Bore War"'; and the second, 'The beginning of cultural policy was a direct result of the repercussions of the Second World War'.[20]

Stating 'initial hypotheses' may not be the best prelude to rigorous historical analysis. It seems to have led Weingärtner to place undue weight on evidence supporting the hypotheses and to ignore, undervalue or fail to look for anything which might undermine them. The book's opening page provides a glaring example: 'Only in the second half of 1939, two articles in *The New Statesman and Nation* [*sic*] indicated that the principle of state neutrality [towards the arts] was facing a serious challenge in Great Britain.'[21] As will be seen, it is totally inaccurate to suggest that before July 1939 'the principle of state neutrality' to the arts was unchallenged.

Among the least satisfactory of Weingärtner's chapters, one particularly relevant to the subject of this book, is devoted to the attitudes in the 1930s of what he termed the cultural elites.[22] Focusing on five members of these 'elites', E M Forster, T S Eliot, Cyril Connolly, George Orwell and J B Priestley, he sought to demonstrate that 'the political principle of cultural laissez-faire ... was complemented by a very similar line of thought by a large number of artists with only few exceptions'.[23] But Weingärtner achieved his purpose only by failing to notice or pursue contrary evidence and by making the heroic assumption that these five somehow covered the 1930s cultural waterfront. As to the latter, he claimed, in a linguistic sleight-of-hand, that they formed 'if not a cross-section of the society, a representative cross-section of the existing political creeds held within that society'.[24]

Furthermore, although Weingärtner used these five commentators to illustrate his hypothesis that pre-war attitudes towards public arts funding were generally negative, every source which he cited from them, without exception, dates from wartime or later.[25] Analysis of pre-war sources, or simple recognition that such sources existed, might have transformed his argument. As it is, he wrongly asserted that two of his five, Eliot and Priestley, took no part in debate on the issues until the war or later. Discussing Eliot, Weingärtner cited only *Notes Towards the Definition of Culture*, published in 1948.[26] He made no reference to a highly relevant essay about the League of Audiences which Eliot wrote for his magazine *The Criterion* in 1938.[27] And he claimed that Priestley 'did not directly contribute to the public debate about state funding before the setting up of CEMA [in 1940]'.[28] This too is simply wrong: as discussed at several points below, Priestley was active in the debate in the 1930s, both publicly and behind the scenes, and was highly supportive of state funding.

There is one historical study which examines some aspects of John Christie's 'Council of Power' and at least mentions the League of Audiences: Richard Witts' *Artist Unknown* (1998), rightly subtitled *An Alternative History of the Arts Council*.[29] This is discussed below. For now it can be suggested that Witts' love of overstatement, appetite for non sequiturs and lack of referencing greatly reduce his book's value; but he is almost the only modern writer to consider any of these movements for government arts subsidy.

## Scope and Aims of This Book

These accounts reach similar conclusions about what preceded CEMA and the Arts Council: almost nothing. They also illustrate a way of thinking about Britain in the 1930s and 1940s which for most areas of social history is now less common, and is seen as less tenable, than it once was. Jose Harris suggested in 1992 that 'Politicians and historians writing both during and after the war continually reaffirmed the image of the war as the cradle of the welfare state . . . .'[30] By the time she wrote, this was changing: '. . . there has been widespread reaction, partly ideological, partly based simply on scrutiny of primary sources, against what Cannadine has called the "welfare state triumphalism" of much post-Second World War British historiography.'[31] As Harris showed, the post-war welfare state had pre-war roots.

This reaction has not extended to historians of the relationship between the arts and the state in Britain. Harris questioned whether wartime and post-war changes to institutions in Britain were 'directly induced by the war, or were . . . part of a much longer-term process of societal change that was occurring anyway, and in which the war was merely a passing episode'.[32] Her answer was nuanced. For those from Keynes onwards who have written about the origins of the Arts Council, the answer has been a crude: 'Induced by the war, obviously.'

This book is in part a critical look at this conclusion. It goes beyond this, because the organizations and campaigns it examines are important in other ways. And in Chapter 2 it provides context for what follows: an assessment of the health of live music and theatre in Britain in the 1930s.

The first organization discussed, in Chapters 3 to 5, is Alfred Wareing's League of Audiences. The League, and Wareing, are now entirely forgotten, but there are several good reasons for researching and writing about them. In the mid-1930s the League attracted much favourable press coverage in Britain and across the Empire. It had high-profile supporters not only from the arts but also from politics and the Church of England, up to and including the Archbishop of Canterbury. It demonstrated that state funding of live music and drama was a subject of public interest and discussion before World War II. Its proposed structure for subsidy – a body at arm's length from the government, distributing Treasury funds to support the arts – was in essence that adopted by the government for both CEMA and the

Arts Council. And several of those most closely associated with the League went on to senior positions at CEMA and the Arts Council.

The philosophical basis of its work is perhaps of most interest. This was the belief that the 'mechanized arts' of cinema, broadcasting and recording posed not only an economic threat to live theatre and music, but a political and moral threat to 1930s Britain as a whole. Leading churchmen and other League supporters feared that the mechanized arts would create a passive and acquiescent population, unable or unwilling to think and act for themselves and inert in the face of an authoritarian government. The League's campaign for subsidy was driven by a desire to see live theatre and music financially supported in order to help fight against this.

The second campaign, discussed in Chapters 6 to 8, was led by John Christie, the founder of Glyndebourne Festival Opera. Its initial, unfortunate, name 'Council of Power' was soon dropped in favour of 'National Council of Music'. Under Christie's dominant leadership, it neither sought nor received press coverage. But at two conferences at Glyndebourne in 1938 Christie gathered leading figures from the worlds of classical music and business to discuss, probably for the first time, some of the issues which were to preoccupy the Arts Council for decades to come. The issues included the role and needs of amateur art, the nature of national art, and – particularly – whether state support for the arts should focus on promoting the highest possible quality or the widest possible availability.

Christie's continuation of this work into wartime was important in two further ways. First, the new supporters he attracted during the war, and the further discussions he held, demonstrate that for years after CEMA was set up it was widely seen as temporary, that its development into the Arts Council was by no means inevitable, and that other models of arts funding by the state were considered viable and possible. Second, Christie's wartime work influenced the government's planning for the Arts Council. But this influence was wholly negative: the Board of Education and CEMA, led respectively by Rab Butler and Keynes, in putting together their ideas for a peacetime funder of the arts were motivated in part by a determination that Christie should not prevail.

The third campaign was that against Entertainments Duty, a tax introduced in 1916 on admission prices to all sporting and entertainment events. The campaign, discussed in Chapter 9, had specific and general aspects. The former was led by the Old Vic and Sadler's Wells, seeking tax exemption as not-for-profit organizations whose work was 'partly educational'. The general campaign was led in the 1930s by the Stage and Allied Arts Defence League, an alliance of all the main providers of theatre, amateur and professional, West End and regional, formed to lobby for the tax on live performances to be abolished or much reduced. The fight against Entertainments Duty was important both positively and negatively. The main negative is that campaigners became actively hostile to the League of Audiences, believing that the two aims – subsidy on the one hand, an end to Entertainments Duty on the other – were in competition with each other. This hostility greatly harmed the League of Audiences' campaign. The main positive is that the Entertainments Duty campaign was largely successful. Commentators at the time saw the removal of tax on 'partly educational' performances as a form of subsidy. And in 1935 and 1939 successive Chancellors of the Exchequer cut the tax on live theatre and music explicitly on the grounds that they wanted to 'do something' to help them compete with the cinema. The tax cuts were larger in terms of lost revenue than any grant to CEMA or the Arts Council before the 1950s, and the second one came into force the day war was declared. Thus the campaign against Entertainments Duty demonstrates not only that the British government in the 1930s was sympathetic to the needs of the arts, but also that, right up to the outbreak of war, it put this sympathy into practice by providing substantial financial help.

* * *

There is rich archival material on all three campaigns. This material, private correspondence as well as official documents, provides rare insights into individuals from the worlds of theatre, music, the church, the civil service and politics. This is particularly the case with what may be seen as the two main characters, Alfred Wareing and John Christie. Of both it can be said that their personalities shine through their written words, and that they evoked extraordinarily strong reactions from friends and collaborators, well-wishers and adversaries. So it is a further purpose of the book to rescue Alfred Wareing from oblivion, reveal little-known aspects of John Christie's life and work, and cast new light on some other major figures of the period.

## Notes

1 'The Arts Council: Its Policy and Hopes', reprinted in *The Listener*, 12/7/45.

2 *Arts and Cultures* (London: Sinclair-Stevenson, 1995), hereafter 'Sinclair', p24.

3 Sinclair, p23.

4 Ibid., pp23–4.

5 Ibid., p26.

6 London: Methuen, 1995.

7 Ibid., ppxiv–xv.

8 Chicago: The University of Chicago Press, 1970.

9 Ibid., p19.

10 Basingstoke: Macmillan, 2000.

11 Ibid., p39.

12 London: Hamish Hamilton, 1977.

13 Ibid., p185.

14 Ibid., p173.

15 '"The Best for the Most": CEMA and State Sponsorship of the Arts in Wartime 1939–45', *Twentieth Century British History*, Vol 1, No 3 (1990), pp289–317.

16 Ibid., p289.

17 London and New York: I B Tauris 2012 [date of revised paperback edition]; hereafter 'Weingärtner'.

18 Weingärtner, Chapters I–IV, pp1–49.

19 Ibid., p5.

20 Ibid., pp5 and 6, respectively.

21 Ibid., p1.

22 Ibid., Chapter III.

23 Ibid., p23.

24 Ibid.

25 Weingärtner in his introduction (p9) suggested that the chapter's purpose was to describe 'the picture "before the war"', in order to assist his task of demonstrating how the war changed things.

26 London: Faber and Faber, 1948.

27 'A Commentary', *The Criterion*, March 1938, pp478–85; see Chapter 4.

28 Weingärtner, p32.

29 London: Warner Books, 1998.

30 Jose Harris: 'War and Social History: Britain and the Home Front During the Second World War', *Contemporary European History*, Vol 1, No 1 (March 1992), p17.

31 Ibid., p20.

32 Ibid., p21.

2

# Theatre and Classical Music in 1930s Britain

## Introduction

The campaigns in 1930s Britain for state funding of live music and theatre were motivated by the belief that the future of these arts was in jeopardy. Much of the perceived threat was economic: those who ran theatres, touring theatre companies and orchestras were concerned about financial viability, those who worked in these industries about their own employment prospects.

There was a further, related belief held by the League of Audiences and campaigners against Entertainments Duty: that the main threat to live performance was from cinema, broadcasting and recording. Chapter 4 discusses the moral and political forms this took – in essence, that these 'mechanized arts' posed a danger to society as a whole. This chapter considers the more practical aspects – the fear shared by many working in theatre and classical music in the 1930s that the cinema and the BBC were seducing audiences away from live performance and thus that the mechanized arts threatened their livelihoods. The chapter considers the evidence behind this belief; it discusses the health generally of theatre and live classical music in 1930s Britain, and the impact on them of the mechanized arts.

## Cinema vs Theatre

Many histories of 1930s Britain present a grey picture of its performing arts scene: theatre-going in decline, plays tailored for the well-heeled and uncritical, music-making and amateur theatre in a trough, and increasing recourse by people of all classes to the canned entertainment offered by 'Hollywood', the gramophone and the wireless. A causal link is often suggested – that cinema's dominance was at the expense of theatre and other live entertainment. A classic, pithy statement of this view came in A J P Taylor's *English History 1914–1945*, published in 1965: 'The cinema slaughtered all competitors.'[1]

Taylor's argument was both quantitative and qualitative: compared with earlier times there were fewer theatres putting on fewer productions to smaller audiences in the 1930s, and what was put before the public was simply not as good. The available statistics and many contemporary accounts tell a different story.

Statistics about theatre productions and performances in the 1930s compared with earlier and later decades are, if not comprehensive, substantial and solid. They do not support Taylor's contention that cinema 'slaughtered' theatre; indeed, they suggest no evident decline in the quantity of theatre (for quality, see below), nor any causal link between the rise of the cinema and the condition of live theatre. The best systematic quantitative evidence is in J P Wearing's sixteen-volume series providing details of every production in each of what he classified as 'the major theatres of central London' for every year from 1890 to 1959.[2] Wearing's work has received some criticism, most relevantly about its geographical restrictions.[3] But the criticism has been minor, and even the critics have acknowledged its unique value: 'I know of no other venture on this scale making available the theatrical riches of a great modern city in this detailed way.'[4] Lack of coverage of theatres outside London and audience numbers are obvious limitations. Production and performance numbers are, however, a reasonable surrogate for audience sizes, and while there was more theatre in London than elsewhere in Britain in the 1930s, this is true of every decade. So Wearing's work is a good quantitative indicator of the health of live professional theatre in Britain over these seventy years.

In brief, it shows that far from the 1930s being a period in which theatre was in decline, it was the busiest of all the seven decades in terms of both active theatres and numbers of productions in London.[5] The next busiest in terms of numbers of theatres was the 1940s and in terms of productions was the 1920s.[6] The only area where the 1930s did not lead was in numbers of performances: fewer than in the 1920s, 1940s and 1950s, but more than in the 1900s and 1910s.[7] This means that theatrical productions had on average shorter runs in the 1930s than in some other decades. The figures provide no other evidence that there was 'less theatre' in the 1930s. On the contrary, with more productions in more theatres in London in the 1930s than in any other decade between the 1890s and the 1950s, live theatre was fairly healthy, and was holding its own despite the rise of cinema.

Taylor also argued that the quality of live theatre deteriorated during the 1930s, in two respects. First, public appetite for 'the classics' declined greatly and companies specializing in this repertoire went under: 'In the nineteen-twenties there were still touring companies: two in Shakespeare, one in Shaw, two ... in romantic plays. These all expired. Shakespeare dwindled to the London Old Vic and the Memorial Theatre at Stratford upon Avon, which was sustained mainly by American tourists and parties of schoolchildren.'[8] Second, 'The London theatres offered fewer new plays of distinction.... Galsworthy died in 1933.... Shaw was in his dotage.'[9]

Contemporary sources cast doubt on Taylor's conclusions. They also suggest what led him to them: he looked in the wrong place for his evidence – primarily in the West End, which, then as now, was not where the best new theatre was found.

Concerning performances of the classics, the theatre producer Norman Marshall published in 1947 *The Other Theatre*,[10] a mixture of memoir and study of what was later called alternative or fringe theatre. It began with an account of Marshall's theatre-going between September 1925 and June 1926:

> I doubt if there can ever have been a season when so many of the classics were to be seen in London.... I saw thirteen plays of Shakespeare, half-a-dozen Elizabethan and Restoration classics, all five of Chekov's full-length plays, and one apiece by Moliere, Ibsen, Gogol, Calderon, Andreyev, Dostoievsky, Turgenev, Hauptmann and Benavente.[11]

He then listed the plays he had seen by modern playwrights, but explained:

> Hardly any of these plays were given within that ramshackle edifice known as 'The West End Theatre'. The theatre which staged most of them was struggling for its existence in strange out-of-the-way edifices such as a drill hall in Hampstead..., a forgotten playhouse in Hammersmith ..., a cramped little cinema out at Barnes..., and a backstreet attic in Covent Garden.... What had the West End to offer to compare with the work of these exiled groups of players?[12]

For Marshall this applied just as much to the 1930s: 'Nearly everything that was most worthwhile in the English theatre in the period between the wars was due to the influence of these rebel organisations.... [This book] is a record of how the English theatre was saved from stagnation and sterility... imposed upon the theatre by the managers and by the Censor....'[13]

Cecil Chisholm's *Repertory* (1934)[14] expressed a similar view of West End theatre: 'Glancing down the list of plays now running in London, I find ... Only five reasonably interesting plays out of thirty-three "shows".... When the commercial manager does produce an interesting play, he does it merely by accident.'[15] Chisholm's view of theatre beyond the West End in the 1930s suggests that what Marshall wrote of London was also true elsewhere. He began his final chapter:

> In twenty years the face of the British theatre has been transformed, particularly in the provinces. We have from thirty to forty repertory theatres and companies at work; a dozen keen amateur repertories, some of which will inevitably develop into professional theatres; a beginning of the building of beautiful modern playhouses.... A situation has arisen of which we dared not even dream twenty years ago.[16]

For Chisholm, as for Marshall, the main problem facing the theatre was a lack not of talent or audience but money. Marshall described the type of theatre producing this new work as 'struggling for its existence'; Chisholm noted that 'Nine out of ten of our repertory theatres live from hand to mouth. They are prevented from doing fine work well within their compass because it may reduce the takings for a single week.'[17] The solution, for Chisholm, was public subsidy. The final page of his book was a plea for the theatre to organize 'a special propagandist body'[18] to campaign for this. In the very year *Repertory* was published, though apparently unconnected with it, the League of Audiences was formed to do just that.

One contemporary writer expressed opinions in some respects similar to Taylor's: the playwright and critic St John Ervine. Ervine was convinced that live theatre was in a bad way. He was a keen supporter of the League of Audiences and a passionate hater of cinema.[19] In *The Theatre in My Time* (1933)[20] Ervine suggested a link between cinema's growth and theatre's perceived decline. But from this point, his views diverged from Taylor's. For Ervine, more fundamentally, cinema's triumph over theatre was a symptom of society's general decay from what he saw as the high point of 1914. By the 1930s, Ervine's views were generally reactionary and misanthropic. They led him to identify the war and its legacy as responsible for all society's problems, of which those of the theatre were a part:

> Soon after the signing of the Armistice, the theatre ceased to have an intelligent and educated audience.... A million men had been killed in the War, and these were, for the most part, the flower of the Nation. Millions of people, half educated and nervously agitated, were growing up without any discipline or training.... restless uninstructed people, whose only notion of entertainment was a frightful noise.... The theatre could not appease this nerve-racked, speed maddened population....[21]

For Ervine the preceding golden age of theatre had itself been only a relatively brief period of light in the prevailing gloom: 'In 1914, the second great period of the English theatre came to an end',[22] but this had followed 'The destitution of the drama in England in the last forty years of the eighteenth century and the first seventy-five of the nineteenth'.[23] It may be relevant that, as *The New York Times*' obituary of Ervine[24] observed, 'Probably his most successful plays were "Jane Clegg" and "John Ferguson," both written before World War I'.

Ervine provided some figures to support his argument: 'Five years ago, there were about five hundred theatres [in Britain].... Now, in 1933, there are about two hundred and fifty'.[25] But he provided no source for this drastic claim of a fifty per cent reduction in just five years, and it is unconvincing when set against the mass of contrary evidence. While Ervine showed a more constructive and enthusiastic side when the League of Audiences was founded, much of his book is best seen as an entertaining rant against the modern world.

Other influential writers on theatre in the 1930s were less anxious than Ervine about the harm done to it by cinema. James Agate was theatre critic of the *Sunday Times* from 1923 until his death in 1947.[26] In the 'Epistle Dedicatory to Mr. Ivor Brown' (the style is typical) in *First Nights* (1934), a collection of his *Sunday Times* reviews, he suggested that any threat had diminished by 1934:

> All theatre-lovers must be concerned with what is popularly called 'the menace of the films'. The phrase has a nineteen-thirtyish ring about it.... Four years ago ... it was thought that they would be in such direct competition with the theatre that one could survive only on condition that the other perished.... [But] the theatre has retained its old public and the cinema has created a new one.[27]

Ivor Brown himself, a strong supporter of the League of Audiences and thus of the cause of subsidy, was more sanguine still. Writing in *Drama*, the magazine of the British Drama League, in 1937,[28] Brown expressed confidence that live theatre would prosper in spite of the cinema. Noting the 'extraordinary hold of the living actor seen and heard in person', he asked: 'Is not this drama with its scenes of sinking ships and savage life knocked sideways by the meanest effort of Elstree [film studios]? The answer, delivered at the box office, is quite simply "No"'.

Agate's suggestion was that the perceived economic danger which cinema posed to theatre was at its height in 1930. The date is significant, given the introduction of talking pictures in the late 1920s; for Agate, apparently, the threat of the 'talkies' had proved exaggerated. As early as 1929 the playwright and later Labour MP Benn Levy (of whom more in Chapter 4), in a memo for the Incorporated Society of Authors, foresaw a rather niche challenge which talking pictures might pose to live theatre. Apart from 'the more general effect upon Theatre business [caused] by the novelty and popularity (temporary or otherwise) of this new type of entertainment', Levy suggested that 'with the "talkie", the Touring Manager is faced with the possibility of his play being presented scene by scene and word by word at an opposition house'.[29] Levy's background was relevant: he was 'dialogue writer' for Alfred Hitchcock's first talking picture (one of the first in Britain), *Blackmail*, released the same year and itself adapted from a play.[30] But the danger seems not to have come to pass.

A final source casts further light on theatre's health in 1930s Britain, its relationship with cinema, and, incidentally, the views of St John Ervine. In December 1935 *The Times* reported that '[the actor] Sir Cedric Hardwicke and Mr. St. John Ervine took part in a debate on "You actors waste your time on films," held yesterday at 45, Park Lane'.[31] According to *The Times*, Ervine argued that 'Actors were being seduced from the art they loved by money to take part in a thing they despised.... He wanted actors to come away from the entertainment of the charwoman, for it was only people with a charwoman's mind who went to the cinema.' For Hardwicke, cinema and theatre were not in conflict: 'The only part of the theatre that the cinema had killed was the provincial touring company, and he viewed its passing with no regret.... The films were not made for people who were able to go to the theatre but for those who for one reason or another were not so able.'

The debate continued in the *Theatre Managers' Journal*.[32] Hardwicke received more criticism than support; but the criticisms, from some leading theatre managers of the time, attacked his views on touring companies rather than backing Ervine's views on cinema. The Managing Director of Moss Empires, which included the London Palladium, the Prince of Wales Theatre and many of the largest regional theatres,[33] argued against every element of Hardwicke's case. About the quality of theatre outside London, Hardwicke 'cannot have had time to see some of the most excellent recent provincial productions'. Concerning its profitability, 'I am sure quite a few West End Theatres will envy the numbers ... [Noel Coward] has played to' on a recent regional tour. And concerning competition between cinema and theatre, 'Some of us have noted a big reaction to "flesh and blood" this year.... [When the public] go to their local city or on their holidays they have a definite desire to see the real stuff "in the flesh"'. The Managing Director of the Howard and Wyndham theatre chain was alone in accepting any of Hardwicke's views, agreeing that cinema had almost eliminated small touring companies. But 'Fortunately there is a decided come back to the Theatre, and Repertory, the real feeding ground of all, has been making vast strides.'

The conclusion from all this is that there was no marked decline in the quality or quantity of theatre produced in Britain in the 1930s, that cinema was not 'slaughtering' live theatre, and that the arguments mounted against cinema by such writers as St John Ervine were more emotional and moral than economic and statistical. They are considered further in Chapter 4.

## Broadcasting vs Live Music

In 1933 the music critic Ernest Newman wrote that 'the musical destiny of this country [is] in the hands of the BBC'.[34] Many agreed that, for better or worse, this was the case. Throughout history it had been possible to hear professionally performed music only in live performance. For economic, social, cultural and practical reasons, the vast majority of the population was excluded. In the inter-war period, for the first time, anyone who could afford a wireless and licence or a gramophone and records could hear such music. Even St John Ervine wrote positively of 'the labourer in a remote hamlet' now being able to hear Beethoven's Seventh Symphony 'as easily as if he were an habitué of the Queen's or the Albert Hall'.[35]

In *The Arts in England* (1949) Mary Glasgow, Secretary-General of the Arts Council, agreed: 'When, during the war, concerts were taken by C.E.M.A. to unlikely audiences in remote districts ... it was discovered that a large and genuine audience for music existed.... The effect of radio music has shown itself to be wide and enduring.'[36] In this, Glasgow was echoing her late Chairman, John Maynard Keynes: '... the BBC has played ... the predominant part in creating this public demand.... I am told that today when a good symphony concert is broadcast as many as five million people may listen to it. Their ears become trained. With what anticipation many of them look forward if a chance comes their way to hear a living orchestra....'[37]

Such views seem uncontroversial, indeed obvious. But there was a surprising number of contrary voices, motivated as much by dislike of the BBC and fear of the damaging effects of the 'mechanized arts' in general as by a genuine belief that wide availability of music was somehow harmful. Among later commentators, A J P Taylor's opinion of the BBC, and of Sir Thomas Beecham, was as clear and lacking in evidence as his opinions of theatre and cinema in the 1930s: '... a single man, Sir Thomas Beecham, did more for British music than was done by the massed battalions of the BBC.'[38] Beecham's own views were more extreme still. In 1934 he suggested that the BBC's 'monstrous monopoly of the air is infinitely more dangerous than the aeroplane menace', and that within twenty years '[we] will depend for every kind of music on the radio and musical reproduction by mechanical devices'.[39] Beecham was not a lone voice. In the *Musical Times*, W R Anderson wrote approvingly: 'Sir Thomas was perfectly just in most of his remarks. We ought to be grateful for a man who is not frightened of anybody or anything.... The monstrous thing is that it [the BBC] is not answerable to anybody'[40] – a surprising comment in a regular magazine column called 'Wireless Notes'.

Even so, aside from his general reputation as a controversialist, Beecham was an unlikely pessimist about the future of live classical music and the effects of broadcasting. As for the former, only two years earlier, in 1932, he had founded one of Britain's finest orchestras, the London Philharmonic.[41] And not only did he work frequently with the BBC, he also lobbied it frequently for more broadcast time (and thus fees) for his own projects. Even so, it is worth considering the evidence behind such arguments as Beecham's. The influence of the arguments is considered further in Chapter 4.

There is no statistical study of classical music as thorough as J P Wearing's volumes on London theatre. But the case made by Beecham and those who thought like him seems based more on gut feeling or prejudice than on hard data. They provided no such data – nothing to suggest that live classical music was at serious risk in the 1930s, still less that the BBC or the recording industry was the cause. As noted above, classical music was for the first time available to millions of potential listeners. It is, to say the least, counter-intuitive that this development endangered live classical music; so it was for those who held this view to make the case for it. Beyond arguing that the radio and gramophone discouraged home and other amateur music-making (a point considered below), they did not even attempt to do so. Perhaps most importantly, examination of what the BBC actually did makes Beecham's position untenable; Beecham himself dismissed the BBC's activity in the phrase 'monstrous monopoly of the air',[42] while Taylor failed to address it at all.

The BBC was the dominant force not merely in broadcast music but in all aspects of professional classical music in Britain in the 1930s other than musicians' training. Ernest Newman recognized this in the quotation above. So did the composer Arthur Bliss, writing in 1932: 'The BBC has grown in ten years to be the greatest music-making machine . . . that has ever existed.'[43] It was the pre-eminent promoter of live concerts, funder of concerts put on by other promoters (through payments for broadcasts), commissioner of new music, creator of new orchestras and employer of musicians. The following examples suggest that in all these areas its effect was positive rather than the reverse.

The Promenade Concerts, perhaps the most famous concert series in the world, were founded in 1895 by Robert Newman and Sir Henry Wood. On Newman's death in 1926, the Proms were on the point of folding until the BBC took them on;[44] they have kept them in being ever since. According to Asa Briggs, 'At the first concert under the new regime Wood . . . told a friend that he was so elated he had never conducted with greater spirit. He also said how wonderful it was to be free at last from "the everlasting box office problem".'[45]

For several years from 1930 the BBC was also responsible for ensuring the survival of opera at the Royal Opera House. Through a complex arrangement not only did the BBC became the controlling shareholder in the Covent Garden Opera Syndicate (1930) Ltd, but the Treasury offered subsidy to Covent Garden, via the BBC, of £5,000 in 1930 and £7,500 for each of the following five years.[46] And Briggs pointed out that during the 1930s 'the BBC gave considerable financial help not only to Covent Garden but to Sadler's Wells and Carl Rosa, and it broadcast opera from Glyndebourne as early as 1935',[47] only its second season of operation. Despite his expressed view of the BBC as a 'menace' and a desperate threat to live music, Sir Thomas Beecham 'continued to press the BBC . . . to give more financial help to Covent Garden' (of which he was then Music Director) through increasing the number of opera broadcasts.[48]

Furthermore, in the 1930s the BBC founded three symphony orchestras – the BBC Symphony Orchestra in 1930 and the BBC Scottish and Welsh Orchestras in 1935.[49] As noted above, the field was, nonetheless, uncrowded enough to permit Beecham to found the London Philharmonic in 1932. Writing in 1935, the BBC's Director of Music, and Principal Conductor of the BBC Symphony Orchestra, Adrian Boult, gave this view of the orchestral scene in Britain before and after 1930:

> . . . the reputation of British music and British musicianship abroad was extremely low. Our capital city contained but one orchestra [the London Symphony Orchestra] and that an inferior one. . . . The formation of the Corporation's Symphony Orchestra was the turning point. . . . With this fine orchestra working under admirable conditions, the Corporation was clearly capable of reaching a standard hitherto undreamt of in this country.[50]

This might be considered special pleading were it not supported by visiting musicians including the famously demanding conductor Arturo Toscanini, who told Boult: 'You have done with the BBC Orchestra in three years what took me with the New York Philharmonic five years . . . you have made it into one of the finest orchestras in the world.'[51]

The BBC's role as commissioner of new music is too large a subject to cover here,[52] but an idea of its contribution can be gained by considering briefly its role in Benjamin Britten's early career. The BBC first broadcast one of Britten's works in 1933, when he was just nineteen.[53] Although Britten was never on the BBC's payroll, his employment from 1935 in the GPO Film Unit resulted from a recommendation by its Music Department.[54] From 1937, appreciating his speed and facility in producing music to order, the BBC began commissioning scores from him; in 1937 and 1938 he wrote incidental music for seven radio plays and features.[55] Also in 1938 the BBC commissioned Britten to write a piano concerto for premiere, with the composer as soloist, in that year's Promenade Concerts[56] – a work reviewed patronizingly by *The Times* as 'one of the most interesting novelties we have had at the Proms for some time'.[57] Later in the same Proms season Britten conducted the BBC Symphony Orchestra in his *Variations on a Theme of Frank Bridge*, written the previous year.[58] And later the same month some of his music for Auden and Isherwood's play *The Ascent of F6* was televised from Alexandra Palace.[59] This was all before Britten had reached the age of twenty-five. Such opportunities for a young composer to write so much for almost immediate performance and to make a living from composing, and for listeners (and viewers) to hear the resulting music, were not only unprecedented but had been impossible at any earlier period.

Some of the most valuable contemporary accounts of classical music in Britain in the 1930s were written by Arthur Bliss, particularly a series of twelve articles in 1935 in the BBC's magazine *The Listener* under the general title *A Musical Pilgrimage of Britain*.[60] This had some similarity to J B Priestley's *English Journey* (1934);[61] while Bliss and Priestley were friends,[62] it is not clear whether it was inspired by Priestley's book. Bliss became the BBC's Director of Music in 1942.[63]

Even before the *Musical Pilgrimage* he had written for *The Listener* about the BBC and music. In the article cited above, describing the BBC as 'the greatest music-making machine that has ever existed', he noted with approval what he saw as the corporation's benignly elitist approach: 'It has obviously decided rightly … to bridge any gulf between the public and itself by enticing the said public to creep up to its own level of taste …'[64] For Bliss, music on the BBC was an unqualified force for good: 'A serious listener can in a year become acquainted with the best symphonic and chamber music of all periods performed sometimes superbly, at all times adequately. It is the equivalent, in painting, of a year's tour round the most famous galleries of the world. No one can fairly ask for anything better … .' Bliss suggested that the BBC was 'achieving on a national scale what

Sir Henry Wood has done with his Queen's Hall audiences – unostentatiously raising the level of musical appreciation'. Wood, of course, had achieved this partly due to the BBC's funding the Proms. Finally, the BBC Symphony Orchestra 'has set a standard of playing high enough to cause a perceptible stiffening and liveliness in other orchestras'.

The *Musical Pilgrimage* looked more broadly at the state of music in Britain, in the form of despatches about musical life, amateur and professional, in places ranging from Cornwall to Glasgow, though excluding London and the south-east. Among the issues Bliss explored were the state of amateur music making and the BBC's influence on this, the only aspect of musical life in which the corporation's critics claimed that it had proved specifically rather than generally harmful. He provided many examples to suggest that the amateur tradition, choral and otherwise, was in good health. Indeed, his conclusions ran totally counter to those of the critics:

> There seems hardly a village which is not touched by some musical organization. In a general way broadcasting has been the most potent cause of this growth. It has awakened the sense of music in vast sections of the population. There is naturally a percentage ... lazily content to take the ready-made article ... but there are other listeners who wish to get into closer touch with music by learning to take part themselves.[65]

Bliss acknowledged two dangers for amateur music: 'Saturation point is being reached.... There are frankly too many societies', and 'probably due to the effect of broadcasting, the public demand superfine performances' – which amateur music societies were rarely able to deliver. But neither point suggests that the BBC had a negative effect on amateur music, let alone on music as a whole.

Indeed, in all the ways discussed above the BBC was doing much to keep classical music and opera in good health in the 1930s. There is one role to which it is worth drawing particular attention. By paying for permission to broadcast concerts and operas, and as a shareholder and regular funder of Covent Garden, the BBC was acting in fact if not in name as a provider of subsidy. This role has been largely ignored by writers about public funding of the arts from Keynes onwards, a failure further contributing to the myth that arts subsidy became salient only on the outbreak of World War II.

It would be tedious to emphasize this theme repeatedly, but the crucial, indeed pre-eminent, role of the BBC in classical music in the 1930s is relevant to much of this book. Contrary to Beecham's and Taylor's views, the evidence stron suggests that largely due to, rather than in spite of, the BBC, the 1930s sa burgeoning in both the quantity and quality of classical music produced, performed and listened to in Britain, live as well as broadcast and recorded.

## Conclusion

This chapter surveying the health of live theatre and classical music in 1930s Britain has been far from comprehensive. It has not, for instance, covered the campaign in the 1930s to create a National Theatre, the role of amateur drama, nor, other than in passing, the recording industry. Its aim was to include sufficient evidence to demonstrate the condition of these performing arts before the war. That evidence shows that they were in better health than is often suggested; that in practice they were not harmed by the cinema and the BBC, indeed, that classical music was thriving because of the BBC; and accordingly that the active and passionate campaigns for state funding of the arts in the 1930s, examined in later chapters, were driven more by politics and principle than by direct economic need.

## Notes

1 Harmondsworth: Penguin Books, 1970 (originally published OUP, 1965), hereafter 'Taylor', p392.

2 J P Wearing: *The London Stage: A Calendar of Plays and Players 1890–1899, 1900–1909, 1910–1919, 1920–1929, 1930–1939, 1940–1949* and *1950–1959* (Metuchen, NJ, USA: The Scarecrow Press, 1976, 1981, 1982, 1984, 1990, 1991 and 1993 respectively), hereafter 'Wearing 1890s', 'Wearing 1900s' etc.

3 See, for instance, Joseph Donohue: 'Review of *The London Stage 1890–99: A Calendar of Plays and Players* by J P Wearing', *Educational Theatre Journal*, Vol 29, No 2, May 1977, pp268–71, and George Dorris: 'Review of *The London Stage: A Calendar of Plays and Players* by J P Wearing', *Dance Chronicle* Vol. 18, No. 3, 1995, pp505–10.

4 Dorris (see above) p506.

5 61 and 4256 respectively; Wearing 1930s, vol 1, pvii.

6 53 and 3980 respectively; Wearing 1940s and Wearing 1920s, respectively, vol 1, pvii, in each case.

7 The figure for each decade is in each case in vol 1, pvii, of that decade's volumes; the 1890s volumes do not provide the equivalent figure.

8 Taylor, pp392–3.

9 Ibid., p393.

10 London: John Lehmann.
11 Ibid., p11.
12 Ibid., pp11–12.
13 Ibid., p13.
14 *Repertory: An Outline of the Modern Theatre Movement* (London: Peter Davies, 1934).
15 Ibid., pp75–6.
16 Ibid., p226.
17 Ibid., pp227–8.
18 Ibid., p237.
19 See below and Chapter 4.
20 London: Rich & Cowan; hereafter 'Ervine'.
21 Ibid., pp177–8.
22 Ibid., p163.
23 Ibid., p65.
24 25/1/71.
25 Ervine, p189.
26 https://www.britannica.com/biography/James-Agate, retrieved 15 October 2018.
27 London: Ivor Nicholson and Watson, 1934, pvi.
28 'Plays of the Month', *Drama*, Vol 16, No 1, October 1937, p1.
29 The Keep (East Sussex Record Office), Benn Wolfe Levy papers, SxMs37/19/1, memo of 2/7/29, 'Talking Picture Versions of Stage Plays'.
30 http://www.samuelfrench.com/author/3342/benn-w-levy and http://www.imdb.com/title/tt0019702/fullcredits#writers, retrieved 30 December 2013.
31 14/12/35, p4, for all quotations in this paragraph.
32 *Theatre Managers' Journal*, January 1936. The relevant pages – not numbered – were pasted into National Archives file CUST153/5: Entertainments Duty Volume 5: The Living Theatre 1932 to 1940, pp154–6.
33 http://www.arthurlloyd.co.uk/MossEmpiresJubilee1949.htm, retrieved 22 March 2018.
34 *Sunday Times*, 15/11/33, quoted in Asa Briggs: *The History of Broadcasting in the United Kingdom: Volume II – The Golden Age of Wireless* (Oxford: Oxford University Press, 1965), hereafter 'Briggs', p171.
35 Ervine, pp197–8.
36 B Ifor Evans and Mary Glasgow: *The Arts in Britain* (London: The Falcon Press, 1949), p16.
37 'The Arts Council: Its Policy and Hopes' (*The Listener*, 12/7/45).
38 Taylor, p299.
39 Quoted in W R Anderson: 'Wireless Notes', *Musical Times*, November 1934, pp990–1.
40 Ibid.

41 https://www.lpo.org.uk/about/london-philharmonic-orchestra.html accessed 25 March 2018.

42 Much of the material in this section is drawn from Briggs, pp169–84.

43 'What Broadcasting has done for Music', *The Listener*, 16/11/32; reprinted in Gregory Roscow (ed): *Bliss on Music: Selected Writings of Arthur Bliss 1920–1975* (Oxford: OUP, 1991), hereafter '*Bliss on Music*', p62.

44 Briggs, pp172–3.

45 Ibid., p173; Briggs footnotes the quotation within the quotation: 'W. W. Thompson in the BBC Programme *Scrapbook*, 18 Jan. 1948'.

46 Ibid., pp178–83; the subsidy was discontinued in 1932.

47 Ibid., p182.

48 Ibid., pp182–3.

49 Ibid., p170.

50 Quoted in Briggs, p184.

51 Quoted in Briggs, p171.

52 See, generally, Jenny Doctor: *The BBC and Ultra-Modern Music, 1922–1936* (Cambridge: Cambridge University Press, 1999).

53 Humphrey Carpenter: *Benjamin Britten – A Biography* (London: Faber and Faber, 1992), p50.

54 Ibid., p63.

55 John Evans (ed): *Journeying Boy: The Diaries of the Young Benjamin Britten, 1928–1938* (London: Faber and Faber, 2010), p316.

56 Ibid., p317.

57 19/8/38, p10.

58 8/9/38; https://www.bbc.co.uk/events/rzhbj5/by/date/1938/09/07, retrieved 8 April 2018.

59 *The Times*, 26/9/38. p19.

60 Published between 2/10/35 and 18/12/35; reprinted in *Bliss on Music*, pp105–55.

61 London: William Heinemann/Victor Gollancz, 1934.

62 Arthur Bliss: *As I Remember* (London: Faber and Faber, 1970), p100.

63 Ibid., pp139–64.

64 Quotations from *Bliss on Music*, pp63–4.

65 Ibid., p152, for this and the following two quotations.

3

# The League of Audiences: (i) 'I am progressing almost beyond my hopes'

## A Forgotten Debate

This and the following two chapters trace the history of Alfred Wareing's League of Audiences.[1] The League enjoyed a high public profile in the 1930s and almost total neglect ever since. Its story demonstrates that before the war, press and public were deeply interested in arts subsidy, and that it was a cause actively supported by many beyond obvious music and theatre lovers.

Any discussion of the League of Audiences must focus on two cultural debates. The first was about whether state funding of the arts would lead inevitably to state control of the arts. Given the examples of 1930s Nazi, Fascist and Communist cultural policies, this concern was understandable. The other – more intense at the time, rarely remembered now – was about the effects on British society of the 'mechanized arts' of film, the wireless and the gramophone. The economic effects of the mechanized arts on live music and theatre were considered in Chapter 2. But there were also fundamental cultural and moral issues associated with them: questions such as whether 'mechanised music and drama [should] be allowed to extend their soulless sway, without protest';[2] how to respond to the threat posed by the cinema, 'where pop-eyed illiterates lie about in heaps, gaping at the Garbo! [*sic*]';[3] and whether, in brief, film, broadcasting and recording were creating a population of passive and inert consumers. It was fear of the effects of the mechanized arts which mobilized many beyond the worlds of theatre and music, particularly senior members of the Church of England, to engage with the League of Audiences.

In a sense both debates arose from a fear of authoritarian government, but they argued from opposite premises to opposite conclusions. The first was about the potential for abuse of arts subsidy by a government seeking to create 'state art'. The second foresaw governments using cinema and broadcasting to create a quiescent population, and argued that subsidy was needed so that live music and drama could combat this. Both may seem exaggerated and unrealistic in hindsight, but the first was important for the League's opponents while the second was central to its mission. This chapter is about the League's rise, from 1934 to mid-1938. Chapter 4 focuses on these two central debates and discusses the Church of England's involvement in the League's work. Chapter 5 examines the League's decline as war approached, and its legacy and significance.

## 'Advancing upon the iron portals of Whitehall': The League Begins

### Alfred Wareing

In October 1934 articles appeared in the British national, regional and imperial press reporting on, and applauding, a new organization. 'Candidus',[4] in the *Daily Sketch*, summarized its key themes:

> I notice with pleasure the creation of a new society for the encouragement of the drama and music. It is called the League of Audiences, and if it succeeds, it will convert audiences, hitherto the passive objects of private commercial speculation, or sometimes of private philanthropy, into genuine assistants at their own entertainment. . . . It will seek to induce our rulers to do as much for . . . [music and drama] as for the more consciously educational institutions of museums and art galleries. . . . Its second object will be to 'preserve and promote interpretation of these arts by persons present in person before their audiences' – a wholesome reaction against the mechanisation of the arts. . . . Someone will say that this will cost money. Of course it will.[5]

For the League of Audiences, live music and theatre, and their audiences, were threatened by film, records and broadcasting, and by commercial interests in general. These arts needed public funding to make the fight more equal, and they deserved funding as much as the art displayed in museums and galleries.

The League was not alone in this view. Even as it was being established, Cecil Chisholm's book *Repertory* (1934),[6] discussed in Chapter 2, argued that without subsidy repertory theatres would fold: 'Manchester failed Miss Horniman [and] . . . Birmingham has twice let down Sir Barry Jackson.'[7] Chisholm did not underestimate the challenge: 'As the normal British cabinet has no electoral spur to foster taste in art, literature or the drama, it can hardly be expected that any Government will ever introduce a bill on the subject . . . an immense amount of educational work would be necessary in the press and on the platform.'[8]

Chisholm's solution, the call which concluded his book, was 'the formation of a special propagandist body to further this vital work. The need for a beginning is urgent; for many years of arduous work lie ahead.'[9]

He might have been describing, or prophesying, the League of Audiences. The League was the creation of one man, Alfred Wareing. Biographical material on Wareing is sparse. The major source is a privately published, overly respectful, biography by Winifred Isaac, who after Wareing's death saw the League of Audiences through its long decline.[10] Wareing was a theatre man through and through. He was born in 1876. Having failed to make his mark as an actor, he founded the Glasgow Repertory Theatre in 1909. In its first year he gave Chekhov's *The Seagull* its first production in English, along with plays by Ibsen, Shaw, Arnold Bennett and John Galsworthy.[11] Wareing's work in Glasgow (from which he had to resign in 1912 due to ill health), and subsequently as Director of the Theatre Royal Huddersfield throughout the 1920s, earned respect from colleagues in the repertory theatre movement and from theatre historians.[12] Apart from the League of Audiences, his final posts were in Stratford-upon-Avon, as Librarian of the Shakespeare Memorial Theatre from 1931 to 1933 and Borough Librarian from 1941 until his death the following year.[13]

But Wareing's character was more notable than his CV. It shines through his writings, press accounts, and the tributes from friends and admirers with which Isaac's book began. Among these was Walter Elliot, Scottish Unionist politician, a member of the Cabinets of the National governments for most of the 1930s,[14] and a friend of Wareing's since Elliot's days as a medical student in Glasgow.[15] Elliot wrote of Wareing's 'direct approach ... which no amount of bludgeoning could knock away',[16] as apparent in the Glasgow days as twenty-five years later, when Wareing 'was advancing, still with the same childlike certainty, upon the iron portals of Whitehall'. Wareing 'was without genius in writing or eloquence in speech. He had simply an innate belief in the good-heartedness and sincerity of those in whose hands lay power; and indefatigable persistence; and a cutting-edge which, though blunt, would in the long run saw asunder mountains.'

Persistence was a quality much associated with Wareing. The theatre critic (and, later, editor of *The Observer* and member of the Arts Council) Ivor Brown, in his foreword to Isaac's book, wrote: 'The persistence which carried this deaf man, quite unknown to the big-wigs of S.W.1, through the barriers is astounding.'[17] It had its downside, as Brown acknowledged: 'The true proof of his zeal was his willingness to drive his friends to distraction for the cause ... I remember a time when I groaned at every ring of the telephone. Wareing again! ... He was after one like the Hound of Heaven, husky, smiling, anxious, indomitable.'[18]

References to Wareing's deafness were also common. The *Daily Herald* chose the headline 'Deaf, But Wants New Music Law' for a story about the League of Audiences.[19] And as Ivor Brown's comments suggest, he inspired love (the word is not too extreme) and exasperation equally, often in the same person. John Christie, founder of Glyndebourne and originator of the 'Council of Power' discussed in later chapters, was particularly ambivalent. Christie described Wareing as 'that damned old fool' and reported to his friend (and League of Audiences Treasurer) Harold Baker that '[Wareing's] answer to me was ... simply not to listen. He is an infuriating old man.'[20] Baker had to remind him that 'His deafness is a great impediment.'[21] Yet, as noted in Chapter 5, Christie contributed anonymously to Wareing's personal expenses when, in 1939, times became hard for him. Baker conceded that 'sometimes he [Wareing] resents criticism (from an excessive enthusiasm for his crusade), but I have never found him obstinate beyond reason.'[22] James Mallon, Warden of Toynbee Hall, reflected a common view when describing Wareing to Cosmo Lang, Archbishop of Canterbury: 'He is a simple and loveable man, handicapped by deafness and perhaps by volubility. But he is so much possessed by his dream of re-awakening England to love music and drama that one hears him stray from the point, or approach the wrong point, without impatience.'[23]

Wareing's optimism was apparent as early as December 1933, before the League was set up, when he wrote to a friend:

> ... (in the strictest confidence and no one but you must know of this) that I am progressing almost beyond my hopes. There are good prospects of heart to heart talks with Mr [Stanley] Baldwin [then Lord President of the Council], the Chancellor of the Exchequer [Neville Chamberlain] and Sir John Simon [Foreign Secretary]. And probably the Premier [Ramsay MacDonald]. ... So that ... we may hope to have some of the most important Cabinet Ministers in favour of relief for the living Theatre.[24]

Devotion to his cause rather than bravado kept Wareing going. In letters of March 1934, he recorded that he had been coached by Walter Elliot for a meeting with Chamberlain's Private Secretary; the meeting, he thought, 'will [not] be anything like the ordeal of that [*sic*] which Mr. Baldwin gave me',[25] and he confessed that 'I dreaded the interview with Mr. Baldwin. That was an ordeal indeed.'[26] No record from the Government side survives of this 'ordeal'.

Optimism prevailed. In an early talk (Wareing was a tireless speaker at theatre clubs throughout Great Britain) he stated baldly: 'It seems pretty certain that this plan will succeed, and in a very short time, for it is the first time that Music and Drama has [*sic*] come together to demand Government recognition.'[27]

## The League and the Press

Such views might seem unrealistically hopeful, but for much of the League's early existence they appeared well-founded. The League received a range and quantity of press coverage which make its subsequent oblivion hard to understand. A little of this was negative – the *Birmingham Mail* commented that 'the "League of Audiences" is the latest alias and device of that active group of persons who are anxious to put music and the drama on the rates or taxes'.[28] But such carping was unusual. The League's press cuttings books[29] contain more than 300 cuttings covering its first fifteen months (October 1934 to January 1936); almost all were highly favourable. And the quotation indicates that, contrary to the views of later commentators, arts subsidy was a familiar subject of campaigning in the 1930s. The *Birmingham Mail* also noted the variety of the League's supporters: 'They are a curiously mixed "League". Beginning with the Archbishop of York and the Bishop of Worcester, they include our revolutionary friend Mr. Maxton ... [James Maxton, Scottish Socialist MP and leader of the Independent Labour Party].'[30]

The *Daily Telegraph*, reporting the League's creation, was not only sympathetic (and remained so) but managed to suggest that seeking government money for the arts was almost mainstream: 'In most other countries music and the drama are recognised as essential to national well-being, and subsidised. In this country they are taxed. To induce our Government to moderate this attitude is the dream of all men who care deeply for these arts.'[31] Apart from the *Telegraph*, newspapers of such varied political persuasion as the *Daily Sketch*, *Observer*, *Morning Post* and *Manchester Guardian* were early, and remained strong, supporters of the League.[32] The regional press was equally enthusiastic: the *Birmingham Post*, *Lancashire Daily Post*, *Yorkshire Post*, *Leicester Mercury*, *Northern Echo*, *Sheffield Independent* and *Glasgow Bulletin* all reported the League's founding at length, mostly favourably.[33]

The regional press provided some of the most detailed analysis. The *Staffordshire Sentinel* included a substantial opinion piece pointing to the paradox that 'the factor which has been most effective in making a State subsidy for music necessary ... is itself a State enterprise, namely, broadcasting' and concluding that 'if nothing is left of the Bill [the League's proposed Music and Drama Bill], if and when it passes through Parliament, but a concession of the general principle of State aid for the arts, much will have been gained'.[34] The paradox, depending on the idea that broadcasting reduced the audience for live music and drama, does not withstand scrutiny. The evidence suggests, on the contrary, that broadcasting did not damage live theatre and much increased the demand for live music – see Chapter 2.

Coverage of the League's founding extended to *The Children's Newspaper*, which told its readers that 'that new and curiously-named body the League of Audiences, which has been launched through the initiative of Mr Alfred Wareing ... intends to make an appeal throughout the Empire ...[to all] who desire to see and hear living interpreters of the drama and music'.[35] Even Wareing's public talks were widely reported. In January 1936, for instance, he delivered at Fort Dunlop, Birmingham, 'a lively attack on London players and playgoers'[36] which argued the case for subsidy to support the best of regional theatre. This talk received not only much local attention ('Mr. Alfred Wareing ought not to need any introduction, because it was he who founded the League of Audiences' – *Wolverhampton Express*),[37] but also reports in *The Times*, *News Chronicle*, *Evening News*, *Morning Post* and even the South African *Cape Argus*.[38]

Indeed, the imperial press was highly enthusiastic, particularly after Lord Bessborough, Governor-General of Canada from 1931 to 1935, became the League's President. Its press cuttings book contains reports from India, South Africa, Canada, New Zealand, Australia, Malaya and Ceylon. The *Natal Advertiser* called for a branch of the League to be established in Durban and the *Adelaide Daily Mail* for the equivalent in Australia ('It is to be hoped that a branch of the League of Audiences is formed in each Australian State'); Wareing himself wrote an article for the New Zealand *Dominion*.[39] The Madras (Chennai) *Hindu* put the League's aims in a broader context: 'The revolt against the machine has broken out in an unexpected quarter'.[40] The *Hindu*, too, wondered: 'When will somebody think of doing the same thing [establishing something like the League] in India?'

## The League's Supporters

In addition to favourable press coverage, the League attracted to its 'Council of Associates' many leading theatrical figures, including J B Priestley, Arthur Wing Pinero, Sybil Thorndike and Lilian Baylis. Its smaller 'General Council', as the *Birmingham Mail* noted, was headed by the Archbishop of York, and included the Bishop of Worcester and James Maxton.[41] Priestley was a particular catch. In 1934 he was among Britain's most successful literary figures, famous for novels, plays and social commentary (his *English Journey* had just been published). In October 1934, the month the League was founded, he offered to include its circulars in programmes at the Duchess Theatre, which he co-managed and where his play *Eden End* was running.[42] In December 1934 the *Montreal Daily Star* reported 'Advocates of State Aid for the Stage in England Gain Supporter in J B Priestley',[43] he spoke at the launch of the League's Music and Drama Bill (see below), and he wrote the postscript to a 1936 League pamphlet 'The Audience Assists'.[44]

Wareing could generally find a wide range of celebrated 'names' to promote the League. A letter in its support published in *The Times* in April 1936[45] included among its signatories Lord Bessborough, the historian R H Tawney, the Archbishop of York, the Director of the Royal College of Music Sir Hugh Allen, the biologist Julian Huxley, the recently retired Conservative MP Sir Gervais Rentoul and the film producer Alexander Korda. And the League's membership, though never above a few hundred strong, was highly distinguished. Among its members, paying an annual subscription of 10s/6d, were the musicians Adrian Boult, Myra Hess, Imogen Holst and Henry Wood; the actors Peggy Ashcroft, Lewis Casson, Gracie Fields and John Gielgud; and some who became notable in the later history of public arts funding, including John Christie, Eric White and William Emrys Williams.[46]

## The League's Programme

As for what the press and these members were supporting, Wareing's original plan was:

> . . . that this Government should . . . vote £50,000 per annum, to be administered by a Commission appointed to disburse this sum to those British enterprises in Drama and Music which stand in need of assistance and are worthy and deserving. The Commissioners would make grants in the form of loans bearing interest, the principal to be repaid if and when profits are made . . . .[47]

The concept was fleshed out and modified, and the projected budget increased, in a draft Music and Drama Bill. The League's legal adviser, without other explanation, suggested the Forestry Act 1919, which had set up the Forestry Commission, as 'certainly . . . the Act most appropriate to use as a basis for the present Bill'.[48] The League's papers include a marked-up copy of the Forestry Act, with 'Forestry' replaced by 'Music and Drama' throughout, the deletion of sections such as that dealing with the prevention of damage by rabbits, and the addition of clauses relevant to grant-making in the arts.[49]

The Bill envisaged the government's providing an initial capital sum plus an annual grant.[50] The Crown would appoint eight Commissioners 'of whom two at least shall have special knowledge and experience – one of Music and one of Drama'. The relative lack of arts expertise among the Commissioners was not explained but may have been intended to prevent special pleading by professional interests and ensure that the League indeed represented audiences. Three of the Commissioners would be paid; a maximum of £4,500 a year was suggested as total salaries for the three. One of the unpaid Commissioners would be an MP. The Bill envisaged the Commissioners having wide powers. These included making grants or loans 'to any person including local authorities to promote or encourage Music or Drama' and managing 'any financially sound undertaking engaged in the production of musical or dramatic work'.

This latter provision was highly unpopular with theatrical managers, who saw it as an excessive power. It contributed to Wareing's failure to achieve regular public subsidy for music and drama by 1939. But what the League was *not* about was, ultimately, at least as damaging. The flipside of Wareing's singleness of purpose and persistence was a failure or inability to form an alliance with anyone whose aims differed even slightly from his own. This was clear as early as November 1934, in an interview published in *The Observer*.[51] Wareing acknowledged that the government's removal of Entertainments Duty from the Old Vic and Sadler's Wells theatres was 'a Governmental recognition that their work is of public importance'.[52] But 'our plan is not primarily or even remotely concerned with the entertainment duty. And it differs from most other schemes, whose idea is to build a National Theatre, and so forth.' Chapter 5 discusses the effects of Wareing's insistence on distancing the League from related campaigns.

## 'A piece of idealistic blackmailing': The League Gains Support

The League's Music and Drama Bill was launched at a 'Drawing-Room meeting at Seaford House' in May 1935, at which speakers including J B Priestley 'strongly advocated State recognition of Drama and Music and the general decision of the guests was that the time had come to approach the Government to that end'.[53] Priestley also 'deplored the anomaly that, while theatre-goers are taxed for their pleasures, novel-readers, via the public libraries, had free access to books bought with public money'.[54] This was another attack on Entertainments Duty, and again suggests that co-operation rather than antagonism between the two campaigns would have been to the benefit of both. The *Liverpool Post* reported that the gathering included Sir Thomas Beecham and Sir Cedric Hardwicke, and noted 'The League of Audiences was well and truly launched'; while *The Observer* commented: 'A powerful and organised League of Audiences might be able to bring off a "piece of idealistic blackmailing", making a Government listen to its mild demands. The chances are high, and the object is good.'[55] At a further 'at home', a few weeks later, Dame Sybil Thorndike gave a 'tempestuous speech' in favour of the League and the Bill.[56]

While the press was mainly favourable, the League tended to exaggerate the enthusiasm within government. Reporting to the League's Council of Management in October 1935, Harold Baker, then its General Secretary, wrote: 'In my opinion, the chances that the next Government ... will ultimately accept it [the Bill] are not merely good but steadily improving .... we already have strong supporters among Cabinet and ex-Cabinet Ministers .... Mr Wareing has secured an expression of opinion, most favourable to us, from the present Chancellor of the Exchequer [Neville Chamberlain].'[57] Baker's colleagues may have seen him as someone who spoke with authority about the political world. At this time he was Warden of Winchester College,[58] but he had been a Liberal MP before 1918 and a junior Minister under Asquith.[59] It was he who persuaded Lord Bessborough to become the League's President.[60]

Baker acknowledged that 'in view of the European situation, it is improbable that the next budget will allow the Chancellor ... to make the provision required by the Bill'. But he failed to note that in any case Chamberlain's support was more personal than political. Writing to Wareing in December 1935, Chamberlain was sympathetic to the League's aims but refused any public association with it: 'Although I believe I was the first to suggest a contribution from the rates to an orchestra in Birmingham when I was Lord Mayor ... it is many years since I have had anything to do with the matter.'[61] A subsequent letter, reported to the League's Council of Management in July 1936, may be seen as generally encouraging or kicking the subject into the long grass: 'I think you are setting about it in the right way, namely, by educating and arousing public opinion. It would be difficult for any Government to act without some organised and vocal backing.'[62] Chamberlain was not alone in seeing the government as following rather than leading public opinion on the issue; but Wareing put much weight on such statements. In his November 1934 *Observer* interview,[63] he said: 'Mr Baldwin was one of the first to be interested in this new movement, and he gave me an interview earlier in the year [the one he privately described at the time as 'an ordeal']... I have a very strong suspicion that the Government would not mind being "coerced" if it could be given proof that any large general body of voters ... were interested in the matter.'

Harold Baker's October 1935 report included some ideas for broadening the League's popular appeal, such as 'encouragement of Local Authorities to start

Open Air Theatres, particularly where there are numbers of unemployed',[64] campaigning against both theatre censorship and Entertainments Duty, and establishing 'offshoots [of the League] in the Dominions and Colonies'. But Baker was half-hearted about cuts in Entertainments Duty, suggesting that 'there is no demand for this, except from managers', and, as noted, Wareing actively opposed mingling the two campaigns. For Baker 'the Music and Drama Bill [should] be considered our main objective'; for Wareing it was the only objective.

Despite the League's limited success with the government, many MPs supported the Bill. In December 1936 eight Conservative, Labour and Independent MPs called a meeting at the House of Commons to 'discuss the formation of a Music and Drama Committee'; they promised an attendance including Laurence Binyon (the poet of 'For the Fallen') and Gracie Fields.[65] The *Daily Telegraph* reported that the meeting was 'presided over by Capt. V. A. Cazalet M.P., and addressed by ... [among others] Lord Bessborough ..., Dr. Malcolm Sargent ... and (the moving spirit) Mr. Alfred Wareing'.[66] The *Telegraph* commented:

> The questions before us were two. Shall mechanised music and drama be allowed triumphantly to extend their soulless sway without protest or defence ... on behalf of 'the real thing'? And.... Is not the time ripe for Laisser-faire to relinquish its grip on music and drama in England, seeing that it has been discredited in its workings in so many other directions, such as tramp steamers, sugar-beet and fat cattle?[67]

The answers provided were a clear 'No and 'Yes' respectively. The *Telegraph* strongly supported the principle of government involvement in the arts:

> On the day this [Music and Drama] bill becomes an Act of Parliament Laisser-faire will be recognised as having suffered defeat in one of its last and remotest strongholds.... The day may surely be hoped for when a repertory theatre in a town of 100,000 population will no more have to fight for existence than the library or museum.[68]

The left-wing *Daily Herald* noted the breadth of political support for the Bill: '... a meeting, arranged by the League of Audiences, supported the Music and Drama Bill – yes, and it is backed by Tory members.... "Fancy leaving that to private enterprise!" said one Tory! We are getting on.'[69]

The League saw further grounds for optimism around this time. A few weeks before the House of Commons meeting, Wareing discussed the League at 10 Downing Street with Sir Geoffrey Fry, Stanley Baldwin's Private Secretary. Fry's view was that 'the present Government would not be able to find the money for the Music and Drama Bill, but he thought the League of Audiences would ultimately come to success'[70] – the sort of 'jam tomorrow' pronouncement on which Wareing thrived. And some saw Neville Chamberlain's appointment as Prime Minister in May 1937 as a hopeful sign. The *Birmingham Post*, Chamberlain's home newspaper, commented: 'Now that we have a Prime Minister whose interest in drama and music is serious . . . we may perhaps look forward to some kind of State support of these intellectually still quite vigorous but materially languishing arts.'[71]

The *Post* had a nuanced view of the issue. It opposed direct government subsidy as 'entirely antagonistic to a democratic rule . . . [leading to] the subservience of art to national propaganda'; but it supported the League's Bill since funding decisions would be taken not by the government but by a Commission 'empowered to grant aid to dramatic companies and to choirs or orchestras which can prove to the satisfaction of experts the social and artistic value of their work and the necessity of some help to assure its continuance'. This description in 1937 of Wareing's proposed Commission is remarkably close to Keynes', eight years later, of the newly created Arts Council: '. . . a semi-independent body . . . provided with modest funds to stimulate, comfort and support any societies . . . which are striving with serious purpose and a reasonable prospect of success to present for public enjoyment the arts of music, drama and painting.'[72] With Chamberlain's appointment, the *Post* concluded, 'we seem to be nearer to the realisation of something of this kind than ever before'.

This optimism continued into 1938. *The Times* reported a further House of Commons meeting in February, which 'attracted Members of Parliament of all parties . . . in support of the Music and Drama Bill'. Little of substance occurred, though 'It was decided to summon a meeting at a later date and to invite the Prime Minister'.[73] Wareing explained to the meeting that 'the Bill came not from vested interests or professions, but from the electorate' and that 'the object of the Bill was to obtain Government recognition of music and drama without setting up a Ministry of Fine Arts'. The claim about the absence of vested interests was all too well-founded: as will be seen, opposition from vested interests in the theatre industry proved seriously harmful to the League.

*The Times* reported extreme claims made at the meeting, it is not clear by whom, for the Bill's effects in Britain and abroad:

> . . . the [Bill's] Commissioners would encourage . . . the organization of companies of the highest standard to produce notable English works of drama and music and present them overseas, where they would help bring a better understanding

> of our national outlook and so help to keep the peace of the world and preserve the spirit of community.

In Britain, the Bill would 'increase the amenities of rural life by visits of performers, orchestras, brass bands ... thus helping to arrest the drift to the towns'. Neither claim had much to do with the Bill's provisions. Both provided ammunition for its critics.[74]

Two other factors fed the League's optimism. The first was the removal of Entertainments Duty from some not-for-profit theatres, on the grounds that their work was partly educational.[75] When the government removed the duty from the Old Vic and Sadler's Wells, the *Sunday Times* suggested that 'for the first time it brought an aesthetic principle into politics.... The remission of a tax is, of course, a form of subsidy, and ... is given on aesthetic grounds.'[76] The issue was more complex than this. The exemption had no aesthetic motivation, and Wareing for one saw a great difference between tax exemption and subsidy – as he had said in his *Observer* interview, 'our plan is not primarily or even remotely concerned with the entertainment duty'.[77] Furthermore, in practice the campaign to end the duty clashed with and damaged the League of Audiences. On the other hand, Wareing saw the Old Vic and Sadler's Wells decision as 'a beginning. It is a Governmental recognition that their work is of public importance.'[78] This change to Entertainments Duty strengthened the view that arts subsidy was gaining support within the government.

The other ground for optimism was the 1937 Physical Training and Recreation Act. This authorized, and quickly led to, large-scale public funding of sports and recreational facilities. In the Act's first six months, forty-two grants were made for capital projects including swimming pools and community centres, plus 'a substantial sum ... placed at the disposal of the National Playing Fields Association'.[79] By November 1938 grants totalling around a million pounds had been made by central government to local authorities, with further grants to voluntary organizations.[80]

In the *Musical Times* in early 1938 Wareing suggested that this demonstrated 'the Government's attention to other forms of entertainment and recreation'.[81] He was not alone in seeing an analogy with funding for culture. Also in early 1938, J H Alden wrote in *Music & Letters*[82] that 'many people imagine the [League of Audiences'] proposals to be either too idealistic or to savour of undesirable Government control ... but ... the scheme bids fair to materialize sooner than the most hopeful at one time thought possible.... The Music and Drama Bill [is] ... complementary to the recent Physical Training and Recreation Act.' Alden reported that the initial capital to launch the physical training scheme was £2.4 million and the annual grant £170,000, figures far larger than those envisaged in Wareing's Bill. He suggested that the government's having made 'physical fitness . . . a subject for the law of the land . . . is evidence of an intention to go to the logical conclusion and to care also for the welfare of the nation's mind'. Alden quoted 'Scrutator', who in the *Sunday Times* in August 1937 had forcefully argued that there was a link between public funding of physical recreation and the League of Audiences' campaign:

> We are organizing the gymnastic of our body with the assistance of the State . . . by the same reasoning we must organize ourselves in the pleasures of the arts. . . . As youth and strength must exercise itself . . . so audiences . . . must organize themselves into a League as Mr. Alfred Wareing exhorts us. The cult of beauty in mind and body must be part of our democratic economy.

In early 1938 there seemed good grounds for believing that this vision could be realized.

## Notes

1 The papers of the League of Audiences are in the Victoria and Albert Museum Theatre and Performance Archives, with file prefix THM/149/; hereafter 'V&A/THM/149/-'.

2 *Daily Telegraph*, 5/12/36.

3 Ervine, p235.

4 'Candidus' was the pen name of Henry Newham (https://wellcomelibrary.org/item/b18228732#?c=0&m=0&s=0&cv=0., retrieved 19 September 2018). Later in the 1930s Newham became editor of the right-wing magazine *Truth* (R B Cockett: 'Ball, Chamberlain and *Truth*', *The Historical Journal*, Vol. 33 No. 1, March 1990, p134).

5 15/10/34.

6 London: Peter Davies, 1934.

7 Ibid., p234.

8 Ibid., pp235–6.

9 Ibid., p237.

10 *Alfred Wareing: a biography* (London: Green Bank Press, 1951), hereafter 'Isaac'.

11 Ibid., pp37–8.

12 See, for instance, George Rowell and Anthony Jackson: *The Repertory Movement: A History of Regional Theatre in Britain* (Cambridge: Cambridge University Press, 1984), pp46–8 and 66.

13 Isaac, p76.

14 http://hansard.millbanksystems.com/people/mr-walter-elliot, retrieved 21 December 2013.

15 Isaac, px.

16 Ibid., pxi, for all Elliot quotations in this paragraph.

17 Ibid., pix.

18 Ibid., px.

19 1/2/38.

20 Glyndebourne Archive, box file 'John Christie – letters re Glyndebourne – Conference of Musicians 5&6/3/1938 and 2/7/1938', Christie-Baker, 4/2/38.

21 Ibid., Baker-Christie, 8/2/38.

22 Ibid.

23 Lambeth Palace archive: Lang Papers L1-L17 1938, Vol 162, p346, Mallon-Lang, 21/4/38.

24 V&A/THM/149/5, Wareing-Selby 29/12/33.

25 Ibid., Wareing-E W Record, 12/3/34.

26 Ibid., Wareing-Billy Rhodes, 9/3/34.

27 Ibid., undated draft talk by Wareing.

28 12/10/34.

29 V&A/THM/149/3.

30 *Birmingham Mail,* 12/10/34.

31 12/10/34; the *Telegraph* had further positive coverage of the League on 2/12/36, 5/12/36 and 3/2/38.

32 For instance *Daily Sketch* 15/10/34, 11/4/35 and 14/2/38; *Observer* 3/6/34, 2/6/35, 29/9/35 and 6/12/36; *Morning Post* 12/10/34, 17/1/36, 5/1/37 and 12/1/37; and *Manchester Guardian* 12/10/34, 28/12/34 and 20/4/36.

33 All between 12 and 19 October 1934.

34 3/1/36.

35 13/10/34.

36 *The Times*, 16/1/36.

37 8/1/36.

38 All 16/1/36 except *Morning Post* (17/1/36) and *Cape Argus* (30/1/36).

39 *Natal Advertiser*, 23/5/36, *Adelaide Daily Mail*, 20/8/38, and *Dominion*, 2/6/36, respectively.

40 8/5/36.

41 V&A/THM/149/1, League's proof annual accounts for 1934/35.

42 V&A/THM/149/5, Wareing's report of 2/11/34 to the League's Executive Committee, for Priestley's offer; http://www.nimaxtheatres.com/duchess-theatre, retrieved 9 December 2013, for Priestley and the Duchess Theatre.

43 22/12/34.

44 BBC Written Archive Centre (hereafter 'BBC WAC') file R44/228: 'Publicity – League of Audiences 1934–1937'.

45 14/4/36.

46 V&A/THM/149/6, the League's membership card index.

47 V&A/THM/149/5, preamble to the League's 'Proposed Plan whereby the British Government may recognise the Arts of Drama and Music' (undated, but late 1934).

48 V&A/THM/149/4, opinion by R J Sutcliffe, Barrister, 21/12/35.

49 Ibid.

50 V&A/THM/149/5, synopsis accompanying printed version of the Bill.

51 25/11/34.

52 The campaign against Entertainments Duty is discussed in Chapter 9.

53 Isaac, p97.

54 Ibid.

55 31/5/35 and 2/6/35, respectively.

56 *Yorkshire Post*, 23/7/35.

57 V&A/THM/149/5, report dated 2/10/35.

58 http://discovery.nationalarchives.gov.uk/details/c/F38062. His letters to John Christie from this period, in the Glyndebourne archive, are on his headed Winchester notepaper. On Baker, see, further, Chapter 5.

59 https://api.parliament.uk/historic-hansard/people/mr-harold-baker/index.html, accessed 13 October 2018.

60 He undertook to do so in the report of 2/10/35 cited above.

61 V&A/THM/149/1, Chamberlain-Wareing, 21/12/35.

62 V&A/THM/149/3, report by Wareing, 10/7/36.

63 25/11/34.

64 V&A/THM/149/5, report of 2/10/35.

65 V&A/ THM/149/3, notice of 1/12/36 meeting.

66 5/12/36.

67 Ibid.

68 Ibid.

69 2/12/36.

70 V&A/ THM/149/7, minutes of League Executive Committee meeting, 5/11/36.

71 28/6/37, and for quotations from the *Post* in the following paragraph.

72 'The Arts Council: Its Policy and Hopes' (*The Listener*, 12/7/45).

73 10/2/38.

74 Including T S Eliot: see Chapter 4.

75 See Chapter 9, pp195–203.

76 7/4/35.

77 *The Observer*, 25/11/34.

78 Ibid.

79 HC Deb, 14/4/38, vol 334 cc1342-3W.

80 HC Deb, 17/11/38, vol 341 cc1052-3.

81 February 1938, p142.

82 *Music & Letters*, Vol 19, No1, January 1938, pp79–83, for all later quotations in this paragraph, including that from 'Scrutator'.

# 4

# The League of Audiences: (ii) Fear of the Machine and Distrust of the State

## Introduction

The League of Audiences' aims were simple – public subsidy for live drama and music, distributed by a body at arm's length from the government. The underlying arguments were more complex. The League was a coalition of practitioners and supporters of theatre and live music, drawn from across the political spectrum. But there were broadly ideological beliefs uniting most of those in favour of subsidy, and similarly ideological beliefs uniting most of those opposed to it.

For supporters, the unifying belief was that 'mechanized entertainment' – broadcasting, gramophone records and cinema – was harmful not only to theatre and live music but to society as a whole, in ways which went far beyond its economic impact. The first section of this chapter considers the origin, nature and extent of this view. The second section considers the involvement in the debate of the churches in general and the Church of England in particular.

The belief shared, or at least expressed, by many of the League's opponents was that government funding could harm artistic freedom, lead to state control of the arts and be misused by an authoritarian government. The final section of the chapter considers how strong, widespread, influential and sincerely held this view was.

## The League and Mechanized Art: (a) 'A sensation of impotence and dumb acquiescence'

The fear of 'mechanized art' in the 1930s, a prominent feature of the decade's cultural politics, has received little academic attention. It was part of a more general fear that people were becoming victims rather than masters of machines. The belief underlay, for instance, Charlie Chaplin's 1936 film *Modern Times*. It can also be seen in a speech the same year to the British Drama League by Elsie Fogarty, founder of the Central School of Speech and Drama, against 'such a movement as tap dancing [which] submitted the whole body to the rhythm of a machine'.[1] The practical aspect was the view that mass distribution of culture via film, recordings and radio would reduce demand for live performance and harm the music and theatre professions. Chapter 2 suggested that this fear was misplaced. Other elements of the campaign against the mechanized arts were moral and political.

## 'Condemned to death by being canned alive': The Scope of the Issue

The fight was fundamental to the philosophy of the League of Audiences from the start. Indeed, earlier still: a draft manifesto from early 1934, when its proposed name was 'The Fellowship of British Audiences', undertook that the Fellowship would provide 'British Audiences with an articulate voice to express the claims of audiences to see and hear living performers actually present in person wherever this just right may be challenged by the mechanical'.[2] And later the League briefly experimented with the Latin motto 'Homo Potior Machina' ('Man is Mightier than the Machine').[3]

The 'challenge of the mechanical' was central to press support of the Music and Drama Bill. An editorial in the *Manchester Guardian* argued that the growth of mechanical reproduction was self-defeating: 'What material will there be for the machine to reproduce if creative effort dwindles? . . . the decadence of creative work in two important arts makes the production of some such plan [as the Music and Drama Bill] one of considerable interest.'[4] Others had more fundamental objections. The *Birmingham Post* was concerned 'at the plight in which serious art finds itself owing to the mechanisation of public entertainment and, what is still worse, the appalling standardisation of this mechanical distribution'.[5] The *Post* warned: 'It will not be long before we shall . . . have lost all sense of the difference between celluloid or shellac and human flesh and blood, if something is not done to save actors and musicians from being, as it were, condemned to death by being canned alive. But the League of Audiences can do it.'[6]

The *Daily Sketch* took a line based partly on equity: central and local government had long funded the visual arts; the performing arts should receive similar treatment, and the threat of mechanized art had increased the need. As already noted, the *Sketch* was an early and consistent supporter of the League, perhaps surprising for a populist and politically Conservative newspaper. In February 1938, the *Sketch*'s commentator 'Candidus' was 'pleased to see that

Mr. Alfred Wareing's Music and Drama Bill continues to gain supporters, both in Parliament and in the country'.[7] 'Candidus' supported the Bill because it was 'no more than an accident of history that has given the pictorial arts a claim on the public purse which is denied to music and drama . . . [and because] the grievance of music and drama would not be so grievous but for the rise of wireless entertainment, . . . [which] enables the Government to say that its patronage of the arts is not confined to pictures'. Unusually, 'Candidus' criticized unsubsidized live as well as broadcast art – and audiences: 'The average commercial play is for people who have dined well and are having a night out. Audiences – whether in theatres or over the wireless – are becoming more and more passive: the practice of the arts of music and the drama is something that is switched on or plugged in.'

As discussed in Chapter 3, the fight against mechanized art was sometimes linked with that against physical passivity, with the government's funding of physical recreation seen as a hopeful sign for music and drama. For some, the analogy went further. Thus 'Scrutator' wrote in the *Sunday Times* in 1937 that:

> . . . there was danger that our democracy would become merely the passive recipients of manufactured pleasures, instead of being the artificers of their own joy. Sport was in danger of becoming something to read about or watch, not to engage in; music of being something you turned on with a handle instead of making; and the vast silent audiences of the cinema took in but never assisted at a performance.[8]

Chapter 2 suggested that this fear too – that broadcasting, for instance, threatened amateur music-making – was misplaced; but the fear seems to have been genuine.

Along the same lines but more generally, writing in the *Yorkshire Post* in April 1936 Sir Gervais Rentoul, ex-MP, founding Chairman of the Conservative backbench 1922 Committee and a member of the League of Audiences' Executive Committee, described 'the new mechanisation' as producing 'a sensation of impotence and dumb acquiescence'.[9] These words may have been written for Rentoul by Alfred Wareing: see below. The same month, the *Glasgow Herald* merely noted that 'In another column today, Mr. Alfred Wareing, whose name and achievements will not be readily be forgotten by friends of the old Glasgow repertory theatre movement, discusses the function of the audience and the part it has to play in saving music and the drama from the evils inherent in mechanical reproduction'[10] – the evils apparently being too obvious to require spelling out. By the late 1930s television was considered alongside cinema, radio and recording as a potential drug for its audiences. Writing to Wareing in July 1939 the Secretary of the Theatrical Management Association (not a supporter of the League)[11] agreed that 'the whole question is one of man v machine, but we want man to control the machine, and not to become its slave as Television will make him if we are not careful'.[12] (It is a picturesque detail that Alfred Wareing's daughter, the actor Lesley Wareing, starred as Lydia Languish in a television production of Sheridan's *The Rivals* broadcast in August 1938 from Alexandra Palace.)[13]

The actor and theatrical manager Lena Ashwell expressed opposition to mechanized art in both a moderate and an extreme form. Ashwell was famous for providing drama productions for troops at the front in World War I and for equivalent work in London boroughs after the war.[14] Her memoir *Myself a Player* (1936)[15] presented this view of the theatre/cinema distinction: '... the theatre demands the co-operation of the audience and establishes a living cord in which the audience give, as well as receive. The cinema is a picture, observed with interest, but necessarily the audience is merely the spectator.'[16] This was a common argument: that film, recordings and radio provided 'product' for passive consumers while inherent in live theatre and music was collaboration between performers and audience – though the nature of the collaboration was rarely spelt out.

Ashwell's other position was starker, linking mechanized art explicitly with political dictatorship: 'no adverse force, whether the limitation of art ..., the Entertainment Tax or the expense which excludes patrons, is half so disastrous to the drama as the influence of the machine.'[17] After arguing that the microphone and film camera had diminished the art of acting, she damned cinema with the very faintest praise as having 'provided amusement as an alternative to drinking'.[18] Then she got into her stride. For her, the defining element of cinema was the producer/director:

> All the creative powers which spring up within the artist are inhibited by being directed, so all spontaneity and freedom of expression are reduced to efficiency .... It is an age of Producer-Directors: Stalin at Moscow, Mussolini in Rome, Hitler in Berlin, conducting a mass-mind and using such instruments as death or ruin as penalties for independent thought or independent action.[19]

## 'Death to Hollywood'?

While Ashwell was rare in drawing a direct parallel between cinema and totalitarian government, she was among many who disliked and distrusted the medium. Some attacked it in general; others focused on the influence of American popular culture via Hollywood in particular – a concern mainly associated with later decades, but strongly present in the 1930s. Writing about the December

1936 House of Commons meeting of the League of Audiences, the *Daily Express* reported the comedian Gillie Potter telling the assembled MPs: 'Simple people in the shires of England are addressing each other in the patois of the middle States of America. This [Music and Drama] Bill will help the British actor to counteract this effect on our people.'[20] Similarly, in J B Priestley's *English Journey* (1934), 'they ['girls' in Boston, Lincolnshire] are almost indistinguishable from girls in a dozen different capitals, for they all have the same models, from Hollywood'.[21]

Hostility to Hollywood could take extreme forms. As was seen in Chapter 2, the playwright and *Observer* critic St John Ervine was among the extremists, inveighing against 'pop-eyed illiterates ... gaping at the Garbo!'.[22] He was better disposed to other aspects of mechanized art (see below), but loathed cinema unreservedly. He feared that theatre was losing out to cinema ('Shall I ever forget my dismay when, on pilgrimage to Bergen to see the little theatre in which Ibsen learnt his craft, I found that it, too, had been given over to the pictures!'),[23] and saw the struggle between theatre and cinema as surrogate for a greater battle: 'The mechanisation of mankind is rapidly being accomplished. We have canned music and canned actors.'[24] But his book *The Theatre in My Time* ended on a note of surprising, indeed inconsistent, optimism: '... some cheerfully announce its [theatre's] imminent demise. But it lives on, and presently, when adult minds prevail again, it will revive.... Even in these days ... a good play will outlast the most popular picture. Can creatures of celluloid prevail over living actors? Not in a world of living men and women!'[25]

Ervine was an early and strong supporter of the League of Audiences. In 1935 he wrote in *The Observer*,[26] in one of his more pessimistic moods, that 'we are in grave danger of rearing up a machine-maddened people who have lost their sight and their hearing and the use of their hands, and have no taste.... [This] is the problem which Mr. Alfred Wareing, this man whose faith moves mountains, is setting out to attack and solve.' Ervine quoted Wareing himself as suggesting that 'the mechanisation of amusement ... produce[s] a feeling of impotence, a dumb acquiescence [the phrase used by Sir Gervase Rentoul in the *Yorkshire Post* article quoted above]'. The *Daily Telegraph*'s report of the December 1936 House of Commons meeting concurred. Two speakers had discussed '"the devouring onrush of mechanical amusement." The devourers, hardly named, but present in the minds of all, were, of course, the B.B.C., the H.M.V., but above all, the cinema.'[27]

John Maynard Keynes made a direct and gratuitous attack of this sort in his 1945 radio talk about the Arts Council, while extolling Englishness in art: 'Let every part of Merry England be merry in its own way. Death to Hollywood.'[28] But there were always powerful voices on the other side. The 1932 report *The Film in*

*National Life*,[29] produced by the Commission on Educational and Cultural Films and funded by the Carnegie UK Trust, provides a contrasting view of the theatre versus cinema debate soon after the arrival of the talkies. The Commission's membership was large and varied, including academics, civil servants, county Directors of Education, St John Ervine and the editor of the BBC magazine *The Listener*.[30] Its aim was to investigate film's educational and cultural value, and the report's major outcome was the creation in 1933 of the British Film Institute.[31] Among the report's starting points was one equally applicable to any technological change: 'It is as idle to rail at the machines, to talk of "mechanised culture" and "canned music," as it would have been to ignore the invention of printing as a cultural influence.'[32] And among its cultural observations was a suggestion that, by 1932, previously snobbish attitudes towards the cinema had relaxed:

> A fellow of an Oxford College no longer feels an embarrassed explanation to be necessary when he is recognised leaving a cinema. A growing number of cultivated and unaffected people enjoy going to the pictures, and frequent not merely the performances of intellectual film societies, but also the local picture house to see, for instance, Marlene Dietrich.[33]

The novelist Graham Greene, film critic for *The Spectator* and *Night and Day* for much of the 1930s,[34] went further in a 1937 essay. For him, film had surpassed theatre in depicting 'Life as it is and life as it ought to be ... The stage of course has long ceased ... [to do so] at all. Mr St John Irvine [*sic*], Miss Dodie Smith, these are the popular playwrights of the moment: they have no sense of life as it is lived.'[35]

Some supporters of the League of Audiences occupied the middle ground between these intensely pro- and anti-cinema positions. They argued that live and mechanized arts were mutually dependent, that each strengthened the other, and that films, broadcasts and recordings both promoted and required a healthy tradition of live performance. Such views led the *The Radio Times*, published by the 'mechanized' BBC, to print articles supporting the League:

> It is only the most prejudiced and near-sighted person who can think there is any essential rivalry between, say, broadcasting and the theatre, or broadcasting and the concert hall.... Broadcasting is not necessary to, but can help, the theatre; the theatre is necessary to, and can help, broadcast drama... a visible audience is an important factor in any healthy art....[36]

And among publicly declared donors to the League were not only the Governors of the Shakespeare Memorial Theatre and Rupert D'Oyly Carte (proprietor of the eponymous opera company, and thus keeper of the flame of Gilbert and Sullivan operettas), but also the film producer Alexander Korda.[37]

Wareing himself did not accept that mechanized art could assist live performance, but saw a relationship of dependence in the other direction:

> This League ... stands for Man versus Machinery. In all such contests hitherto man has lost, but if he wakes up and joins the League of Audiences he will not lose now; for ... the machine needs man and cannot function without him.... Makers of mechanized amusement depend upon a constant flow of creative artists.... So the big men in the mechanical amusement industry were among the first to come forward and aid this movement...[38]

## Opposition to 'Mechanized Music'

In assessing the health of live classical music in the 1930s, Chapter 2 considered the role of the BBC, the dominant force in classical music in Britain. Supporters of subsidy tended to be less hostile to the BBC than to the film industry. By contrast with the views about cinema of those in the theatre world, generally negative and rarely warmer than neutral, commentators such as Arthur Bliss and Mary Glasgow acknowledged that broadcast music positively encouraged both amateur music-making and attendance at live music.

Even some of League's fundamentalist cinema haters were well disposed to the BBC and the gramophone. St John Ervine was almost gushing: 'Mechanisation has undeniably achieved great results and done great good. The labourer in a remote hamlet, who had no expectation of ever hearing Beethoven's *Symphony No 7* ... now hears ... [it] as easily as if he were an habitué of the Queen's or the Albert Hall. The world has been widened for millions of men and women by the B.B.C.'[39] J B Priestley wrote in 1937, of broadcasts and recordings, that 'now I make my own programmes at home, and though the performances are not quite so vivid and exciting, I can choose them myself, and they are free from that prima donna silliness ... which still runs riot in big concert halls.'[40] He painted a fairly accurate view of a future which may have appeared dystopian to opponents of mechanized music: 'What we need now is a tiny portable instrument, to which one listens through earphones, so that it does not disturb anybody else, and whole symphonies and concertos and operas recorded on miniature rolls of film so that they could easily be carried about with us. Then we could lie in our bed at sea or in the desert, and still have our music.'[41]

Nonetheless broadcast music was by no means exempt from the sort of attacks which the League mounted against cinema. Most originated within the musical world. Sir Thomas Beecham's diatribe against the BBC's 'monstrous monopoly of the air' is one example.[42] The composer, conductor and critic Constant Lambert provides another, rather more interesting. At twenty-one Lambert had composed a ballet score for Diaghilev's Ballets Russes,[43] and he was still in his twenties when, in 1934, his book *Music Ho!* was published.[44] It remained influential for many years; a reviewer commented on a 1960s reprint that 'There can be no disputing the fact that *Music Ho!* 'has achieved the status of a classic', as the publisher's blurb goes'.[45] *Music Ho!*, subtitled '*A Study of Music in Decline*', was primarily an attack on trends in modern music; but Lambert devoted several chapters to what he called 'The Mechanical Stimulus'.[46]

Lambert's argument was that 'Since the advent of the gramophone, and more particularly the wireless, music of a sort is everywhere and at every time; in the heavens, the lower parts of the earth, the mountains, the forest and every tree therein. It is a Psalmist's nightmare.'[47] Lambert's was a subtler and less elitist version of T S Eliot's 'more means worse' argument in his post-war *Notes Towards the Definition of Culture* (see below). For Lambert, the wider availability of music, primarily due to the radio, meant a dilution of the *intensity* of musical experience. He saw this happening both in people's homes ('the more people use the wireless, the less they listen to it')[48] and in public. As to the latter, he wrote:

> In the neighbourhood where I live ... there is a loudspeaker every hundred yards or so, and it is only rarely that they are tuned in to different stations ... It would not matter so much were the music bad music but, as the B.B.C. can boast with some satisfaction, most of it is good. We board buses to the strains of Beethoven and drink our beer to the accompaniment of Bach.[49]

... which may have been an exaggeration to bolster and dramatize the argument.

Lambert objected on grounds of monotony and unsuitability, novel arguments in 1934. He also argued that the BBC exercised undue influence on the creation of popular artistic taste – that 'the whole of London ... is made to listen to the choice of a privileged few, or even a privileged one'.[50] The 'privileged one' was Christopher Stone, 'whose well-modulated voice has doubtless given pleasure to millions'.[51] Stone was (according to Asa Briggs) 'the first of the British "disc jockeys" and thereby "founder of a very exclusive profession"'.[52] Lambert noted that 'at certain hours of the day it is impossible for anyone to escape from his breezy diffidence. That he is a benevolent autocrat I am sure is true. ... But the fact remains that he enjoys a position of dictatorship as fantastic as anything in Aldous Huxley's *Brave New World*'.[53]

Lambert reiterated his concern at the high quality of the music now so widely available: '... we are fast losing even the minor stimulus of genuine healthy vulgarity. In the present age it is impossible to escape from Culture.'[54] He feared that this would 'eventually produce in us, when we hear a Bach concerto, the faint nausea felt towards a piece of toffee by a worker in a sweet factory'. Lambert considered the situation 'even more trying for the musical than for the non-musical'. Such views were ahead of their time. Even thirty years later, in 1964, Benjamin Britten attracted controversy for saying something similar:

> [Music] can be audible in any corner of the globe, at any hour of the day or night, through a loudspeaker, without any question of suitability or comprehensibility.... If I say the loudspeaker is the principal enemy of music, I don't mean that I am not grateful to it as a means of education.... But it is not part of true musical *experience*.... Music demands more from a listener than simply the possession of a tape machine or a transistor radio.[55]

Britten later suggested that 'I may have slightly overstated the case'.[56]

## The League and Mechanized Art: (b) The Involvement of the Churches

Lambert's and Britten's objections to 'mechanized music', stated a generation apart, were primarily cultural: both were concerned about its effects on music and listeners rather than on society as a whole (despite Lambert's reference to Huxley's *Brave New World*, published only two years before *Music Ho!*). But as discussed above, the issue of live versus mechanized art was also seen as a battle to preserve values believed threatened by an increasingly regimented and uniform way of life. It is in this context that the Catholic and Anglican press, and Anglican Church leaders, became involved. As early as May 1935, *Christian World* reported on the League of Audiences' 'campaign to save music and drama in this country from the curse of too much mechanization ... The League's proposals seem to have a real social importance.'[57] The following month, the *Catholic Herald* gave substantial coverage to what it called 'A Society for the Protection of "Personal" Arts'.[58] Under the subheading 'Danger of Mechanism', the *Herald* argued the case for government support, and cited a precedent: 'Everyone will remember that the B.B.C. came to the aid of the promenade concerts at Queen's Hall a few years ago, for even they were in financial difficulties.' This was a rare acknowledgement that the BBC was itself a major public funder of the arts.

The involvement in the League of senior members of the Church of England, led by William Temple, Archbishop of York, particularly caught the attention of the religious press. From the League's earliest days, Temple headed the names on its General Council[59] and was one of its Vice-Presidents.[60] Temple, who was to succeed Cosmo Lang as Archbishop of Canterbury in 1942, had long been active in social and political causes (he had been a member of the Labour Party and was the first President of the Workers' Educational Association).[61] In June 1937 he planned to address the Church Assembly in favour of a motion supporting the League.[62] For reasons not easy to discern the debate did not take place, but in early 1938 Temple revived the motion and wrote an article for the *Daily Telegraph* promoting the League and the Music and Drama Bill.[63] It took up most of a page, with the headline 'Mass-produced Entertainment Is Not Enough – Now the Nation Must Support Human Elements'. Under the subheading 'Peril to Whole Spiritual Life', Temple wrote that the Bill 'should be able to claim the support of all who appreciate the deep unity of a people's culture and spiritual life .... We do well to welcome the wireless and the film; we shall do ill if we allow them to obliterate the creative work of musical and dramatic artists in living touch with the audiences which they bring together.' *The Quiver* magazine noted: '. . .it testifies to the change in public opinion that a leading dignitary of the Church should be pleading for the better recognition of drama. May we not ... say that the effort of the Archbishop ... is but a sign of the very healthy reaction from the mass-production which is threatening all of us?'[64]

In a story headed 'Archbishops Disagree About State Subsidy', the *Manchester Guardian* reported on Temple's motion for the Church Assembly.[65] The motion urged the government to 'recognize' music and drama as it did libraries, museums and galleries, and pledged the Church Assembly's support for the principles of the Music and Drama Bill. It suggested that live performance created a greater sense of community than broadcasts or films ever could; that a reduction in professional live performances harmed amateur music and drama; and that 'there would be a danger for the film industry itself if there should be no adequate supply of actors trained in direct intercourse with an audience'. The *Guardian* reported that Cosmo Lang opposed the motion on the grounds that 'the Assembly was not sufficiently informed about the proposed bill to justify passing the motion ... [and] libraries and museums were public institutions different from private enterprises like theatres'.[66]

The *Church Times* devoted an equivocal editorial to this disagreement.[67] On the one hand, 'Gramophone, film and radio have brought entertainment in abundance ... there has probably been a valuable gain in aesthetic appreciation, and a considerable advance in musical education.' On the other, 'amateur music-making and drama could not be expected to thrive against the competition of the singing and playing of the most gifted artists of the day broadcast into every home.' Furthermore, the price of mechanized art was that 'thousands of actors, actresses, musicians and variety artists have been put out of employment ... [and] it has induced a passivity unknown at any former age'. Chapter 2 cast strong doubt on the former assertion, and it is not clear how the latter squared with the alleged gain in aesthetic appreciation. In any case, despite its concerns about mechanized art, the *Church Times* thought the cure proposed in the Music and Drama Bill more dangerous than the disease: it 'seems to us to smack ominously of Fascist methods ... once let Commissioners ... have a footing in the theatre, and much of that spontaneity and creativeness that the Archbishop [of York] desires to foster will be destroyed' – a concern explored below.

The *Catholic Herald* reported on the Archbishops' disagreement and the *Church Times*' 'Fascist' gibe: 'What, then, is one to make of the opposition of the Archbishop of Canterbury on the feeble pretext that the Church Assembly did not know enough about the Bill (its provisions have been before the Assembly for three sessions)? What is one to say of the *Church Times*' suggestion that parts of the Bill smack of Fascism (not Socialism, mind you)?'[68] The *Herald* left these questions hanging. But less than three months later the disagreement seemed resolved: on 5 May 1938 Cosmo Lang presided at a meeting at Toynbee Hall to promote the Music and Drama Bill.[69]

A likely cause of Lang's change of heart was a typically direct letter (using equally typical moral blackmail) from Alfred Wareing.[70] This claimed that 'your [Lang's] statement "that the Church Assembly was not sufficiently informed about the proposed Bill to justify a Motion" is unfair to the League and to me personally ... such damage as this statement has already done should be repaired as soon as possible'. Lang's Chaplain, the Rev. A C Don, noting that Wareing seemed 'much distressed' by Lang's words asked the Secretary of the Church Assembly whether the motion might be reinstated.[71] The reply was discouraging: '... it is obviously not [a subject] in which the Assembly as such is particularly interested.'[72] But the campaign for Lang's support spread.

First, Don and William Temple agreed between them that a new Church Assembly motion supporting the Bill should be tabled.[73] Second, Lord Rathcreedan (from whom no other record survives of interest in the League) requested that Lang support a motion in favour of the Bill in a possible House of Lords debate.[74] Don replied that Lang could not propose the motion, but 'is genuinely interested in the subject and is anxious to do what he can to help'.[75]

And third, George Gordon, Vice-Chancellor of Oxford University and Lord Bessborough's successor as President of the League of Audiences, wrote asking Lang to help the League in any way he could.[76] The League was apparently on Lang's mind: replying to Gordon he reported that he had 'had a long talk with [James] Mallon of Toynbee Hall today on the subject of the League of Audiences and the proposed Bill.... [because] it is always awkward if one introduces a subject without having considered all possible objections to it'.[77] The outcome was Lang's decision to chair the Toynbee Hall meeting.[78]

Preparing for the meeting, Lang again consulted Mallon. Mallon's reply (describing Wareing as a 'simple and loveable man') was quoted in Chapter 3. Mallon also undertook to consult 'the Treasury official who advised on the form of the [Music and Drama] Bill ... [and who] thought that the Forestry Commission was closely analogous'.[79] (Lang's papers contain no results from this consultation.) In addition, Alfred Wareing met and provided written briefing for Lang.[80]

An invited audience of around a hundred, including five MPs, attended the Toynbee Hall meeting.[81] Among the speakers was the critic James Agate, who, according to Wareing's disciple Winifred Isaac, 'gave a glowing account of what the Works Progress Administration was doing to help music and the stage in the United States'.[82] Agate himself recorded in his diary: 'The important points are how much the people can afford ... what balance of loss that must leave, and whether the government can afford to make up that loss. The vital thing in this question is not eloquence but data. Yet I'll bet that tomorrow morning the Times reports only the Archbishop.'[83] He was broadly correct.

John Christie of Glyndebourne, whose relationship with the League is discussed in Chapters 5 and 6, also spoke. Isaac suggested that he did little to advance the League's cause: 'Mr Christie obviously favoured a more selective encouragement.... [He] asserted that there was no demand for what was good; there was only a demand for what people were accustomed to see, which in these days was films.'[84] Cosmo Lang himself recorded: 'I expressed my general sympathy with the objects of the League and the meeting. But I was careful to point out that I could not be expected to approve of all the content of the Music and Drama Bill.'[85] *The Times*' report of the meeting[86] was less nuanced: Lang had noted that 'the first difficulty was the increasing mechanization of both music and drama'; had suggested that 'there was precedent [for state subsidy of music and drama] in the museums, libraries and picture galleries'; and had 'express[ed] his cordial sympathy with the [Bill's] general principle'.

Thus by May 1938 the Archbishops of Canterbury and York appeared to be on the same side as the *Catholic Herald*. The aim of the Music and Drama Bill, according to the *Herald*, was to persuade the government to protect live music and drama 'in an age when both are rapidly succumbing to mechanisation . . . by means which enable the public to be a purely passive recipient needing only to press a button to be doped by entertainment. . . . As the age of leisure develops, so will the evil of mechanised entertainment.'[87]

These images are closer to Huxley's *Brave New World* than was Constant Lambert's description of the 'position of dictatorship' enjoyed by a BBC presenter.

## 'Under the shadow of a new State obligation': Opposition to the League of Audiences

The League of Audiences argued that without government subsidy for live performances, the public would respond with 'dumb acquiescence . . . [to] the devouring onrush of mechanised amusement'. At the same time an argument with similarly loaded imagery reached a very different conclusion: that subsidy itself would lead artists and public to respond with dumb acquiescence to an over-powerful government. As discussed in Chapter 1, writers such as Andrew Sinclair and Jörn Weingärtner have ignored the former view and focused on the latter alone, to bolster their case that support for arts subsidy was almost non-existent in the 1930s, or that subsidy was regarded with active hostility, or both. They have exaggerated the extent of opposition to subsidy in the 1930s, but it did exist.

Sir Thomas Beecham presented it in characteristically niche form. Beecham, a large, unpredictable and often mistrusted force in the arts at the time, was an ambivalent supporter of the Music and Drama Bill. Writing to Alfred Wareing in March 1937, he expressed general agreement, but was concerned that 'out of eight Commissioners to be appointed [under the Bill], only two are required to have any special knowledge and experience of the subject'.[88] He feared that the Commission would be a body 'selected upon the plausible principle that, knowing nothing whatever about the subject it has to administer or deal with, it is thereby enabled to preserve an open mind about it. My experience is that in all artistic matters, an open mind is the same as a vacant one.' Beecham continued: 'I am from beginning to end against the inclusion among the Board of Commissioners of political "duds" and departmental "washouts", and any attempt to provide . . . places for the more conspicuous failures in our political world will meet with the most strenuous opposition . . . from one representative at least of the musical profession.'

Other commentators presented more 'classic' statements of the view that state subsidy, and the Music and Drama Bill in particular, would open the way to state control of the arts. It is worth considering three of them – one from the political left, one from the right and one probably disingenuous and motivated largely by self-interest.

The last of these was expressed by the British Drama League (BDL) in private correspondence and in the pages of its magazine *Drama*. The BDL was an important organization in the theatrical world, its Director, Geoffrey Whitworth, skilled at forming alliances and securing influential backers. But its argument against the Bill had an ulterior motive, as part of Whitworth's larger campaign against the League of Audiences and seeking an end to Entertainments Duty.[89] The issue emerged first in a letter of March 1937 from Whitworth to Wareing,[90] a solemn counterpart to Beecham's more cavalier correspondence.

Whitworth paid glowing tribute to Wareing ('You have yourself worked so long and so nobly for the Theatre'), as prelude to criticizing the Bill. While 'it would be fantastic to assume that you would willingly associate yourself with any movement which might have an opposite result to that which you and we desire', Whitworth felt that Wareing had not properly considered the arguments against the Bill. Among these was one about state control. Whitworth claimed to support subsidy in principle. His work with the Carnegie UK Trust had convinced him of its value, and 'An extension of that policy, under the permanent control of the State, could do an immense amount to preserve the living Art of the Theatre'. But for Whitworth, the Bill went damagingly far beyond this, giving the Commissioners power 'to engage in theatrical management on their own account … which might easily end in control of the entire entertainment industry by the State'. Whitworth's argument then took a surprising turn: he suggested that Wareing was 'presenting the Government of the day with a weapon they could use … with a universality scarcely second to that of the British Broadcasting Corporation itself'. So – according to Whitworth – while there were deep objections of principle to the Bill, the BBC already embodied these objections in a more extreme form.

This is one reason why one might doubt Whitworth's apparent concern about the Bill. The BDL's role, position and public statements suggest other reasons. The BDL represented a wide range of interests, including those of commercial theatre managers. Whitworth's letter included the comment that 'Interference with private enterprise should surely be forbidden' (his emphasis), suggesting that his concern was with political influence on the business side of theatre at least as much as with state control of content. Furthermore, elsewhere he and the BDL repeatedly argued that abolishing Entertainments Duty on live performances, sought particularly by the commercial theatre sector, was a higher priority than subsidy, and indeed that the campaign for subsidy was a damaging diversion from this. Finally, Whitworth's letter reported that 'having had opportunities for first-hand study of the Theatre both in Soviet Russia and in Germany, I have come to the conclusion that although State control has undoubtedly given opportunities for theatrical production on a scale unknown in non-totalitarian States, the result has been unfavourable to dramatic expression'. Given this tame criticism of cultural practice in totalitarian states, it is reasonable to doubt Whitworth's apparently intense opposition of principle to the modest and arm's length state involvement envisaged in Wareing's Bill.

That was a private communication. Whitworth and the BDL also dealt with the issue in the magazine *Drama,* which Whitworth edited. In 1937 and 1938, *Drama* reported several times on state arts funding abroad. It gave positive coverage to the US Federal Theatre Project, part of President Roosevelt's Works Progress Administration and a programme far larger, and more directly under government control, than anything envisaged by the League of Audiences. In July 1937 *Drama* printed a long, eulogistic article about 'the true National Theatre of America' which was 'springing into being with all the vigour of a giant'.[91] The writer was optimistic that if current progress was maintained, 'the W.P.A. Theatre ... will undoubtedly prove the most impressive theatre in the world'. He noted that since it 'originally came into being to deal with the problem of the many players who were literally starving due to the depression ... the trend of the theatre is definitely and understandably "left"'. Yet in three highly positive pages there was just one reference to the danger that 'being Government controlled it can be used as a powerful political weapon, a fact which the Anti-Roosevelt group are not slow to point out' – but a fact which did not otherwise appear to trouble the writer.

There was a further article on the Federal Theatre Project, by its Director, Hallie Flanagan, in November 1938. This made no reference to the danger of government control; indeed, there was little mention of the Project's politics beyond Flanagan's opening claim that 'Government support of the theatre brings the United States into the best historic theatre tradition'.[92] The accompanying editorial was equally silent on the issue, noting merely that 'we are pleased to be able to print an authoritative account' of the Project.[93]

More startling was an article in the January 1937 issue, 'The Theatre in Berlin'.[94] This contained no hint of concern about state control. Instead it reported: 'Last season the National-Socialist Government subsidised the German theatre to the extent of thirty-six million marks. Out of the twenty-three important theatres in Berlin, thirteen are still privately owned, five are under the direction of General Goering; while another five are protected by Dr. Goebbels.' The author went on to note that 'National Socialism's main contribution to drama has been the construction of a number of open-air theatres which have been built with the help of the compulsory Labour Service'.

Given the extraordinary tone of this article, the absence of articles in *Drama* expressing critical views of theatre in Nazi Germany, and *Drama*'s dismissal of the political dangers of the Federal Theatre Project, it is hard to take at face value Whitworth's concerns that the Music and Drama Bill would damage artistic freedom.

Despite the views Whitworth expressed to Alfred Wareing, the BDL delayed adopting a formal public position on the Bill. *Drama* gave Wareing space in its November 1937 issue to write about it.[95] He began with a question based on a doubtful premise: 'Does it make you uncomfortable to know that . . . ours is now the only Government in the whole world which does nothing for Drama?' He sought to deal with the concern that government funding might lead to government control by distinguishing between direct funding by a Ministry of Fine Arts ('people . . . know about the evils which lurk in these Ministries') and the Bill's proposed Commission at one remove from the government.

Wareing's belief that direct government funding would threaten freedom of expression seems to have been sincere. A copy of the Bill in the Lambeth Palace archive contains his manuscript note: 'It is the general opinion that a Ministry of Fine Arts would establish a Dictatorship, would become a hot-bed of intrigue, and a dangerous instrument of propaganda.'[96] But Wareing's distinction between direct and arm's length funding failed to reassure the BDL. In April 1938 *Drama* announced: 'The time has come when it seems only right that readers of "Drama" should be informed of the official attitude of the Drama League to the League of Audiences and to the Music and Drama Bill.'[97] The attitude was not positive. *Drama* paid tribute to Wareing's 'indominatable [*sic*] courage' and noted that he had gone 'further than any of his predecessors in obtaining State aid for the theatre'. But while conceding (unlike Whitworth, writing to Wareing a year earlier) that 'the Bill itself is . . . contrived on a sound principle', it concluded 'with the utmost regret' that the BDL could not fully endorse it. It put forward two main reasons. The first, that ending Entertainments Duty on live performances was a higher priority than gaining subsidy, is discussed later. The other was that 'A Government of propagandist tendency might easily, through subservient Commissioners, gain ideological control of the theatres benefiting by their grants ... A National Theatre is one thing. The nationalisation of the theatre another. It seems to us that the objection has only to be stated to become conclusive.'

Given the approving articles in *Drama* about state-funded theatre in the USA and even Nazi Germany, it is difficult to see why the BDL saw this objection as 'conclusive'.

There were others whose opposition to state subsidy on such grounds was more clearly sincere. One was the playwright Benn Levy. Levy became an MP, on the left of the Labour Party, in the Attlee administration, and – surprisingly, given his pre-war views – a member of the Arts Council and of its Executive Committee from 1953 to 1961.[98] Levy had been at the House of Commons meeting of February 1938, discussed in Chapter 3, and wrote to Wareing about the Music and Drama Bill a few weeks later.[99] For Levy, 'this question of freedom, especially in these times, is of over-riding importance, and I hoped to persuade you [that] ... you and your enthusiasm would serve the theatre much better by pressing for its emancipation from its present control instead of putting it under the shadow of a new State obligation.' He suggested that if Wareing 'should still believe that money is more important to the theatre than freedom ... abolishing the Entertainment Tax ... is obviously a far better form of subsidy in that it admits of ... no possibility of even indirect State interference'. He concluded: '... much as I hate to be, I am definitely against you, and with the friendliest goodwill in the world I shall do my best either to oppose your plan or, better still, convert you to mine.'

Levy next went public, in the Society of Authors' journal *The Author*.[100] He insisted that he had no wish 'to start a dog fight with the League of Audiences, which happens to be that rare occurrence in the world of the theatre, a body forceful, well-organized and effectual'. Instead, he hoped to persuade it 'to reconsider the highly debatable means by which it proposes to seek an objective that is not debatable at all'. He argued for remission of Entertainments Duty in almost identical terms to those in his letter to Wareing. But direct state subsidy was very different: '... if we are to pipe for State payment, we will probably be expected ... to pipe a State tune.' The Bill would mean 'that playwrights and managers would then have to steer a course so circumspect as to avoid offending not only the Censor's undefined susceptibilities, as at present, but also the undefined susceptibilities of any [person or group] ... powerful enough to make things difficult for the unfortunate Commission administering the Government subsidy'. There were several pages more in this vein. Levy was repelled by 'this proposed additional premium on mediocrity':

abolishing entertainment tax doesn't require state interference

> . . . now especially, when freedom everywhere is on the retreat . . . when hundreds of thousands of children are being trained . . . to grow up with the mentality of fighters, haters, bullies and slaves . . . a passionate holding fast to the idea of England as a rallying point for the free . . . even in what may seem such secondary branches of the national life as its theatre, is the purest . . . form that patriotism can take.

Levy continued his campaign in the pages of the film and theatre magazine *The Era*. Interviewed 'about some strong criticism of the League of Audiences which he expresses in the current issue of "The Author"', Levy said: 'What the theatre needs is freedom, not cash.'[101] Levy presumed that the production plans of theatres seeking help would be presented to the Commissioners: 'Then the fun would begin. One member would think a play a bit too Left, another that one was rather too violent, or too Right, or likely to offend the Church.' Levy considered that the League's 'objective is sound and its motives pure. But it is trying to help the theatre in an entirely wrong-headed way.'

The following week, *The Era* interviewed Alfred Wareing.[102] With uncharacteristic asperity Wareing attacked Levy for his lack of positive ideas, but did not deal directly with Levy's concerns: 'What is biting Benn Levy? . . . He is . . . unhappy about the current state of the theatre . . . He thinks something should be done about it. But though he presents not even the foggiest notion of what or how, he attacks the movement which aims to put things right.' The disagreement continued in the following issue. In a letter to *The Era*, Levy summarized his case (public subsidy would put theatre under an obligation to the state; the profession should campaign against censorship, not for additional state control; and if money was crucial, an end to Entertainments Duty was the better approach), and attacked Wareing's method of discussion: '. . . it is a time-honoured resort in debating societies to ignore your opponent's arguments and to attack him for a case that he never advanced.'[103] Levy returned to the subject once more, in *The Era* in October 1938, replying to an article criticizing the failure of the theatrical profession to get behind the League of Audiences. He opposed subsidy, he said, because 'the only theatre guaranteed to stimulate no opposition anywhere is a dead theatre'.[104] And there Levy's statements on this issue rested – until, in 1953, he became a member of the Arts Council.

Fear of 'mechanized art' was expressed by people from a wide variety of political backgrounds; so was fear of state control. T S Eliot was a far more conservative opponent of state funding than Benn Levy. Eliot was one of the five members of the 'cultural elites' on whom Jörn Weingärtner based his argument in *The Arts as a Weapon of War* that fear of state control of the arts caused intellectual opinion in the 1930s to be generally hostile to state subsidy.[105] Weingärtner's use of Eliot was problematic in three respects. First, he cited only Eliot's *Notes Towards the Definition of Culture*,[106] published in 1948, nearly ten years after the period under discussion. Second, that book's main argument against state funding of the arts was that it would lead not to undue state influence but to poor quality. For Eliot more meant worse: '... to aim to make everyone share in the fruits ... of culture ... is to adulterate and cheapen what you give'; '[it is an] essential condition of the preservation of the quality of the culture of the minority, that it should continue to be a minority culture'; and 'in our headlong rush to educate everybody, we are lowering the standards'.[107] This has nothing to do with artistic freedom.

Third, Weingärtner did not cite an essay by Eliot which did support his case and was published before the war.[108] In his quarterly magazine *The Criterion*, Eliot considered at length the campaign of the League of Audiences, 'an organization from which in the past I have received leaflets which I fear I have treated with inadequate attention'. He had been alerted to it by the *Church Times*' editorial of February 1938, discussed above: '... the Editor of the *Church Times* ... devotes a leading article in his issue of 11th February to arousing dubiety in the minds of his readers on the subject of the Music and Drama Bill ... I am happy to be at one with the Editor of the *Church Times* in this matter.' He also relied on *The Times*' report of the League's House of Commons meeting of February 1938, discussed in Chapter 3.

Eliot recalled that in the previous issue of *The Criterion* he had 'suggested the possibility that the creation of a National Theatre was a step which might lead to the eventual creation of a Ministry of Fine Arts'. He now suggested that, even if it was not Wareing's intention, it was possible 'once the Government takes an active and overt part in the cultivation of the Arts, such confusion will ensue that in time there will be a call for a "dictator of the Arts" (will it by that time be Mr. Hore-Belisha or Mr. Duff-Cooper?) to put things to rights'. In his view, more thought had gone into the mechanics of setting up a Commission to spend money on the arts than into 'the problem of *how* to spend the money. It is a pity that action should take precedence over thought.... the more the State takes over, the less will be the private initiative.' He concluded by suggesting that the state might come to treat the arts as another branch of public administration. Rather obscurely, Eliot cited a proposal by the writer G D H Cole that a National Investment Board be created. He adapted Cole's description in order to suggest how the Music and Drama Bill would operate:

> ... socially undesirable forms of music or drama (... according to the opinion of the eight Commissioners appointed by the Crown – i.e. nominally by the Prime

> Minister but actually by civil servants whom no-one will ever be able to trace) could be *prevented* from crowding more useful music and drama out of the market. ... the State can begin to guide music and drama into the right channels ... What should be produced in the way of music and drama depends on what the people is [*sic*] willing to have imposed on it....

Alfred Wareing may not have taken Levy's and Eliot's views seriously enough. But he sincerely opposed the establishment of an Arts Ministry and saw the appointment of independent Commissioners as a safeguard. This was in essence the model the government adopted for CEMA and subsequently the Arts Council. Even in the1930s the League was not alone in distinguishing between direct government funding and funding at one remove. As noted in Chapter 3, the *Birmingham Post*, for example, made this distinction the subject of an editorial in June 1937.[109] Direct subsidy would be 'entirely antagonistic to democratic rule', and a government 'that runs, let us say, a group of national opera-houses ... can only be ... despotic in its executive practice'. But with a semi-independent Commission, while there would have to be 'constant critical vigilance on the part of the public and the Press ... its control ... will not be insuperably difficult'.

There were probably three reasons why Wareing paid relatively little attention to arguments about the dangers of state control. First, he believed that his proposed Commission largely neutralized the dangers. Second, pragmatically, the performing arts needed money, and the government was the only likely source. Third, the Eliot/Levy arguments seemed less important to argue against than those to the effect that the performing arts were simply a low priority for public funding.

Jörn Weingärtner argued, without mentioning the existence of the League of Audiences, that the main attitude towards subsidy among the 'cultural elites' before the war was opposition, due to fear that 'the state will take over everything'.[110] Examination of the evidence shows that this attitude was not widespread. Few expressed it with the force of Benn Levy or T S Eliot. Furthermore, the case of Geoffrey Whitworth and the BDL suggests that in some cases this argument against subsidy may have been used as a mask for more commercial, less principled, concerns.

## Conclusion

The view that public subsidy was necessary to combat the menace of mechanized art was expressed far more widely in the 1930s than the view that subsidy should be opposed because it would limit artistic freedom.

As Geoffrey Whitworth (perhaps unwittingly) conceded in his letter to Wareing of March 1937, and as Constant Lambert argued in *Music Ho!* in 1934, the BBC already offered the government a means of exerting, if it chose, strong and direct influence on cultural life in Britain. If Whitworth had been genuine in his concerns, he should have publicized the dangers of the BBC as passionately as 'Scrutator' did in the pages of the *Sunday Times*: 'For the first time, the State set up in the business of entertainment ... It made a monopoly of arts and pleasures ... it risked creating a tyranny all the more monstrous and dangerous because it was exercised over men's minds.'[111] The arm's length monopoly state broadcaster of news, light entertainment and 'high culture' was a far more powerful tool in the hands of a determined and malevolent government than the modest arm's length funding organization envisaged in the Music and Drama Bill; but Whitworth was silent on this.

The next chapter discusses the decline and fall of the League of Audiences. Fear of mechanized art helps explain both the League's rise and support for state arts subsidy generally in the 1930s. The fear that such subsidy would lead to state control of the arts was of far less importance in the League's history and in its failure to achieve its aim by 1939.

## Notes

1 *Drama*, Vol 15, No3, December 1936, p42.

2 Undated (but early 1934) draft in V&A/THM/149/5.

3 Lambeth Palace archive: Lang Papers, L1-L17 1938, Vol 162 (hereafter 'Lang papers'), p324, undated copy of League of Audiences leaflet.

4 20/4/36.

5 28/6/37.

6 Ibid.

7 14/2/38.

8 Quoted in *Music & Letters*, Vol 19, No1, January 1938, pp79–83.

9 27/4/36.

10 14/4/36.

11 See, generally, Chapter 5, pp68–72.

12 V&A/ THM/149/7, Horace Collins-Wareing, 22/7/39.

13 http://genome.ch.bbc.co.uk/a22abe624c714eec9a1f292c2e92e02a, retrieved 4 January 2016.

14 https://www.britannica.com/biography/Lena-Ashwell, retrieved 14 October 2018. See also Chapter 9, p192.

15 London: Michael Joseph, 1936; hereafter 'Ashwell'.
16 Ashwell, p265.
17 Ibid., p257.
18 Ibid., p258.
19 Ibid., pp259–60.
20 2/12/36.
21 London: William Heinemann/Victor Gollancz, 1934 (1937 cheap edition), pp366–7.
22 Ervine, p235.
23 Ibid., p190.
24 Ibid., p197.
25 Ibid., pp247–8.
26 22/9/35.
27 5/12/36.
28 'The Arts Council: Its Policy and Hopes' (*The Listener*, 12/7/45).
29 London: George Allen and Unwin, 1932.
30 Ibid., ppv–vii.
31 Toby Miller: 'Who Are These People?', *Cinema Journal*, Vol47, No4, Summer 2008, pp121–2.
32 *The Film in National Life*, p10.
33 Ibid.
34 See David Parkinson (ed): *The Graham Greene Film Reader* (New York: Applause Books, 1995).
35 'Subjects and Stories', in Parkinson (ed), p409.
36 Filson Young: 'The League of Audiences and "The World We Listen In"', *The Radio Times*, 14/2/36.
37 *The Times*, 14/4/36, letter from Lord Bessborough (President of the League) and others; see Chapter 3, pp30–1.
38 'The League of Audiences' Music and Drama Bill' (Letter to the Editor, *The Musical Times*, Vol 78, No 1130, April 1937, p355).
39 Ervine, pp197–8.
40 *Midnight on the Desert* (London: William Heinemann, 1937), p160.
41 Ibid.
42 Chapter 2, pp17–18.
43 https://www.britannica.com/biography/Constant-Lambert, retrieved 15 October 2018.
44 London: Faber and Faber, 1934.
45 Ian Kemp: 'Let's to billiards', *Musical Times*, Vol 107, No 1486, December 1966, pp1059–60.
46 *Music Ho!*, pp233–74.
47 Ibid., p233.

48 Ibid.
49 Ibid., pp234–5.
50 Ibid., p235.
51 Ibid.
52 Briggs, p77, quoting from an interview with Christopher Stone from 1952.
53 *Music Ho!*, pp235–6.
54 Ibid., pp 237 and 238, for this and the two following quotations.
55 http://www.aspenmusicfestival.com/benjamin-britten/,retrieved 29 September 2013.
56 http://www.gramophone.co.uk/features/focus/90th-anniversary-interviews-benjamin-britten, retrieved 29 September 2013.
57 9/5/35.
58 22/6/35.
59 V&A/THM/149/1, League of Audiences' draft annual accounts for 1934/35.
60 *Birmingham Post*, 28/6/37.
61 https://www.britannica.com/biography/William-Temple and www.wea.org.uk (retrieved 15 October 2018), respectively.
62 *Birmingham Post*, 28/6/37.
63 3/2/38.
64 May 1938, pp725–9.
65 11/2/38.
66 It is not clear whether this was a quotation from Lang or a paraphrase.
67 11/2/38.
68 18/2/38.
69 *The Times*, 6/5/38.
70 Lang papers, p328, Wareing-Lang, 16/2/38.
71 Ibid., p332, Rev A C Don-Sir Philip Wilbraham, 22/2/38.
72 Ibid., p333, Wilbraham-Don, 23/2/38.
73 Ibid., pp334, 335 and 338: respectively, Don-Temple, 8/3/38, Temple-Don, 8/3/38 and Don-Temple, 10/3/38.
74 Ibid., pp339–40, Rathcreedan-Lang, 30/3/38.
75 Ibid., p341, Don-Rathcreedan, 31/3/38.
76 Ibid., p342, Gordon-Lang, 9/4/38.
77 Ibid., p343, Lang-Gordon, 11/4/38.
78 Ibid., p345, Wareing-Gordon, 14/4/38.
79 Ibid., p346, Mallon-Lang, 21/4/38.
80 Ibid., p349, Wareing-Don, 25/4/38.
81 Ibid., p357, Toynbee Hall meeting attendance list.
82 Isaac, p126.
83 https://archive.org/stream/in.ernet.dli.2015.173789/2015.173789.E-G-O-3_djvu.txt, retrieved 26 December 2017 – Agate's diary entry for 5/5/38.

84 Isaac, p126.
85 Lang papers, p354.
86 6/5/38.
87 18/2/38.
88 V&A/THM/149/4, Beecham-Wareing, 10/3/37.
89 Chapters 5 and 9.
90 V&A/THM/149/4, Whitworth-Wareing, 12/3/37, for all quotations in the following two paragraphs.
91 Shirland Quin: 'The Theatre in America', *Drama*, Vol 15, No10, pp161–3.
92 Hallie Flanagan: 'The Federal Theatre', *Drama*, Vol 17, No2, pp19–22.
93 Ibid., p24.
94 Marie Seton: 'The Theatre in Berlin', *Drama*, Vol 15, No4, pp50–2.
95 'The League of Audiences and the Music and Drama Bill', *Drama*, Vol 16, No 2, pp27–8.
96 Lang papers, p364.
97 'The Music and Drama Bill', *Drama*, Vol 16, No 7, pp103–4.
98 https://archiveshub.jisc.ac.uk/search/archives/47d32228-2700-3c79-89f8-b2b615534fc9, retrieved 18 October 2018, and Arts Council of Great Britain: Eleventh Annual Report 1955–1956: '*The First Ten Years*' (London: ACGB, 1956).
99 V&A/THM/149/4, Levy-Wareing, 2/4/38.
100 Vol XLVIII, No4, Summer 1938, pp105–9.
101 *The Era*, 23/6/38.
102 30/6/38.
103 7/7/38.
104 27/10/38.
105 Weingärtner, Chapter III; Eliot is discussed at pp29–31. See Chapter 1.
106 London: Faber and Faber, 1948.
107 Ibid., pp106, 107 and 108, respectively.
108 'A Commentary', *The Criterion*, March 1938, pp478–85, for all quotations in this and the following paragraph.
109 28/6/37.
110 Weingärtner, Chapter III, *passim*; the quotation (from Cyril Connolly, from a 1940s, not pre-war, essay) is on p31.
111 7/4/35.

# 5

# The League of Audiences: (iii) Decline, Fall and Legacy

## Introduction

The Toynbee Hall meeting of May 1938, chaired by the Archbishop of Canterbury, proved to be the high point of support for the League of Audiences. After this it went quickly downhill, though its formal ending was much delayed. This chapter examines what happened to the League from spring 1938, the reasons for its decline and its importance in the history of public funding of the arts. But it begins earlier, by examining Alfred Wareing's relationship with the BBC – a graphic illustration of Waring's inability to understand people and organizations not sharing his total commitment to arts subsidy. The chapter then examines Wareing's relationship with the theatrical establishment. His failure to work with key organizations in the theatre world, indeed his incurring their strong opposition, was central to the League's decline. These case studies help explain why the League failed to secure central government subsidy for music and drama by 1939. The following sections examine the League's extinction as war approached and later. The chapter ends by considering its legacy: its influence on CEMA and the Arts Council, and Wareing's place as a forgotten pioneer of arts subsidy in Britain.

## 'Mr Wareing is filled with something of the crank ingredient': The League of Audiences and the BBC

Despite influential supporters and widespread and positive press coverage, the League of Audiences and Alfred Wareing were far from universally popular. Wareing's dealings with the BBC demonstrated a failure to get his message across that became typical of the League's later history.

The relationship began well. Despite Wareing's views on mechanized art, the BBC's *Radio Times* printed approving articles about the League.[1] Their author was Filson Young, an external adviser who provided views to the BBC on individual programmes and the balance between them.[2] In February 1936 Young, noting that the League was 'industrious and ambitious enough to draft a Bill', feared that 'the likelihood of such a Bill being passed is so small that for the moment it would be a waste of time to discuss its proposals in detail'.[3] Four weeks later he had changed his mind:

> ... the more I study them [the League's objectives], the more I am convinced of their importance. The effort to organise this demand [for arts subsidy] is long overdue.... in matters of the spirit British Governments are not likely to move, except in response to a very clear and urgent public demand ... The names of those who are supporting the League ... promises well for the organisation of a public demand.[4]

Richard Lambert, editor of the BBC's other main publication, *The Listener*, was equally enthusiastic. He and Wareing had a cordial exchange of letters in July 1934, before the League's launch. Lambert welcomed Wareing's request that the BBC publicize his cause: '... please be sure that you let us in on the ground floor [of the League's plans], and we will do our best to help it forward.'[5] But Lambert's enthusiasm was not shared by BBC senior management. In November 1934, after further exchanges with Lambert, Wareing sought a meeting with the Director-General, Sir John Reith. Reith's secretary requested advice from Gladstone Murray, BBC Director of Information and Publications (and Lambert's boss), but made her own position clear: 'This seems to be rather a silly sort of thing. I don't suppose ... there would be any reason for the D.G. giving his name to it.' Murray agreed, recommending 'the accustomed formula in declining'.[6]

Wareing continued to make no headway with the BBC's upper echelons. An internal BBC account of its dealings with him, produced in 1936, recorded that 'During the autumn [of 1934], Mr Wareing asked that the D.G. should be on the [League's] General Council and the Editor of the Listener on the Executive Council. But in neither request was he successful.'[7] Wareing was not put off. He continued corresponding with Lambert, apparently the only member of the BBC hierarchy to view him positively: a June 1935 memo from Lambert to Gladstone Murray makes clear that Lambert had refused Wareing's invitation to join the League's Executive Committee 'in accordance with your [Murray's] direction', not through Lambert's choice.[8] In general, attitudes to Wareing were less positive the higher one went in the BBC. When Murray sought the views of his boss, the Controller of Programmes Alan Dawnay, on Wareing's latest request for a meeting with Reith, Dawnay wrote: 'I am sure DG will not want to receive these people [*sic*]. Cannot Editor Listener reply suggesting that they shd come & unburden their hearts to you [Murray]?'[9]

Murray accepted the responsibility. His note of the subsequent meeting began: 'You asked me to deflect Mr. Alfred Wareing from the D.G. This I did, spending most of an afternoon in his company.'[10] Murray dropped the bored Mandarin tone long enough to express mild enthusiasm for the League's objectives: '... its success would be definitely advantageous to our work.... [It] would mean widespread development of intelligent listening and active participation in drama and music. It bears socially on the problem of leisure.' But he lapsed back into it when describing Wareing himself: '... mild, idealistic, and pleasant mannered, filled with something of the crank ingredient which is normal to protagonists of the kind.'

At this stage, while the BBC was at best condescending towards Wareing himself, it was not hostile to the League's aims. Indeed, as Murray's comment indicated, it was modestly in favour. Cecil Graves, soon to take over as Controller of Programmes and later as BBC Deputy Director-General,[11] commenting on Murray's meeting with Wareing, doubted 'if there is any urgency about Mr. Wareing's scheme' and advocated a policy of wait-and-see: 'I think it will be some time before we do anything about such a scheme (if ever) ... We come in, I think, if we think the show is a good one... .'[12]

This condition was never met: the BBC hierarchy exhibited throughout its dealings with Wareing an aversion to inappropriate enthusiasm. Although Wareing managed to get a meeting with Sir Stephen Tallents, the BBC's Controller of Public Relations, in December 1935,[13] this was clearly the BBC going through the motions. Tallents reported to Reith's private secretary: 'My own impression of Mr Wareing was that he was an honest, decent man, promoting bona fide a perfectly hopeless scheme.'[14] In 1936, as noted above, an internal BBC document was prepared, summarizing its dealings with the League of Audiences.[15] In essence it was an account of approaches by Wareing and polite rebuffs by the BBC: 'It was explained to him ... that this could not be done...'; 'He was told that [the BBC's active assistance] was extremely unlikely'; 'He was told ... "it was not felt appropriate for the B.B.C. to join the initial subscription list".' After a further request by Wareing to see Reith, in September 1936, Tallents reported to Reith on enquiries he had made:

> When Mr. Wareing came to see me in December 1935, he produced a holograph letter of the previous August from Mr. Neville Chamberlain to himself, which

> seemed to indicate official support. I have now ascertained privately that ... Mr. Chamberlain was feeling a little uneasy about his previous reference to possible support.... [Chamberlain's private secretary] thought there was no possible chance of Government support.[16]

But as ever Wareing was persistent. He enlisted the help of Walter Elliot, Minister of Agriculture and Fisheries, a friend since before World War I, who had coached Wareing for meetings in Whitehall. Soon after Tallents' dismissive note, Elliot wrote to Reith (on Minister of Agriculture and Fisheries notepaper):

> .... to introduce to you Mr. Alfred Wareing, a personal friend of long standing who is working very hard to arouse greater interest in the Drama and Music ... I have no doubt your attention has already been called to this movement in which a good deal of interest is being taken.... Wareing ... is anxious to secure your personal interest, and I should be most grateful to you if you could spare him a few minutes of your time.[17]

Not even Elliot's intervention secured Wareing a meeting: Reith refused, citing pressure of work.[18] In early 1937 Elliot also tried to secure for Wareing a further meeting with Sir Stephen Tallents. Here too he failed. Tallents responded starkly: 'I have seen him once, and do not think he would gain either satisfaction or practical advantage by seeing me again.'[19] Tallents reported that Wareing had 'tried, after seeing me, to get at Sir John Reith'. Since the League's proposals appeared to Tallents 'impractical and nebulous', he had advised Reith against meeting him. Although 'I liked him when we met, and of course would see him again if you really wished it ... I do not see how I can possibly give him practical help.'

The archives record no further attempts by Wareing to see Reith. It is perhaps surprising, with the League attracting both favourable press coverage and high profile supporters, that the BBC was so resistant; equally surprising that its attitude was due not to hostility to the League's ideas but to the belief that the ideas were 'impractical and nebulous' and doomed to fail. The final exchanges between Wareing and the BBC are noted below; but from mid-1938, the BBC was far from alone in its negative attitude towards the League.

## The League of Audiences and the Theatrical Establishment

Among the League of Audiences' papers is a letter from February 1939.[20] It is unsigned, though was probably a copy of a signed original, being headed '(Name and Address confidential)'. It begins: 'I suspect you have been wondering for some time why I have not become a member of the League of Audiences, since you know that I agree whole-heartedly with what it is trying to do.' The writer continued:

> When I first became interested in the League, I told all my friends in the Theatre about it, and was exceedingly surprised when several of them warned me not to have anything whatever to do with it.... They then told me that certain West End Managers were violently opposed to the League..., and would not dream of employing a young actor or actress who was known to be associated with it.

Well established actors could support the League openly, since 'Their value at the Box Office makes them quite safe as far as West End Managers are concerned.... [Many young actors] have starved and cannot afford to lose an engagement... It is from the well-known people that a lead must come!'

The writer did not explain the hostility of West End theatre managers; but it was real, was due to Wareing's failure to work with the theatre establishment, and was a key factor behind the League's decline. Geoffrey Whitworth, Director of the British Drama League, identified the problem when writing to Wareing in March 1937.[21] The letter was discussed in Chapter 4 for its probably disingenuous arguments about the dangers of state control of the arts. But it ranged more widely. Whitworth, a skilled networker, advised Wareing that 'any "endorsement" to be of value at the present moment should include that of ... British Actors Equity, the Society of West-End Theatre Managers, the Touring Managers' Association, the Association of Repertory Theatres, the League of British Dramatists and the like'. Whitworth noted that 'while on the musical and social sides you have already obtained a large measure of support, none of the above specifically dramatic institutions appears to be on your list of supporters ... ultimately the success of the scheme will depend on harmonious working with the "providers" [of drama]' – a lesson which Whitworth himself lived by.

Wareing's relationship with the BBC demonstrated the problems caused by his persistence (or obstinacy) and lack of political acumen. These weaknesses were apparent, more damagingly, in his dealings with the organizations listed by Whitworth, and with the BDL itself. The BDL was probably the most important theatre organization in Britain between the wars (the writer on theatre Clive Barker described it as 'underlying the fabric of inter-war British theatre').[22] Its aims were 'To assist the development of the Art of the Theatre and its right relationship with the life of the Community' – this at a time when, as Whitworth's successor, Martin Browne put it, 'the theatre was still thought of by the average

Briton as entertainment pure and simple – a "night out"'.[23] Thus the BDL's aims were close to those of the League of Audiences. But as noted in Chapter 4, the BDL not only failed to collaborate with the League, it actively opposed it. Its differences with Wareing went beyond the apparent disagreement about state funding and state control. They stemmed from the BDL's membership and role, Whitworth's mission, and Wareing's obstinacy and tactical failings.

The BDL was an umbrella body of umbrella bodies, representing theatre interests from amateur and community groups to professional 'little theatres' to drama schools and commercial theatre management. Whitworth himself led the campaigns to remove Entertainments Duty from live performances and to found a National Theatre. Wareing's exclusive focus on subsidy was always likely to put him on a collision course not only with Whitworth and the BDL, but with other theatre trade bodies. Wareing's attempt to recruit a representative from the Theatrical Management Association to the League's Executive Committee, for example, failed because 'members are still of the opinion that they must confine their support to ... [the campaign] to abolish the Entertainment Tax.... It is regretted, therefore, that we cannot help your movement until the Entertainments Tax has been removed.'[24]

Indeed, each side was ready to damage the other in pursuit of its own aims. Wareing was so focussed on the campaign for subsidy that he was prepared to make trouble, and lose supporters, when the press confused it with the movement against Entertainments Duty. Early in the League's history he reported to its Executive Committee that 'a misleading cartoon appeared in the Sheffield Independent, Nottingham Journal, Yorkshire Observer, Birmingham Gazette [and] Northern Echo'.[25] The offending cartoon, entitled 'His Master's Voice?', depicted the League (personified as a small man) 'backed by film and theatre interests' (personified by large men making such comments as 'Marvellous little feller' and 'He'll put it over') sending a message by loudspeaker 'with the object of bringing pressure to bear on the Chancellor [Neville Chamberlain] to reduce the entertainment tax'.[26] Wareing noted that 'A letter from our Solicitors was sent to the Editors concerned, who published corrections'.

The theatrical establishment behaved similarly. The umbrella organization in the Entertainments Duty campaign was, in 1938, the Stage and Allied Arts League (previously 'Defence League').[27] Writing to the Chancellor of the Exchequer in February 1938, its Chairman, Walter Payne, treated subsidy and relief from Entertainments Duty as a zero-sum game, and dealt with Wareing's work as with an obstacle, albeit an insignificant one:

> An attempt has been made recently to secure Parliamentary support for a Bill entitled 'The Music and Drama Bill', the object of which is to secure a Government grant to subsidise certain forms of dramatic and musical enterprise selected according to the whim of Commissioners. . . . We feel sure you will agree that any such subsidy ... would be premature and indefensible until the fundamental obstacle to progress for British dramatic and musical enterprise – i.e., the entertainments duty – has been removed.[28]

The conflict harmed both causes. Theatrical managers and Geoffrey Whitworth could have tried harder to work with Wareing. The League of Audiences counted among its supporters theatrical stars, leaders from the world of music and senior figures from the Church of England. Their support could have strengthened Whitworth's various campaigns. But the League of Audiences' isolation harmed the League itself more. Wareing apparently never recognized that subsidy for some professional theatre might not be a high priority for amateur drama enthusiasts, commercial theatre management or National Theatre campaigners. His failure to work with representative theatre organizations became an increasing problem as time went on. The coalition of theatre interests campaigning for the end of Entertainments Duty became, consciously or not, a coalition against the Music and Drama Bill.

The behind-the-scenes tensions were also played out publicly, in the BDL magazine *Drama*. The April 1938 article in *Drama* about the Music and Drama Bill[29] was considered in Chapter 4, in the context of the Bill's alleged threats to artistic freedom. The article also reported that, to 'take advice' on the Bill, the Council of the BDL had 'set up a special Committee, who in turn summoned a special Conference of the leading theatrical organisations in this country'. This had resolved that theatre, professional and amateur, 'was suffering, very unjustly, under the tax on living entertainment [Entertainments Duty was payable on admission prices to all theatre, amateur as well as professional]'; that the Bill's aims could be better met by removing Entertainments Duty than by introducing subsidy; but that when that had been achieved, it would be 'prepared to support the underlying principle of the Bill'. *Drama* commented: 'It appears to us that the Drama League [*Drama*'s publisher!] has done a service in obtaining this expression of opinion from a conference so representative of the theatre both in London and in the Provinces, and also of the amateur movement.'

Wareing may have been unimpressed by the article's conclusion: '. . . when the time comes, the Resolution should prove a powerful advantage to the prospects of the Music and Drama Bill. We hope that members of the Drama League will throw their whole weight behind the Bill if and when the preliminary conditions mentioned above [the abolition of Entertainments Duty] have been satisfied.' This was support so qualified as to be indistinguishable from opposition; though the suggestion, however tenuous, that BDL members should at some future point campaign for the Music and Drama Bill suggests that the BDL's objections to it were less conclusive than the BDL publicly, and Whitworth privately, suggested.

Late in the League's history this hostile theatrical alliance still existed. In February 1939 Lord Esher, Chairman of the BDL, wrote to Wareing to report that at a further meeting of all the main theatrical umbrella bodies 'the view was unanimously expressed that the representatives would not be in a position to support the Bill in any form unless and until the Entertainments Tax on the Living Theatre was remitted'.[30] The meeting also decided that even then, support would be conditional on the removal from the Bill of all of the Commissioners' proposed powers other than that of making grants. These points were repeated almost verbatim several months later in a letter from Geoffrey Whitworth to George Morrison MP, Chairman of the League of Audiences' Parliamentary Music and Drama Committee.[31] Whitworth added: 'The amateur movement, so far as it is represented by the British Drama League, is at one with the professional theatre in regarding the abolition of the Entertainments Tax as the chief reform to be worked for at the moment.' The letter added a further condition for support: that the Music and Drama Bill's proposed Commissioners should include representatives of theatre managers, dramatists and amateur theatre.

Some commentators saw this attitude by the theatre establishment as highly damaging. *The Era* magazine began an October 1938 article in some exasperation: 'Why in the name of all that is reasonable is the theatre, always crying out about its financial hindrances, so fiercely opposed to plans for its being helped?'[32] It reminded readers of Cecil Chisholm's call in his 1934 book *Repertory*[33] for a campaigning movement for theatre subsidy, and noted: 'The movement has started. The League of Audiences exists.... [But] what support does this movement get from the theatre? ... When did West-End managers ever co-operate except against somebody or something that they regard as a usurper of their rights? ... Why is the theatre so determined to fight its own best interests?'

## The End of the League of Audiences: (a) Decline

Briefing Sir John Reith on the League of Audiences, Sir Stephen Tallents of the BBC had reported that Neville Chamberlain 'was feeling a little uneasy' about his expressions of support to Alfred Wareing.[34] But Chamberlain continued to make encouraging noises. In December 1935 he helped arrange a meeting between Wareing and the Lord Mayor of Birmingham,[35] and the following month, acknowledging Wareing's thanks, wrote again to 'hope your plans will go forward'.[36] Wareing continued to lobby Chamberlain. Writing to him in the summer of 1938, Wareing used his own health as an aid to moral blackmail:

> My heart is giving trouble and makes me anxious about the future of our movement. . . . In this past week there have been signs that I am almost at the end of my physical strength . . . I am not afraid of anything except the future of our cause. I am only concerned that you should know how much has been done. It would hearten me to tell you, will you please let me?[37]

Chamberlain's reply, though sympathetic ('I was sorry to have your letter of 17th July and to hear of your troubles'), was non-committal.[38] This may have been due to Chamberlain's having higher priorities at the time; but just two months after the Toynbee Hall meeting, and despite continuing positive press coverage, the League was on a downward slope.

Having held successful meetings in the House of Commons in 1936 and early 1938, Wareing considered that the next step should be a House of Lords debate on the Music and Drama Bill. In May 1938, the month of the Toynbee Hall meeting, he asked the Archbishop of Canterbury to move the motion for a debate.[39] To strengthen his case, he passed the Archbishop letters from other peers apparently in favour of the motion. These letters are not in the League's archive, but those that remain, and records of telephone messages, suggest that Wareing had overreached himself and that the climate had changed. Lord Leverhulme wrote: 'If the purpose of the motion is to ask the Government to give some form of financial support to Drama, I do not see how such a request is for one moment likely to be considered at a time when the nation is carrying a peak load of taxation.'[40] There were telephone messages, brutal from Lord Swaythling ('he . . . is not interested in the project; he rather thinks it is a waste of time and would not care to take part in a debate'), less so from the Marquess of Carisbrooke ('He is in sympathy with your work . . . at the same time he regrets it is not possible for him to allow his name to be used'; this message has a note added in pencil: 'Not sent to A[rchbishop] of C[anterbury]').[41]

The Archbishop was unimpressed with the letters he did receive. On 8 June he wrote to Wareing that he had decided against moving the motion.[42] The letter is characteristic of many that Wareing received – disappointing in substance and anguished in tone, as if causing pain to Wareing caused the writer more pain still:

'I am compelled to inflict on you what I fear will be a real disappointment.... Believe me, I dislike exceedingly disappointing your wholehearted and single-minded enthusiasm.... I fear I have no alternative. I am very sorry.' He pleaded pressure of work, but cited further reasons: lack of support from the peers whom Wareing had approached ('When they speak of "supporting the Archbishop", it seems to me often to mean support by their presence rather than by their votes'); and that 'when taxation has been increased and the Government is faced with enormous expenditure' the time was wrong to seek a further call on public funds. Wareing's reply no doubt increased the Archbishop's discomfort: 'Your kind, long letter of Wednesday did not arrive until yesterday, and even now I can do no more than write this acknowledgement....'[43]

In July 1938, the month Wareing wrote to Chamberlain about his heart problems, George Morrison MP secured a meeting for himself and Wareing with Sir John Simon, Chamberlain's successor as Chancellor of the Exchequer. Wareing's report of this meeting recorded that Simon, as his predecessor had done, 'made it clear that we must obtain stronger backing from the Electorate'; but a footnote added: 'Sir John Simon said "We can't afford it!". He did not ask how much it would cost.'[44] As with Wareing's previous meetings with Ministers, no government record of this encounter seems to survive in the National Archives.

From this point on, there were only a few hopeful signs for the League of Audiences. Some high profile supporters spoke up for it. J B Priestley included the League in a speech at the 1938 Malvern Festival, though he concentrated on the campaign against Entertainments Duty.[45] In January 1939 Sir Thomas Beecham addressed the Incorporated Society of Musicians, noting that 'The arts of Music and Drama need more secure foundations.... The Music and Drama Bill ... for which the consideration of Parliament will be asked when times are more propitious, sets out a possible plan.'[46] And as late as August 1939 the Bishop of Worcester devoted his annual Malvern Festival sermon to promoting state subsidy for the arts in general and the work of the League in particular.[47]

But the League, as a public campaigning body, needed not only influential supporters and positive publicity but also money. By late 1938 its lack of cash was causing many League loyalists to lose heart. Its Executive Committee appointed a committee to consider the future. Its report, of December 1938, concluded:

> ... (a) adequate financial support has not been forthcoming from members of the League to sustain the work. (b) ... having regard to the present commitments of the Government under its rearmament programme there can be no hope that

> the Music and Drama Bill . . . can be acceptable to the Government at the present time or in the immediate future.[48]

Its proposals were equally downbeat. It was 'unable to recommend that any appeal should be made to the public in support of the work of the League'. What it did recommend was that until 'it appears prudent to revive the effort to secure Government support', the League should become a body simply encouraging concert- and theatre-going; though the committee 'finds it difficult to believe that this cultural objective ... will be strong enough in itself to gain financial support'.

Money had always been a problem for the League, even when at its most successful as a campaigning organization. St John Ervine saw Wareing as 'this man whose faith moves mountains'.[49] But Wareing's optimism, as well as his persistence, had its disadvantages, particularly in relation to finance. His draft budget for the League's first year, 1934, had projected income of £8,000 and spending of £7,663.[50] The anticipated income was made up of £3,000 in membership subscriptions and £5,000 in 'Donations from persons pecuniarily interested in the prosperity from increased audiences'.[51] In practice the League's annual income never exceeded £1,900, and in the year ending September 1938 – during which it had gained so much positive press coverage and public attention – its income was £543 against spending of £1,240.[52]

Given its financial situation, the views of the special committee, the increasingly difficult political climate and the hostility (in effect) of the theatre establishment, it is surprising that the League was not dissolved at this point. But it took several weeks for this thought even to surface. Two letters to Wareing from Wilfred Stephenson, a member of the Executive Committee, are illuminating in this respect. Stephenson, an Inland Revenue Commissioner, showed the same mixture of devotion, guilt and pain at causing pain which Wareing evoked in many supporters. The day after the League's Executive Committee discussed the special committee's report, in December 1938, Stephenson wrote in encouraging terms (beginning his letter 'My dear wonderful friend', and signing off 'Kindest regards and unbounded admiration'): 'I hope you took courage by yesterday's meeting: courage, did I say? God knows you couldn't hold any more of that ... I know that all the work is done by yourself and Hodgkinson and Baker – and more power to your elbows.'[53] But his mood had changed by the following month, when a colleague on the Executive Committee tabled a motion to wind up the League. Stephenson (in a letter ending 'In all personal sympathy')[54] attempted to spell out the realities for Wareing:

> Your enthusiasm and tireless work during these years have been . . . little short of a miracle. . . . We have, in fact, a tremendous body of spiritual backers and less, much less, than no money at all with which to carry on the Gospel. When . . . you ask us, the Committee, to continue this indefinite liability, you are merely deferring, and certainly increasing . . . the assessment when the inevitable end comes.

Stephenson believed that the winding-up motion would pass and a liquidator would be appointed. If so, 'we members will be assessed by that Liquidator at anything between thirteen and fifteen pounds a head. I am prepared to face that. But no more. And, frankly, I shall be very much astonished if the other members come to any other conclusion. One doesn't talk of "being sorry" when a tragedy like this occurs.'

## The End of the League of Audiences: (b) Fall

But Stephenson was mistaken, mainly due to Jo Hodgkinson, Chairman of the League's Executive Committee. Hodgkinson had joined Toynbee Hall in 1930 as James Mallon's deputy, and organized its orchestra, choir and 'Little Theatre'.[55] He was important in John Christie's 'Council of Power' conferences, discussed in the next chapter, and despite his work for the League was among the few participants in the conferences to gain Christie's respect. He was later described as 'one of the best known figures in the post war theatre world', serving as Arts Council Drama Director from 1954 to 1970.[56] Hodgkinson wrote optimistically to the committee before its meeting on 17 January 1939: if the decision was to close down, committee members would be personally liable for debts totalling £200; but 'we are making more contacts daily and getting more encouragement. And if we are able to keep going, we can perhaps expect real and active support . . . when the present situation calms down.'[57] The motion to wind up the League failed even to secure a seconder. Instead the committee accepted a suggestion by one of its members, Eric White, that he seek help for the League from the National Council of Social Service (forerunner of the National Council of Voluntary Organisations), for which White then worked.[58] White later spent nearly thirty years working at CEMA and the Arts Council, and wrote a history of the Arts Council: see below.

The committee reconvened a week later. White had failed to persuade his employer to fund the League, but the winding-up motion was not revived. On the contrary. Wareing tabled a 'put up or shut up' resolution: the Executive Committee was 'bound in honour to put forward its united utmost endeavours to carry on the work of the League as at present', and those who disagreed should 'be invited to resign and their offers to discharge their proportion of the debts... [should] be accepted'.[59] Discussion on this was adjourned and the resolution was withdrawn; but the meeting accepted a proposal by J G Wilson, Chairman of the booksellers Bumpus, that members should seek a total of fifty pledges of £5 each to provide enough money for the League to continue until the end of the year.[60]

Serious fundraising ensued, though Wilfred Stephenson was among several Executive Committee members who took Wareing's ultimatum at face value and resigned.[61] In February 1939 many League members received requests for a £5 donation, including Sir Henry Wood (who paid) and J B Priestley (who sent £10).[62] The most generous donor was John Christie of Glyndebourne.

Christie's role was ambiguous. As discussed in the next chapter, he saw the League's proposals as in many ways in conflict with his own; and as noted in Chapter 3, in a letter of February 1938 to Harold Baker, the League's Treasurer and Honorary Secretary, he described Wareing as 'an infuriating old man' and the League as 'a number of little people with small minds'.[63] Yet he gave the League a total of £160 between February 1937 and July 1938.[64] Christie's correspondence with Baker is revealing about the League at this time, Baker's role as mediator, and Christie himself. Alongside its insults, Christie's February 1938 letter illustrated his key differences with Wareing: 'Wareing's purpose, he tells me, is to defeat the machines.... His method of defeating the machines (which I do not wish to do), is ... to produce on a large scale stuff of a lower value than the machines give'.[65] Baker replied: 'When we are stronger we can sort the chaff from the wheat – meanwhile we should enlist all the support we can for "Government action"'.[66]

Christie's criticisms of Wareing were more measured by late 1938, when Baker sought further financial help for the League: '... old Wareing has come a bit too soon.... The right time to work up the audience side is when you can deliver the goods and, at present, music is not organised to do this.... I think that but for Wareing, the Audiences League would be shelved for a bit'.[67] But Christie continued his financial support of the League – and of Wareing himself: in January 1939 he took over the role of personal benefactor from another donor. Just after the League's meeting at which the winding-up motion failed to find support, Baker wrote to Christie's secretary that '[Mr. Christie] will make no further contributions to the League, but will give Mr. Wareing £50 for his personal subsistence.... I think that for every reason, Mr. Christie's name should be concealed (Mr. Christie agrees).... if you will arrange for the cheque to go to Dr. Mallon [Warden of Toynbee Hall], he will pay it to Mr. Wareing as though it came from the previous benefactor'.[68] It is unclear who the previous benefactor was.

When the approach to the National Council of Social Service came to nothing, Baker again asked Christie for help. This time Christie contributed £25, with the offer of a further £25 if a total of £250 (presumably the fifty £5 stakes) was raised.[69] A later scribbled note from Baker to Christie records that this £250 target was not reached, but that the League's Executive Committee had decided to carry on for another month: 'Enough money has been given unconditionally to do that & no more . . . the optimistic members (of whom I was not one) think they may achieve [the £250 target] before the end of March.'[70]

While these transactions continued, in part without Wareing's knowledge, he too was shameless in seeking money for the League. A thank-you letter from him to C E Lawrence, editor of the *Quarterly Review*, began: 'I hate to take your money, but I love the League more.'[71] Lawrence himself was apparently under Wareing's spell, at one stage writing to him that 'You are at once something of Greatheart, an elf and a pirate'.[72] Wareing seems not to have acknowledged how close to extinction the League was by early 1939, beyond thanking J G Wilson, whose idea of seeking £5 contributions from supporters 'not only averted a great danger but rallied the whole group'.[73] Instead, Wareing talked and wrote with apparently undiminished energy. In January 1939 he met and then corresponded with Kenneth Lindsay, Parliamentary Secretary to the Board of Education.[74] Lindsay asked Wareing which local authorities were most active in supporting the performing arts; Wareing suggested Birmingham, putting this down to Neville Chamberlain's efforts when Lord Mayor.[75] Later in 1939, despite the League's fragile state, he recruited to its Executive Committee representatives of six organizations, including the Workers' Educational Association, the National Association of Head Teachers and the Incorporated Society of Musicians,[76] though none from the theatrical world. With the WEA, at least, there were pre-existing connections: the Archbishop of York William Temple, James Mallon and R H Tawney, all League Vice-Presidents, were respectively the WEA's founding President, its Treasurer and its current President.[77]

Even in these difficult times, Wareing's persistence was generally tempered by extreme, almost cloying, courtesy. But on occasion he could be petulant if feeling snubbed. In November 1938, Janet Quigley, a BBC producer, asked him to suggest an 'extreme critic' of the campaign for a National Theatre to take part in a programme on the subject.[78] (It is noteworthy in itself that Wareing was approached to nominate an anti-National Theatre speaker.) The relationship soured when Quigley failed to maintain the correspondence, prompting an apparently sarcastic letter from Wareing: 'I fear you must be ill, and hope when this comes to hand it finds you restored so that you will be able to give attention to my letters.'[79]

This was a rare crack in the façade. In general he accepted the League's reverses with extraordinary outward calm, appearing to believe that the situation of the League, and in the wider world, was about to take a turn for the better. In April 1939, responding to Jo Hodgkinson's noting 'the difficulty of asking for money after the recent crisis', Wareing 'replied that he would start writing letters again after the Easter holidays, when he hoped there would be calmer conditions and more confidence'.[80] In May he wrote a combative article for *The Musical Times*,[81] chiding musicians' organizations for not informing their members about the Music and Drama Bill, urging united action, and reproving Sir John Simon for responding 'We can't afford it!' when he met Wareing the previous summer: 'I thought it queer that he did not first ask us "How much will it cost?".... who is it finds the money the Chancellor says he can't afford? Is not that money provided by you and me?'

That he was not a lone voice even at this stage is shown by *The Musical Times*' making space for him, and by its strong editorial support in the same issue: 'The apathy of the musical profession towards the League and the Music and Drama Bill is both astonishing and discreditable.... there is a strong and growing support for the Bill amongst members of Parliament of all parties.'[82] *The Musical Times* used the recent reduction of the rate of Entertainments Duty on live music and drama,[83] 'despite the present fantastic outlay on armaments', as a further argument that if the political will were there, the money could be found.

Wareing's 'Carry on regardless' approach during 1939 included requests to Sir Adrian Boult, Chief Conductor of the BBC Symphony Orchestra, to address the orchestra, and to the BBC for air-time for a talk on the Music and Drama Bill.[84] Both were politely rebuffed. By July 1939 James Mallon, among Wareing's most loyal supporters, felt 'bound in honesty to express my view that at the present moment any attempt to obtain money from the Government is entirely hopeless'.[85] Mallon cited 'terrific struggles between the Treasury and the B.B.C. about inconsiderable sums' (he was a BBC Governor)[86] to demonstrate the futility of seeking public funding. But Wareing did not moderate his efforts, and did not appear discouraged when, in the summer of 1939, the League lost its London office and began operating out of 'Temporary Offices'[87] – Wareing's home in Stratford-on-Avon.[88] Even in August 1939 he was writing to the Secretary of the Theatrical Management Association: 'I expect you are on holiday now.... Do let us meet when you return – I'd like you to see what we are doing here.'[89] He still hoped for a House of Lords debate on the Music and Drama Bill, enlisting Walter Elliot's help to broker an introduction to Lord Elgin. Less than three weeks before war was declared he was pressing Elgin to open it ('I hope with all my heart that you will tell me that you will be able to consent').[90]

Wareing further demonstrated his extreme resilience on the outbreak of war. Winifred Isaac, Wareing's disciple and biographer, reported his writing in his diary after war was declared 'the words of the Premier in the House of Commons on 2nd September: "Everything that I have worked for, everything I have hoped for, everything I have believed in, during my public life, has crashed in ruins." They were the echo of his [Wareing's] own thoughts.'[91] This was typical of Isaac's insistence in her biography on dwelling on the pathos of Wareing's final years. A different picture emerges from a letter later in September 1939 from Wareing to the Archbishop of York.[92] While he wrote 'I am in a maze – all is crashed to smithereens', within a few sentences apparent despair gave way to fresh resolve: 'I feel it is up to me to build again. What do you think? I believe we shall be needed more than ever when this madness passes.' Also contrary to the view Isaac sought to convey, Wareing's November 1939 report on the League's work over the previous year showed no sign of waning hopes and no record of the League's reverses.[93] Indeed, given the timing, it seems either brave or delusional.

It claimed that 'steady progress' had been made over the period, and that all would have been well but for the outbreak of war. Plans had continued for the House of Lords debate 'which the Archbishop of Canterbury in the previous year had contemplated introducing'. By March 1939 'there were reasons for hoping this Debate might be opened by the Marquess of Lothian. But when our Government declared its intention to aid Poland, the War clouds lowered again. . . . We then interested the Earl of Elgin, but the situation worsened and he rightly decided the time was inopportune.' Waring had also 'worked for some months upon plans for a great representative Public Meeting' to be addressed by the Archbishop of York, claiming also that 'The Premier gave his consent to the appearance of a Member of his Cabinet'. But the meeting was scheduled for 20 October 1939, 'when our movement . . . was halted by the outbreak of war'.

The view that the war caused the League to founder is only superficially plausible. Its financial troubles were discussed above, and other causes are considered below; but it is relevant to note here that Wareing's report was dated a few weeks before CEMA was established, which in many ways realized the League's ambitions, and that the League's decline was evident from mid-1938. By September 1939 it was clearly not viable. Nonetheless, in November 1939 Wareing was already looking forward to the post-war world. It was vital to win the war, but 'it falls to . . . others as an equally important duty to prepare for Peace. . . . our movement has become more than ever vital. . . . We must not be caught napping when Peace comes.'[94] In the same month, the playwright James Bridie, a strong supporter of the League and of Wareing personally, argued in a letter to *The Times*[95] that the outbreak of war made government support of music and theatre more urgent:

> ... the League of Audiences recently secured a measure of Parliamentary support for a commission ... whose function was to be the encouragement and patronage of music and the drama. The objection ... that it was Utopian does not apply to such a commission now, when the Arts are no longer able to proceed under their own power and emergency measures are necessary if they are to be saved.

This was an argument in effect accepted by the government when a few months later it began to fund CEMA.

## The End of the League of Audiences: (c) Lingering Death

The remaining history of the League of Audiences can be briefly told, though despite its near-death experiences in 1939 it continued to exist, in shadow form, for thirteen more years. Wareing appeared unimpressed when CEMA was set up, in January 1940 describing it to George Gordon, the League's President, as 'like pouring water into a sieve'.[96] (See below for Winifred Isaac's maudlin account of Wareing's response to CEMA's creation.) In June 1940, Jo Hodgkinson, the assiduous Chairman of the League's Executive Committee, attempted again to close the League down. Hodgkinson's letter to Wareing does not survive, but Wareing's reply is recorded in the League's 'Letter Book'.[97] Much was in his familiar style: 'It is heartbreaking to know that what has taken more than six years of the utmost I cd give in building up has been smashed to pieces.' But he appeared to bow to the inevitable: 'I must ... accept yr decision as the only practical one we can take.' Indeed, he became uncharacteristically practical, noting that he was the League's largest creditor: 'I hope that part of the sum, which totals abt. £740, will be refunded to me as one of the outstanding liabilities.'

Even this was not the end. In summer 1940 Wareing sought and received funds for the League from, among others, the Bishop of Worcester ('I can't resist your plea even though it may be the last time I shall be able to manage it.... I send you a guinea. I am sorry that this war should have come and knocked your work on the head').[98] He also received two encouraging letters in August 1940, responding to a further report not in the archive. One was from Wilfred Stephenson, who had resigned from the League's Executive Committee in January 1939.[99] Stephenson was 'amazed to see you and the League still alive. Indeed I have often wondered this year when I was going to get the winding-up notice.' He harped on this theme of amazement: '. . . here you are and indeed here it is, at the end of a year of much the most ruinous war we British have ever been involved in. . . . – that is extraordinary under all the impossible circumstances.' Stephenson reflected, as an Inland Revenue Commissioner, on the League's failure in the period leading up to the war: 'No wonder [Sir John] Simon waved his hands about in so helpless gesture [*sic*] when you went to him for money! . . . When I look upon National finance I am really appalled.' He offered Wareing 'warm encouragement and a genuine blessing on your wonderful pluck and perseverance'. The other letter, enclosing his subscription, was from Daniel Lipson, Independent Conservative MP, who 'agree[d] that it was necessary to keep the League in being so that when the War is over . . . Drama and Music may be able to play the part they ought in our National life. We shall then remember, with gratitude I hope, all you have done . . .'[100]

This was almost the League's, and Wareing's, last hurrah. In her biography, Winifred Isaac wrote that 'his friends and supporters became more and more scattered and engrossed in important war work. The final death-blow to his hopes came with the blitz of 1940.'[101] She did not note that by then several of these friends and supporters were working for CEMA. Indeed her biography at this point conveys two apparently incompatible messages: that by summer 1940 Wareing had suffered 'the final death-blow to his hopes', but that in CEMA 'most of *his* ideas were being used'.[102] The inconsistency is explored below. Wareing himself did not long survive the end of the League's active life. He died in April 1942, aged 66. Funeral reports in the local press[103] recorded a 'Tribute to the late Librarian', Wareing having spent his final year as Stratford-upon-Avon's Borough Librarian, but mentioned neither his pioneering work for the repertory movement nor the League of Audiences. A brief obituary in *The Times*[104] did describe him as 'founder of the League of Audiences, and a repertory theatre pioneer'. The League itself remained dormant until ten years later, finally and formally, it was wound up.

The copy of Winifred Isaac's biography of Wareing in the Special Collection of Senate House Library has a manuscript note in Isaac's hand that the League's winding-up was 'because its objects would seem to have been achieved in the work of the Arts Council of Great Britain'.[105] The same words occur in the minutes of the League's final meeting, held, appropriately or not, at the Arts Council's offices, in August 1952.[106] It was chaired by Jo Hodgkinson (by 1952 Drama Director at the Arts Council), and included among others Harold Baker (the longest-serving of the League's office holders, still listed as 'Treasurer'), Eric White (since 1942, Assistant Secretary to CEMA and then to the Arts Council), and Winifred Isaac. Hodgkinson set out the reasons why, finally, the Executive Committee had decided that the League was 'unable to carry on with its objects': first, 'lack of support and finance'; second, 'because its objects would seem to have been achieved in the Arts Council of Great Britain'. He paid tribute to the 'great work done by the late Alfred Wareing . . . as a result of which the way had been prepared for the setting-up of C.E.M.A and the Arts Council of Great Britain'.

But the link between Wareing and the League on the one hand and the creation of CEMA and the Arts Council on the other was at the time a matter of controversy and has since been wholly forgotten.

## The Significance and Legacy of the League of Audiences

From one point of view, the League of Audiences was a failure: the government did not set up an agency in the 1930s to distribute public money for live music and theatre, and the League itself has since been written out of history. Among the causes were the government's unwillingness to devote money to this cause as war approached (though it reversed its attitude once war was declared, and even before the war it did support live music and theatre by other means – see Chapter 9); Wareing's lack of political acumen, in particular his failure to make common cause with those campaigning for the removal of Entertainments Duty; the consequent hostility of the 'organized' theatre sector; and (discussed in the following chapters) the at best ambivalent attitude of John Christie.

But a far more positive case can be made for the League. For several years from 1934 it achieved widespread and favourable press coverage; numbered among its active members many notable writers, critics, musicians and actors; attracted the support of MPs and senior churchmen; made the cause of state funding of the performing arts a familiar topic for public discussion; was the centre of an intense campaign against the effects of 'mechanized art'; and created a belief that the issue was not if but when arm's length government funding of theatre and live music would be introduced in Britain. Two further points can be made in the League's favour. First, several of those most closely associated with it went on to key positions in CEMA and then the Arts Council. James Bridie and Ivor Brown became members of the Council; Jo Hodgkinson and Eric White were among its senior staff. The League was where their ideas were formed (though see below for their differing views of this heritage). Second, the way the government chose to provide subsidy, via CEMA and then the Arts Council, was essentially that advocated by Wareing: '... a semi-independent body ... provided with modest funds to stimulate, comfort and support any societies ... which are striving with serious purpose and a reasonable prospect of success to present for public enjoyment the arts of music, drama and painting', as Keynes described the Arts Council.[107]

It is paradoxical that the government accepted both the principle and the League's model of state arts funding at a time when the League itself, after steep decline, was a spent force. After Wareing's death, it was mainly those who had known him personally who celebrated his role. They did so with striking intensity. Winifred Isaac, Wareing's deputy and disciple, saw CEMA as embodying Wareing's vision, but this, for her, merely underlined the pathos of his last years. This is her account of the announcement of CEMA's plans: '... we found that most of *his* ideas were being used, and *no* acknowledgement was made of their origin. When I exclaimed at the injustice of his name not being mentioned, he kept silence. There are some griefs too deep for words. The neglect of those responsible ... "quite vanquished him". "This was the unkindest cut of all".'[108]

Others managed to praise his achievement less sentimentally. Reporting the creation of the Arts Council in June 1945, *The Observer* noted that it 'would have delighted Alfred Wareing.... Smooth, smiling, very deaf, very devoted, very persistent, and not afraid of wearying the opposition into agreement, Wareing was the kind of man who starts things: when others complete them, this type should have honourable remembrance.'[109] And in 1952, when the League of Audiences was finally wound up, the *Manchester Guardian* recalled Wareing's 'passionately cherished obsession' on behalf of state subsidy, and quoted Ivor Brown's recollection of the period 'when I groaned at every ring of the telephone. Wareing again!'[110] The *Guardian* commented: 'But Wareing was not so mad after all, and he and his league did much to prepare the way for C.E.M.A. and then for the Arts Council, which is, in fact, the realization of his dream and on a grander scale than he could have thought possible.'

The citing of Ivor Brown is apposite. He was closely involved in the League in the 1930s, became CEMA's first Drama Director in 1940 (from which he moved to become editor of *The Observer* in 1942), and was also, from its foundation, a member of the Arts Council.[111] In his foreword to Isaac's biography,[112] Brown recognized Wareing's unique role ('Nobody else could or would have done it'), and suggested that CEMA owed much to Wareing: 'But this time what he had planned came true. C.E.M.A.... was founded.' But he then stated an apparent contradiction, without recognizing or resolving it: on the one hand, in Brown's view, 'war blew up what he [Wareing] was so laboriously building'; but on the other, CEMA, which realized his aims, was created only a few months into the war. The contradiction can be resolved if – as the evidence shows – the 1930s is seen as a period generally sympathetic to the concept of arts subsidy, a sympathy embodied in the League of Audiences. On this reading, Wareing's dreams were close to realization possibly several times and were undone not in September 1939 but earlier, due to the *threat* of war, the international crises and the focus on rearmament of the later 1930s.

Brown was clearer still about the debt that the Arts Council rather than CEMA owed to Wareing. CEMA was a wartime organization; the Arts Council, like Wareing's proposed Commission, was intended for peacetime. The Arts Council Charter of 1946 'was really Wareing's Music and Drama Bill in a larger and more lavish form. That fight was over.' But Brown believed that even before his death in 1942, Wareing 'knew that the theatre in Coketown was getting a better chance and that the good things of the arts were being decently dispersed instead of centralized. And that was what he cared about.'

The writers of the other forewords to Isaac's biography, James Bridie and Walter Elliot, were more explicit still in presenting the Arts Council as Wareing's legacy. Bridie, playwright, founder of Glasgow Citizens' Theatre, Chairman of the Scottish Committee of CEMA from 1942 and member of the Arts Council and Chairman of its Scottish Committee from its foundation,[113] considered that 'the Arts Council was formed on almost precisely the lines he had worked out.'[114] Bridie was as outraged as Isaac at Wareing's lack of recognition: 'In none of the literature of C.E.M.A. or the Arts Council has his name been so much as mentioned. But there is no doubt that he is its "onlie begetter". The Arts Council rests on his dreams, on his hard work, and on his martyrdom.'[115]

Bridie was not alone in applying to Wareing terms like 'martyrdom'. Some were hostile to him, some (such as John Christie) were ambivalent, some (including the BBC hierarchy) regarded him as an impractical dreamer. But in his friends he inspired a combination of loyalty, protective love and almost biblical awe. This is clear from the pain people close to Wareing expressed when having to give him bad news – see, for instance, the letters to him from the Archbishop of Canterbury and Wilfred Stephenson above. Walter Elliot's foreword to Isaac's biography[116] accorded Wareing clear prophetic status. Elliot, Baldwin's and Chamberlain's Cabinet colleague, was certain, as James Bridie and Ivor Brown were, that Wareing had paved the way for CEMA and the Arts Council. Wareing 'set himself to confer upon the theatre that which it had completely failed to get for itself – a twentieth century patron . . . the rank and file citizenry of Great Britain. . . . He did it.' Elliot continued:

> There was no C.E.M.A. then; there was no Arts Council. There were just ideas; ideas in Wareing's head, or printed in rather shabby memoranda. There was no Lord Keynes; subtle, renowned, arrogant, to argue down the cleverest and beat up the proud. Only a little, small man, full of faith and determination. He battered away at these enormous barriers. All the barriers broke up.... others walked through to enter into the kingdom. Wareing did not go through.... Such is the reward of prophets.... There is a fairly heavy responsibility on those who are to carry on the work; because it is built upon an ordinary savage, propitiatory, human sacrifice.

Such extraordinary imagery may have been partly a response to the failure, in particular the failure of Keynes and the Arts Council, to recognize Wareing's contribution. James Bridie's comments suggest this, and the Arts Council's attitude contrasts starkly with these extravagant tributes. While Bridie and Ivor Brown became closely associated with CEMA and the Arts Council, the organizations themselves never acknowledged Wareing's role. The Arts Council's review of its first ten years[117] made passing reference to the League, in a section headed 'The Climate of the 'Thirties'; but this was in a list of more than a dozen organizations, including the National Council of Social Service, the Women's Institutes and the Townswomen's Guilds, which helped to create 'the climate of opinion and interest in which CEMA and the Arts Council were subsequently able to flourish'. The list was almost identical to that in Andrew Sinclair's 1995 history of the Arts Council, discussed in Chapter 1,[118] except that Sinclair did not even mention the League.

Jo Hodgkinson and Eric White, like James Bridie and Ivor Brown, were closely associated with the League, CEMA and the Arts Council; they were senior bureaucrats at the Council, retiring in 1970 and 1971 respectively. White's attitude, however, contrasted starkly with Brown's and Bridie's, and also changed markedly over time. His correspondence with Winifred Isaac in 1950 and 1951 about her biography of Wareing is tantalizing. In January 1950 he acknowledged Wareing's contribution generously, if unclearly: the League's 'attempt to promote a music and drama bill was unexpectedly near success ... [as] was shown later when the war-time work of CEMA led to the establishment of the Arts Council'.[119] When he received Isaac's biography in March 1951, he recalled his time on the League's Executive Committee: '... much of what I learnt has stood me in good stead during the period when I have been working for CEMA and the Arts Council.'[120]

For reasons hard to discern, his view was far less generous by that autumn. Isaac wrote to White in September 1951 to report on the notice her book had attracted, pointing out positive views not of the book itself but of Wareing's contribution to arts subsidy.[121] She cited reviews from *The Observer*, the *Times Literary Supplement* and others to the effect that 'Wareing's greatest achievement came after his death with the formation of CEMA and the Arts Council',[122] contrasting these tributes with the Arts Council's silence about Wareing and the League. She appealed to White 'as a member of the Executive Committee of the League of Audiences, and one who has admitted the personal debt you owe to AW ... to suggest a means by which the grave omission of the Arts Council can be remedied'. Her own modest proposal was an article in the Arts Council Bulletin. She even suggested an author for this, since if she wrote it herself 'it would look as if I were advertising my book'.

In response Eric White sought to diminish this view of Wareing's contribution.[123] He suggested that Wareing's meeting with Sir John Simon, Chancellor of the Exchequer, in July 1938 showed that the League of Audiences was doomed to fail. Given Simon's negative attitude, 'it was only to be expected that progress ... would have to come from a completely different direction. As you know, it was the initiative of men like Lord De La Warr, Lord Macmillan and Dr. Tom Jones that a practical system of State aid for the arts was worked out.' White did not specify in what respects their work was in a 'completely different direction' from Wareing's. He claimed that he wrote 'not to belittle Wareing's work ... but to put the League of Audiences and the Arts Council into correct perspective', and paid him somewhat neutral tribute: 'Anyone who was in contact with Wareing knows only too well how whole-hearted was the fervour with which he devoted himself to the cause of trying to secure State aid for Music and Drama.' Then, in a clear reference to James Bridie's and Ivor Brown's strong support for Wareing, he distanced the Arts Council from the League: '... members of the Arts Council ... have been quite prepared to testify to this [Wareing's contribution] in public.... But it should always be remembered that such statements are made by them in their personal capacity.'

This letter raises several questions: why White's views of the League, or at least his expression of them, changed between early and late 1951; why he was so anxious to dissociate the Arts Council from the League, and from statements in Wareing's support from Council members 'in their personal capacity'; and whether this represented Council policy, formal or informal, or simply White's personal view. While Jo Hodgkinson was more sympathetic than White, a letter from him to Winifred Isaac[124] fails to answer these questions. Isaac had written to Hodgkinson after receiving White's discouraging letter, renewing her request that the Council publish a tribute to Wareing in its Bulletin. Hodgkinson replied:

'I am very much in sympathy with your idea ... and I shall do my best to bring this about.... no one has a greater admiration for him [Wareing] than I have.' But he advised her not to overstate her case: it would be unwise 'to press for the Arts Council to state categorically ... that everything it is doing now all arises from the original work of Mr. Wareing'. Hodgkinson suggested that Isaac take the line 'that his work had played an important part ... in establishing the right atmosphere for the formation of C.E.M.A. and the Arts Council'. This may have been intended as helpful advice, but in practice the Arts Council failed to acknowledge Wareing's role at all. Examination of the Arts Council's papers casts no light on what lay behind its attitude to Wareing and the League.

Eric White's own view hardened over the following quarter-century. In 1971 he retired. Andrew Sinclair suggested[125] that this was part of a 'policy of artistic cleansing' by the then Chairman, Lord Goodman, who, according to Sinclair, saw White as 'an inadequate and retrograde man'. Sinclair himself described White as someone who 'particularly enjoyed refusing the requests of those he did not like'. In 1975 White published his own history of the Arts Council,[126] a curious, lopsided document. Its 320 pages include, for instance, just five references to Mary Glasgow, Secretary to CEMA throughout its existence, and Secretary-General of the Arts Council for its first five years (thus the chief executive of both organizations and White's boss for ten years). Only one, recording her replacement by William Emrys Williams in 1951, is longer than a sentence, and three merely include her name in a list of staff.

But unlike most other writers about the Arts Council, White discussed Alfred Wareing and the League of Audiences. He devoted to them half of his opening five-page chapter, 'The Struggling Thirties'.[127] His treatment of Wareing suggests that Sinclair assessed White fairly. Certainly, one would never infer from White's book that the League had had a high public profile and numerous celebrated supporters, nor that White himself had been a member of its Executive Committee, actively seeking money to secure its survival in 1939. He noted that the League 'succeeded in enlisting the support of a number of men and women of good will', but concluded that it was 'a quixotic enterprise.... it cannot be maintained that the League became an important or powerful force'.[128] As for Wareing, 'Like so many intensive idealists, he seemed slightly daft at times.'[129]

This was a mean-spirited and inadequate epitaph for a man who made public funding of live music and drama not only the mission of his life but also a topic of widespread public and press discussion in the 1930s, and who was regarded by some as the 'onlie begetter' of the Arts Council. But White's is the most substantial discussion of Wareing and the League of Audiences since Winifred

Isaac's biography of 1951. The League, though not Wareing by name, was the subject of a few tendentious and inaccurate passages in Richard Witts' 'Alternative History of the Arts Council', *Artist Unknown* (1998).[130] More recently Euan McArthur, in *Scotland, CEMA and the Arts Council, 1919–1967* (2016),[131] also without mentioning Wareing by name, made passing references to an unspecific connection between 'the failure of the Music and Drama Bill' and CEMA's funding policies. But apart from these scattered mentions, since Eric White's dismissive summing-up in 1975 Alfred Wareing and the League of Audiences have remained undiscussed, unrecognized and forgotten.

## Notes

1 See also Chapter 4, p46.
2 Briggs, p71.
3 *Radio Times*, 14/2/36.
4 Ibid., 13/3/36.
5 BBC Archives, file BBC R44/238: 'Publicity: League of Audiences 1934–1937' (hereafter 'BBC R44/238'), Lambert-Wareing, 5/7/34.
6 Ibid., memo Nash-Murray and manuscript reply Murray-Nash, both 30/11/34.
7 Ibid., 'The League and the BBC', undated (but early 1936).
8 Ibid., memo Lambert-Murray, 21/6/35.
9 Ibid., manuscript responses by Gladstone Murray (24/6/35) and Alan Dawnay (undated) to Lambert's 21/6/35 memo.
10 Ibid., memo Murray-Controller (P) (Dawnay), 15/7/35.
11 Briggs, p19.
12 BBC R44/238, memo Graves-Murray, 19/7/35.
13 Ibid., aide-memoire for Sir Stephen Tallents, 19/12/35.
14 Ibid., Tallents-DG's private secretary, 9/9/36.
15 Ibid., 'The League and the BBC'.
16 Ibid., Tallents-DG's private secretary, 9/9/36.
17 BBC R44/238, Elliot-Reith, 21/9/36.
18 Ibid., Reith-Elliot, 2/10/36.
19 Ibid., Tallents-Elliot, 2/2/37.
20 V&A/THM/149/4, unsigned letter to Wareing, 14/2/39.
21 V&A/THM/149/4, Whitworth-Wareing, 12/3/37.
22 Clive Barker: 'Theatre and society: the Edwardian legacy', in Barker and Gale (ed): *British Theatre between the Wars* (Cambridge: Cambridge University Press, 2000), p15.
23 E Martin Browne: 'The British Drama League', *Educational Theatre Journal*, Vol. 5, No. 3, October 1953, p203.

24 V&A/THM/149/7, Collins (TMA)-Wareing, 21/5/37.
25 Ibid., Report to League Executive Committee, 2/11/34.
26 *Northern Echo* (and other newspapers), 13/10/34.
27 See Chapter 9.
28 National Archives file T172/1338, Payne-Sir John Simon, 14/2/38.
29 Vol 16, No7, pp103–5.
30 V&A/THM/149/4, Esher-Wareing, 8/2/39.
31 Ibid., Whitworth-Morrison, 30/5/39.
32 *The Era*, 13/10/38.
33 See Chapter 2, pp13–14.
34 BBC R44/238, Tallents-DG's private secretary, 9/9/36.
35 V&A/THM/149/1, Chamberlain-Wareing, 21/12/35.
36 Ibid., Chamberlain-Wareing, 22/1/36.
37 Ibid., Wareing-Chamberlain, 17/7/38.
38 Ibid., Chamberlain-Wareing, 19/7/38.
39 This letter is missing from the archive; the Archbishop's reply survives – see below.
40 V&A/THM/149/4, Leverhulme-Wareing, 11/5/38.
41 Ibid. for both; messages dated 10/5/38 and 1/6/38, respectively.
42 Ibid., Cosmo Lang-Wareing, 8/6/38.
43 Lang papers, p363: Wareing-Lang, 11/6/38.
44 V&A/ THM/149/5, September 1938 'Report of the Honorary Organising Secretary'.
45 *Birmingham Post*, 3/8/38.
46 *Manchester Guardian*, 4/1/39.
47 *Malvern Gazette*, 19/8/39.
48 V&A/THM/149/5, Report of League of Audiences' Special Committee, December 1938.
49 *The Observer*, 29/9/35.
50 V&A/THM/149/5, 'Draft Budget For First Year'(undated, but 1934).
51 Ibid.
52 Ibid., figures from the League's annual accounts for the relevant years.
53 V&A/THM/149/7, Stephenson-Wareing, 9/12/38.
54 Ibid., Stephenson-Wareing 12/1/39.
55 Asa Briggs and Anne Macartney: *Toynbee Hall: The First Hundred Years* (Abingdon, Oxon: Routledge, 2011 [reprint of 1984 edition]), p117.
56 John Pick (ed): *The State and The Arts* (London: City University, Centre for the Arts, 1980), p119, for quotation and dates.
57 V&A/THM/149/7, undated note (but January 1939) from Jo Hodgkinson to League's Executive Committee.
58 Ibid., minutes of League Executive Committee meeting, 17/1/39.
59 Ibid., minutes of League Executive Committee meeting, 24/1/39.
60 Ibid.

61 Ibid., minutes of League Executive Committee meeting, 22/2/39.
62 V&A/THM/149/6, League's membership card index.
63 Glyndebourne archive: box entitled 'John Christie – letters re Glyndebourne Conference of Musicians 5&6/3/1938 and 2/7/1938' (hereafter 'Glyndebourne 2'), Christie-Baker, 4/2/38.
64 V&A/ THM/149/6, League's membership card index.
65 Glyndebourne 2, Christie-Baker 4/2/38.
66 Ibid., Baker-Christie, 8/2/38.
67 Ibid., Christie-Baker, 7/11/38.
68 Ibid., Baker-Edwards, 18/1/39.
69 Ibid., Christie-Baker, 1/2/39.
70 Ibid., Baker-Christie, 6/3/39.
71 V&A/THM/149/7, Wareing-Lawrence, 4/4/39.
72 Ibid., Lawrence-Wareing, 31/1/39.
73 Ibid., Wareing-Wilson, 25/1/39.
74 Ibid., Wareing-Lindsay, 30/1/39.
75 Ibid.
76 V&A/THM/149/5, November 1939 'Report of the Honorary Organising Secretary'.
77 See, for instance, the League's and WEA's letter headings, in V&A/THM/149/7.
78 V&A/THM/149/5, Quigley-Wareing, 24/11/38.
79 Ibid., Wareing-Quigley, 21/12/38.
80 V&A/THM/149/7, minutes of League Executive Committee meeting, 4/4/39.
81 May 1939, pp336–7.
82 Ibid., p374.
83 See Chapter 9.
84 V&A/THM/149/5, Boult-Wareing, 16/3/39, and Christopher Salmon (BBC)-Wareing, 22/6/39, respectively. In both cases, Wareing's letter is not on file.
85 V&A/THM/149/7, Mallon-Wareing, 21/7/39.
86 Briggs, p434.
87 So described in V&A/THM/149/5, November 1939 'Report of the Honorary Organising Secretary'.
88 Isaac, p149.
89 V&A/THM/149/7, Wareing-Collins, 15/8/39.
90 Ibid., Wareing-Elgin, 16/8/39.
91 Isaac, p149.
92 V&A/THM/149/7, Wareing-Temple, 22/9/39: extract from Wareing's 'Letter Book'.
93 Ibid., November 1939 'Report of the Honorary Organising Secretary'.
94 Ibid.
95 1/11/39.
96 V&A/THM/149/7, Wareing-Gordon, 30/1/40: extract from Wareing's letter book.

97 Ibid., Wareing-Hodgkinson, 15/6/40.

98 Ibid., Bishop of Worcester-Wareing, 31/7/40.

99 Ibid., Stephenson-Wareing, 26/8/40.

100 Ibid., Lipson-Wareing, 16/8/40.

101 Isaac, pxx.

102 Ibid.

103 *Stratford-upon-Avon Herald*, 17/4/42; *Evesham Journal*, 18/4/42.

104 13/4/42.

105 Manuscript note on p149.

106 V&A/THM/149/1, minutes of League Special General Meeting, 25/8/52.

107 'The Arts Council: Its Policy and Hopes', *The Listener*, 12/7/45.

108 Isaac, pxx; emphasis, quotation marks and punctuation in the original.

109 17/6/45.

110 27/8/52.

111 For Ivor Brown's CEMA and *Observer* roles, see entry on Brown in the *Oxford Dictionary of National Biography*. For his Arts Council membership, see its first annual report, 1945–6 (London: ACGB, 1946).

112 Isaac, ppix and x, for all quotations in this and the following paragraph.

113 http://www.theglasgowstory.com/story.php?id=TGSEH05, retrieved 15 January 2013.

114 Isaac, pvii.

115 Ibid.

116 Ibid., pxiii; the odd punctuation is in the original.

117 ACGB: Eleventh Annual Report 1955–1956: '*The First Ten Years*' (London: ACGB, 1956), pp6–7.

118 *Arts and Cultures: The History of the 50 Years of the Arts Council of Great Britain* (London: Sinclair-Stevenson, 1995), hereafter 'Sinclair', p23; see Chapter 1.

119 V&A/THM/149/6, White-Isaac, 13/1/50.

120 Ibid., White-Isaac, 22/3/51.

121 Ibid., Isaac-White, 23/9/51.

122 Quoting the *Yorkshire Observer*, 30/8/51.

123 Ibid., White-Isaac, 4/10/51.

124 V&A/ THM/149/6, Hodgkinson-Isaac, 17/10/51.

125 Sinclair, p166, for the following three quotations.

126 *The Arts Council of Great Britain* (London: Davis-Poynter, 1975).

127 Ibid., pp17–22.

128 Ibid., p18.

129 Ibid., p19.

130 London: Warner Books, pp27–30.

131 Abingdon: Routledge, 2016, p132; see also pp24 and 28 of McArthur's book.

6

# John Christie and the 'Council of Power': 1936–9

## Introduction

Alfred Wareing's League of Audiences was a very public campaign to secure state funding for the arts. This chapter considers a contrasting initiative with a similar objective, John Christie's 'Council of Power'. The following two chapters discuss Christie's attempts during the war to establish what by then he called the National Council of Music.

Christie's approach differed from the League's in methods, principles and issues. The League aimed to be a popular movement, requiring and receiving much favourable publicity. Christie neither sought nor received public or press attention for his work to 'organise music'. He was proud to call himself an autocrat. Involvement in his campaign was by invitation only. But many leading cultural figures of the period did become involved, and it was the forum in which debates were first aired which were to be, and to remain, central to CEMA and the Arts Council.

The issues preoccupying supporters and opponents of the League of Audiences became less relevant or changed their form after World War II. Benn Levy, among the most active pre-war opponents of state arts funding, joined the post-war Arts Council. And far from using music and drama subsidy as a weapon in a fight against the 'mechanised arts', CEMA and the Arts Council saw no reason to fight them. For them, radio and recordings were positive forces for the arts and for society; they believed that as funders they existed partly to satisfy a demand for live music in particular which the gramophone and the BBC had helped to create.[1] By contrast, matters discussed at John Christie's 1938 Glyndebourne conferences remained current and contentious for decades: whether the main priority of arts funding should be higher standards or increased availability ('raising' or 'spreading', in Arts Council language), and whether amateur or only professional artists should be supported from public funds.

What Christie's work shares with the League is neglect by almost all who have written about CEMA and the Arts Council or more generally about the state and the arts in Britain. Even Christie's only full-length biography[2] does not mention his pre-war campaign for public funding of the arts. Only Richard Witts, in *Artist Unknown*,[3] has discussed it. But Witts' unsubstantiated assertions, doubtful judgements and affection for non sequiturs make his work of limited value.

## The Beginnings: 'I want to form a Royal Society of Music'

These qualities are on full display in Witts' opening sentences: 'John Christie enjoyed the company of Nazis, while Maynard Keynes preferred the fellowship of boys. That is precisely why we have an Arts Council and not a Council for Music and the Arts.'[4] This grabs the attention and suggests that Christie was in some way important in the history of arts funding. It has no other value.

John Christie was the founder in 1934 of Glyndebourne Festival Opera.[5] He was born in 1882 into a prosperous but unhappy family. Christie's biographer Wilfrid Blunt reported that Christie's father 'was insanely jealous of his son, who had to be kept, so far as was possible, out of his sight'; that for three years of Christie's infancy his parents were separated; and that it was due only to his mother's possessing 'the highest sense of duty' that she moved back to the family home when Christie was four years old.[6] After an undistinguished school career at Eton and a spell in the army ended by a riding accident, Christie read sciences at Cambridge. He graduated in 1906 and spent sixteen years, with a break for war service in the army, teaching science at Eton. He had an early and long-lasting passion for the operas of Wagner, but at this stage no other connection with music or the arts in general.[7]

The Glyndebourne estate had been in Christie's family, not always in direct line of descent, from the fourteenth century.[8] In 1913 Christie's father (presumably having overcome his jealousy) handed it over to his son, though it became John Christie's in law only in 1920[9] and his main residence in 1922.[10] Christie's idea of building an opera theatre at Glyndebourne dated from just after his marriage to the opera singer Audrey Mildmay in 1931.[11] He intended that from its first season Glyndebourne should provide '"superb performances" which the public would treat with respect and not attempt to "sandwich between business interviews and a society party"'.[12] He achieved this. The Press was 'unanimous that this was a venture to be taken seriously', and from the start the BBC was 'clamouring for permission to broadcast some of the performances'.[13] This ensured a hearing for Christie's views on the arts and arts funding; as will be seen, he often failed to make good use of these opportunities.

Christie's ambivalence towards Alfred Wareing and the League of Audiences was explored earlier. He dismissed Wareing as 'an infuriating old man', but in late 1938 and 1939 he was not only the League's largest donor but also, anonymously, a personal benefactor to Wareing himself. The aspects of his character which this reveals – irascible, quixotic, generous, determined, irrational, overbearing – were apparent too in his work on arts funding. Isaiah Berlin wrote of Christie's 'peerless personality... the single-mindedness of a secular visionary... boldness, indomitable will and total independence'.[14] These qualities were a huge asset in creating the Glyndebourne Festival, given that opera 'was not part of the British cultural heritage'.[15] But their corollary was obstinacy, rudeness, myopia and unconcealed contempt for those who did not share his views.[16]

All this was clear from the start of his 'Council of Power' initiative, in February 1936. A letter to the critic Herbert Read contains the earliest record of his ideas.[17] Opening with 'Once more I need your help, in fact it is now impossible to get on without you', Christie set out his opinion of the musical establishment:

> I want to form a Royal Society of Music. There are only three musical bodies at the moment in England:-
>
> (1) The Musicians Union – ignorant and hopeless.
> (2) The Incorporated Society – nearly as bad.
> (3) The Musicians Company – which as far as I know only dines and sleeps.

Equally characteristic was his view of musicians themselves: 'It is necessary to include leading musicians in the country, such as Donald Tovey... Most of the others will have to pull up their socks before they are admitted'; his wish for royal patronage; his lack of clarity about the aims of the proposed organization: 'I want your help in setting out the purposes of the Society and its ideals'; and his vanity: 'The Society has got to be authoritative. In coming from Glyndebourne, it would, perhaps, have behind it the only authority which at present seems possible.' Christie proposed that 'it should be called:- "THE ROYAL SOCIETY OF MUSIC (BRITISH EMPIRE)"'. He did not at this stage envisage that the society should receive and distribute government money. Rather, 'if Music had an effective Society it would be able to command respect' from government; and, somehow, this would lead to 'help – financial and otherwise – for Music'.

It would be easy to dismiss this as buffoonery; it was certainly woolly-minded and vague. No reply is preserved in the archive. But alongside Glyndebourne's growing reputation, which made it difficult to dismiss Christie's views, he had well-informed, influential and supportive advisers. Among these was Sir Alan 'Tommy' Lascelles, between 1935 and 1953 assistant private secretary or private secretary to all monarchs from George V to Elizabeth II.[18] On 13 February 1936, a week after writing to Read and less than a month after George V's death, Christie wrote to Lascelles seeking royal support for his ill-defined 'Royal Society of Music'.[19] Lascelles was realistic but not totally discouraging: 'The King… cannot be publicly associated with any new venture until it is actually in being and stands securely on a solid basis, of which financial security and public approval are the two obvious corner-stones. The King's name cannot be associated with anything about which there is any danger of its being a "frost"'. But the King's name might be associated with an organization which 'has justified its claim to exist and can show it has the backing of a body of people really representative of the cause for which it is working'. This set a high bar.

Over the following eighteen months Christie devoted himself mainly to Glyndebourne. He made several unsuccessful approaches to the BBC for regular subsidy in return for broadcasting performances, the BBC paying instead a fee per broadcast, and to the Treasury for remission of Entertainments Duty on Glyndebourne performances.[20] Christie returned to his broader aims only in November 1937, in a long letter to the playwright, novelist and Independent MP A P Herbert setting out his ideas for 'what I call, at the moment, a Council of Power'.[21] This is the earliest traceable reference to the phrase; its origin is unclear, though it is characteristic of Christie. The letter suggests that Christie did not know Herbert well other than as an MP with artistic credentials, deeply involved in the campaign to repeal Entertainments Duty. Christie wanted a parliamentarian on his side, and 'of all the people in the House, I would rather have you'. This regard may not have been reciprocated: the Glyndebourne archive contains no reply from Herbert, and as will be seen below, Christie soon turned his attention to another MP.

Christie wrote to Herbert that 'we are trying to create a new industry, and we are trying to provide for the increased leisure of the people in time to come'. Achieving these aims should be masterminded by the Council of Power, consisting of 'several people who may be musical but who are essentially wise and experienced'. They would not be musicians: 'The advice I have been given by leading musicians has patently been colossally bad – I have not taken it'. This small council would be 'supported by a much larger and more or less ubiquitous Council', but the smaller 'should not be appointed by the larger Council'. Indeed, while the role of the smaller Council of Power was, as Christie expressed it, obscure, that of the larger council was clear: window-dressing.

By now Christie was hoping for public funding, but from local more than central government: 'My scheme avoids throwing more than a nominal expense on the Exchequer, but does throw an expense on the rates until the local people accept and use a new feature in their lives.' He expressed opposition to subsidized ticket prices, despite seeking subsidy for Glyndebourne, because 'The curse of modern life seems to be cheapness, which in Art or in Law is equally fatal.' The cost for central government would be 'the expenses of headquarters, plus some special feature, such as the engagement of Toscanini... etc., for continuous periods of six months, or a year, or several years etc.'. There would also be 'the salaries of say a dozen British conductors who would be working under the autocratic control of the world's greatest conductors.' The emphasis on autocracy and on Christie's concept of high standards, and the expressed dislike of subsidy, were typical. And his focus was always on music, though he did 'believe that Drama must be included.... But there again... the problem is to achieve the supremely good and to show up the bad commercial work with which the public is satisfied.'

Christie hoped that the prestige of the Council of Power would persuade local authorities to provide guarantees against loss for concert series, one of his few specific proposals: '...local authorities would be failing if they did not make the scheme go.' The Council of Power would provide 'the inspiration and education of the local authorities', but Christie also saw a need for tactical schemes and (vaguely defined) legal powers. Concerning the former, 'I should use dodges, such as allocating certain seats of honour to certain local magnates, in order... to obtain local glamour for the concerts.' As for legal powers, the League of Audiences' Music and Drama Bill would be useful, though it would require 'modification... because neither you nor I nor anyone else have any power to influence the local authorities, who are at present ignorant and ready to remain ignorant.'

## The Glyndebourne Conference of March 1938

### Christie Prepares

Throughout this phase of his work Christie combined obsessive interest in ancillary detail, such as the constitution and composition of the Council of Power, some tactical ideas of possibly reasonable quality, such as the 'seats of honour' for local business people, and a lack of strategic grasp. He never managed to explain, for instance, why, except under legal compulsion, local authorities should accept his plans. By contrast with his focus and skill in creating a world-class opera house from very little, Christie's pre-war campaign for public funding of the arts was in many respects remarkably inept. But its significance became apparent in its next phase: two conferences at Glyndebourne, in March and July 1938. These, as noted above, discussed, probably for the first time, issues which were to be central to CEMA and the Arts Council: whether the primary purpose of public funding should be raising standards or reaching as many people as possible, and whether it should assist amateur music and drama or professional work alone.

Christie's key helper at this period was 'one of John's most loyal and devoted assistants',[22] his secretary W E Edwards. Edwards came to Glyndebourne in 1920 as an accountant for Ringmer Building Works, a large building business which Christie ran from the house.[23] He eventually became responsible for administering most of Christie's business activities, working for him until 1953. In 1968, when Wilfred Blunt's biography was published, Edwards was still a director of Ringmer Building Works.[24] Papers in the Glyndebourne archive show that at this period Edwards as much as Christie led the thinking on the proposed Council of Power, a term of which Edwards was fond. He seems to have believed as strongly as Christie in the need for autocratic control exercised by Christie himself.

The March 1938 conference originated in Edwards' view, expressed in a letter to Christie,[25] that there were several unco-ordinated initiatives seeking government funding for the performing arts, notably the League of Audiences and the campaign to found a National Theatre (which 'continues with apparently no kind of solution to the problem of how it is to live'), and that there would be serious but unspecified problems 'unless a strong centralising lead comes along fairly early in the New Year [1938]'. Christie's reply was mainly an attack on the principle of subsidy: 'The cure must come by Music and Drama being fashionable... rather than by subsidizing people's absence [*sic*] and pretending that anyone who listens to Music and Drama must be poor. You can have cheap seats but you must also have expensive ones for people who can pay.... cheapening it... will make it unfashionable.'[26] Despite not addressing Edwards' points directly, and despite Christie's apparent dislike of subsidy, in essence they agreed. The same day Edwards wrote to Christie, Christie himself wrote to his friend Robert Forbes, Principal of the Royal Manchester College of Music, that 'The Country and the politicians pay little heed to musicians because they do not think them sensible. I believe very strongly that the solution of the problem lies in organization.... Intrigue and plotting at present prevent most of the advance that could be made.... Life is complicated, but I am absolutely sure that I am right.'[27]

Edwards sometimes outdid Christie in vague, grandiose and authoritarian language. Responding to Christie's comments on subsidy, Edwards suggested that it was of 'far-reaching importance... to find out whether the promoters of The Music and Drama Bill are intent upon only obtaining a "subsidy" or whether they are willing to have the Bill drawn up into a much higher category, as being the means by which your [Christie's] National Control could be established'.[28] But Edwards also attempted, mainly unsuccessfully, to prevent Christie pursuing vendettas. One was against a highly connected member of the BBC Music Department, Owen Mase, who was also director of the London Music Festival and, in effect, the representative in Britain of the conductor Arturo Toscanini.[29] Christie was offended not to have been invited to join the festival committee: 'I think they have shown great discourtesy to Glyndebourne and to me.'[30] But Edwards saw Mase, and particularly the festival's Chairman Sir Hugh Allen, as important potential allies.[31] Allen, the recently retired Director of the Royal College of Music, remained an influential figure in the British musical establishment. Edwards advised Christie that 'little good could come of a direct attack with regard to the omission of a gesture to you or to Glyndebourne'.[32] Fruitlessly: Christie had written to Mase the day before, to complain of a 'wholly unnecessary act of discourtesy'.[33] Mase played no part in Christie's work, and Allen became something of a hate-figure to Christie.[34]

Edwards' attempts to ensure that the conference dealt with drama as well as music also foundered on Christie's sensitivity to perceived slights. At Edwards' suggestion, Christie invited Lord Lytton, Chairman of the Board of the Old Vic and Sadler's Wells, to nominate a representative. Lytton's nominee was Muriel Gough, a Sadler's Wells governor. Christie's response was graceless: 'I was hoping to get from you a representative whose contribution would be... [more than as] a mere protagonist for Sadler's Wells.'[35] Though Gough attended the March conference, no further contact is recorded between Lytton and Christie.

At this stage, however, relations appeared cordial between Christie and John Maynard Keynes, who as Chairman of CEMA and subsequently the Arts Council became the key figure in arts funding in Britain during the war. Richard Witts claimed in *Artist Unknown* that Christie and Keynes had an 'aversion for each other', and that this somehow explained 'why we have an Arts Council and not a Council for Music and the Arts'.[36] The two fell out spectacularly after Keynes became Chairman of CEMA in 1942, but Witts provided no evidence of earlier animosity, failed to explain how an Arts Council differed from a Council for

Music and the Arts, and offered no reason why any such difference might stem from Keynes' and Christie's mutual aversion. In 1937 their relationship was sufficiently positive for Keynes to invite Christie to a performance of Moliere's *The Misanthrope* at the Cambridge Arts Theatre, starring his wife Lydia Lopokova.[37] Furthermore Keynes respected Christie's work at Glyndebourne. In a private letter to Sir Stephen Tallents, BBC Controller of Public Relations, in 1937,[38] he urged more broadcasts of opera from Glyndebourne, and also 'in the long period of the year when there is no opera, why not give the whole sequence of the Glyndebourne records?'.

Relations were still satisfactory at the time of Christie's conferences. As will be seen, Christie and Keynes held similar views on the type of 'high art' which deserved and needed government funding; and before the March conference Edwards recorded: 'Mr Christie also wonders whether he should endeavour to get Mr. Keynes for this meeting; I thought it would be an excellent thing. . .'[39] Keynes was invited, but replied: 'I am sorry to say that I am still out of health and unable, for the present, to accept any engagements.'[40] Given Christie's chronic inability to conceal his feelings, the absence of overt hostility in his pre-war correspondence with Keynes strongly suggests an absence of underlying hostility.

Christie suffered a disappointment before the conference. He wrote to his wife, on operatic tour in Italy, that he was 'a bit depressed about the result of my interview with the P.M.'s Secretary. He says that there is. . . no money for anything owing to Rearmament. So that my schemes however good or however bad can get no support.'[41] The papers contain no other reference to this meeting, but it influenced Christie's tactics for the conference. The aim 'must be to formulate the scheme, put our house in order'. Once this was done, 'if in such circumstances it is not fed [by government funding], it is being starved to death. The destruction would then be by the Government.'

Attendance at the March conference was varied and distinguished,[42] though all but one of those present were men. There were more musicians than might have been expected from Christie's writings, including the composer Ralph Vaughan Williams, the conductor Malcolm Sargent, and Sir Hugh Allen, despite the correspondence about the London Festival of Music. Their presence is the more surprising given Christie's notes for his opening remarks, which included: 'Ineffectiveness of musicians, shown by Entertainment Tax [presumably their failure to have it abolished]. Inability to use a musician or group of musicians – jealousy – temperament – training on too small lines.'[43] But he was selective about the musicians he invited, being adamant, for instance, that Sir Thomas

Beecham should not attend: 'I am told that Beecham is hostile to me, and... he does nothing to suggest that he isn't.... I think it is better to regard him as a conductor and that's that! In every other connection he seems to fail.'[44]

Most non-musicians at the conference had some connection with music, though they also included the King's private secretary Sir Alan Lascelles.[45] One participant particularly sympathetic to Christie's approach was Robert Mayer, a businessman who in 1923 founded a highly successful and long-running series of children's concerts, conducted by Adrian Boult and Malcolm Sargent, and in 1932 co-founded (with Beecham) the London Philharmonic Orchestra.[46] He wrote to Christie before the conference:

> The time is ripe to turn England into a musical Mecca.... There are other similarities between you and us [*sic*]. We both created something where nothing existed before. We, like you, belong to the small minority which is building and never satisfied, in contra distinction to the mediocre and self-satisfied man [*sic*] from which our profession is suffering badly.[47]

The sentiments and their expression might have been Christie's own.

Although, as Edwards wrote to Christie, 'the League [of Audiences] policy would not coincide with your own,'[48] the League could not be ignored. Edwards proposed that Alfred Wareing should not be invited, but this needed careful handling: '... you will need to have some right of interest in the [League's] Music and Drama Bill, and... you can hardly by-pass Wareing, unless you get him willingly to agree that either, or both, Mr. Baker or Mr. Hodgkinson should be at the conference.'

So both Jo Hodgkinson, Chairman of the League's Executive Committee, and Harold Baker, its Secretary and Treasurer, were invited.[49] Wareing was not. Hodgkinson was used as a bridge between the League and Christie. In the note in which he discussed inviting Keynes, Edwards recorded 'the desirability of the most careful consultation with Mr. Hodgkinson' to discover the League's view of 'Mr. Christie's projected revision of the Music and Drama Bill'.[50] Later, after 'a long and interesting conversation with Hodgkinson', Edwards decided that 'he has a growing regard for your [Christie's] scheme'.[51] Given the vagueness and shifting nature of Christie's scheme, Hodgkinson may have been expressing general rather than specific support, but he was to be an important participant at the conference. Harold Baker, unlike Hodgkinson, was a friend of Christie.[52] Christie's letter to Baker describing Alfred Wareing as 'an infuriating old man' dates from just before the conference.[53] Even by Christie's standards this letter was insensitive to his own weaknesses and to its recipient's feelings. As noted in

Chapter 5, Christie wrote of 'that damned old fool Wareing' that 'he listens to no one' and described the League of Audiences as 'the gathering together of a number of little people with small minds'. Baker took no apparent offence.

Preparing for the conference, Edwards produced for Christie a comparison between the League's proposals and his own.[54] This was not an objective document (unsurprising, given his devotion to Christie and enthusiasm for the Council of Power) but nor was it wholly unfair. It accepted that under Christie's scheme 'the benefit will not be quickly apparent', and its statement of aims was reasonable. The Council of Power sought 'To Raise the standard of Music and Drama throughout the Country.... To use and develop latent talent in the country... [and] create a larger listening public for first-class music by proper organisation and representation'. The League, by contrast, aimed 'To combat mechanisation by increasing living music and drama.... To promote the arts of music and drama by means of a Government subsidy... [and] Popularise music and drama "More, better, cheaper"'.

Then Edwards' objectivity slipped. Under the League's proposals, 'a subsidy is going to enable second-class performances to continue', while with Christie's proposals 'the money cannot get into the pockets of the wrong people, because it will be spent directly by the Council of Power'. The League would cause standards 'to be lowered throughout', whereas 'Mr. Christie's scheme works from the top – the initiative and activity comes from the leaders'. Christie and Edwards always assumed that a top-down system, with Christie at the top, would inevitably lead to higher standards. The leaders – the Council of Power itself – would be 'a self-appointed voluntary body of people... [acting as] the executive in organising music and in particular setting up permanent orchestras'. It would 'be supported by a larger body of musicians who would be able to present their point of view to the Council of Power.... The Government should grant loans through the Council of Power.... Municipalities would be required to support the scheme.'

Before the conference, Christie also discussed his ideas with Adrian Boult. In a follow-up letter,[55] he revealed surprising insecurity: 'I know that I have got to put my case with much greater feeling and inspiration on March 5th than I did yesterday'; but he concluded, more typically: '... simple honesty of purpose will win rather than intrigue.... I am inclined to ignore the alleged tales of hostility one hears because they seem so silly.' Boult sought to reassure him: '... the people you mentioned as coming to Glyndebourne for your Conference will be whole-heartedly out to help matters. I do not think you need fear intrigue.'[56]

## Discussion at the Conference

Christie's introductory remarks to the conference were delivered 'in the ORGAN ROOM – 9.30p.m. (Port on the tables)'.[57] The highly detailed minutes contain only brief references to international tensions. Christie himself commented that 'There is no Government subsidy likely to be forthcoming until the re-armament question is over'.[58] Jo Hodgkinson disagreed, suggesting that 'The Government was rushed into finding millions for the Physical Training and Recreation Act,[59] and such a distinguished body as yourselves could soon rush them into finding money for music'. This view was more typical of the conference than Christie's: discussion centred on where, how and by whom public money should be spent, not on how to persuade the government to part with it.

The most important issue at the March 1938 conference was whether the top priority for arts policy and subsidy should be raising standards or widening availability. Alfred Wareing rarely addressed this explicitly. Christie's and Edwards' view (see the briefing above) was that Christie aimed at 'better', the League at 'more'. In practice, this tension existed from the early days of CEMA and has continued throughout the Arts Council's existence. Keynes as Chairman of CEMA was in Christie's camp: in his study of CEMA, Fred Leventhal described Keynes as 'unashamedly elitist'.[60] But both CEMA and the Arts Council for decades sought to paper over the cracks by using the formula 'the best for the most'. According to Leventhal the phrase was coined by Wareing's friend Ivor Brown, who edited CEMA's bulletin. Leventhal commented that Brown 'was, perhaps not unwittingly, seeking to reconcile two divergent currents'.[61] The phrase fails in this aim. In a situation of limited resources choices have to be made, and 'the best for the most' avoids rather than assists such choices.

Jo Hodgkinson recognized the issue during the March conference: 'Supposing the State is willing to find money for Music and Drama, it will be limited in any case. Supposing you had to judge how that money should be spent. Would it be concentrated in first-class Opera Houses, first-class Orchestras and first-class Theatres, or to be spread over the whole Country [*sic*].' He had no answer to the dilemma: 'It is not unlikely that the Government will find money for this.... When we have got the money there will be important things to decide – whether the money should be spent on the masses in the state or on standard. Personally I cannot make up my mind on this...' ('Standard' was a common usage at the time for what would now be 'standards'.)

Christie had no such hesitancy. Excellence – as defined by himself – always came first: 'I quite agree that we should let the mob hear Opera... there should be some performances which are reserved for the poor (our dress rehearsals)... In working for a higher standard of music, of course we want to get the mob interested.... what I am alarmed at is that the mob should control music, because their taste is so bad.' Ralph Vaughan Williams intervened here: 'Could I ask Mr Christie what he means by "the mob"?' Christie explained: 'The cinema crowd.' Vaughan Williams was the strongest advocate for the contrary view: 'We want to make opera popular and the thing that everyone wants to go to, from the richest to the poorest. We may have to leave out perfection to get popularity.' Malcolm Sargent agreed: 'I think that if we cannot get the standard of Glyndebourne everywhere it is better to have a lower standard than none at all, for the ordinary person.'

Also relevant to the future CEMA and Arts Council, Vaughan Williams sought to discuss support for music-making by amateurs. In a 1932 lecture[62] he had connected this with concern about 'machine-made music': 'Gramophones and wireless have brought the world's riches to the doors of the humblest, but if we all become listeners, there will soon be no one left to listen to. Modern invention is tending to make us content only with the cream of music, but where will the cream come from if there is no milk to skim it off?' At the Glyndebourne conference he argued that 'it is important that we shall become, not a Nation of music listeners, but of music makers'. He saw no contradiction between this and Christie's campaign for high standards. Amateur music-making, for Vaughan Williams, was not only good in itself, but also raised professional standards by creating a discerning and critical audience and acting as the soil from which future professional musicians would grow: 'When people start making music they discriminate for themselves. We have magnificent orchestras at the moment, but they will get past their best. Who is to take their place?'

The argument that educated and critical amateurs helped maintain high professional standards was current also in the musical press. In August 1937, for instance, a *Musical Times* article had suggested that:

> People who can do something for themselves are better able to judge the merits of other people's performances.... the League of Audiences... points out the paradox that in this mechanized age the survival of personal interpretation in music and the preservation of the inspiration of sophisticated audiences have become imperative.[63]

No one responded to Vaughan Williams' arguments, but the issue of amateur art featured more strongly in Christie's July conference.

Vaughan Williams also raised the issue of national art. This was a recurring theme for him in the 1930s: his 1932 lecture had been one of a course of lectures on the subject delivered at Bryn Mawr College, Pennsylvania.[64] At the conference he said: 'We all admire your performances [at Glyndebourne], but it is only through your personal initiative that these performances are taking place in England. . . . They might have been in any other part of the world. . . . We must aim at an art made by our own people.' Again Sargent agreed, explicitly linking this with the question of artistic standards: 'I admire Glyndebourne very much; it is the best opera I have ever been to and I admire you [Christie] for creating it, but I would admire you much more if you did not care what the Foreigner thinks.'

Aside from these issues of principle, discussion at the conference focused on how to structure government support of the arts. Ideas ranged from some which remained current in the Arts Council for several decades to others either trivial or prejudiced. Among the former were Malcolm Sargent's thoughts on the role of local government, in particular the potential for matched funding challenges to coax local authorities to spend:

> More good could be done by the local Corporation than the State with regard to local music. They know local artists. . . . The combination of the State with the Corporation would be the easiest method. . . . If it were known that if £500 would be given from the Corporation and £500 from the State funds, it would be a grand thing. The more they give, the more they will get, and the ratepayers will feel that they are getting something from the State.

Sargent had previously proposed this in a letter to *The Times* in June 1937, suggesting that among its advantages would be the provision of subsidy for music without 'the dangers which can result when any form of artistic enterprise is controlled by a Government department'.[65] But as with Vaughan Williams' case for supporting amateurs, it went unanswered at the conference, Sargent asking plaintively: 'I should like to know what is the snag in my idea of a £ to £ basis, which seems to me very good.'

Jo Hodgkinson attempted to summarize and reconcile the conference's main lines of discussion: wider availability or higher quality; support for amateur art or for professionals only; local funding or a central distributing body, in Christie's words, 'autocratic and protected from abuse by politicians and the public'. Despite his role in the League of Audiences, Hodgkinson was remarkably willing to cede leadership, suggesting that 'Mr. Christie should call together some men to form a National Council. . . . What we want is a National Body, without money, which could act in pulling together all interests. . . The Government won't do anything until such a body is formed and has respect and trust all round.' Hodgkinson was even ready to surrender control over the League's Music and Drama Bill: '. . . it has been decided to redraft the whole Bill. It has been decided to call representatives of all organizations, which might be said to have a personal interest, round a table to state their opinions. Could Mr. Christie send representatives from this Conference to this meeting, and could we agree to work together?' Hodgkinson may have been carried away by the moment: there is nothing in the League's papers to suggest that Alfred Wareing had agreed to or even knew about this offer, and Wareing was as little inclined to compromise as Christie himself. In any case, the proposal went nowhere.

Even with Hodgkinson's diplomatic skills, consensus was likely to be either impossible or empty of substance. In this case it was the latter – a resolution both vacuous and obscure:

> The Conference passed the following resolution:-
>
> > 'A Committee should be appointed to consider whether they could appoint some Body who would gain the respect of the whole Country.'[66]

In a considerable overstatement, Richard Witts claimed of the March 1938 conference that 'In that astonishing weekend the group defined all the basics of the Arts Council'.[67] This was not so. Important topics were raised (like Sargent on matched funding, and Vaughan Williams on the support of amateur arts) but not pursued; and Christie's obstinacy and obsessions did the event no favours. But the conference deserves more attention than it has received. It aired crucial dilemmas, practical questions and philosophical issues around state funding of the arts, and demonstrated, contrary to the views of most commentators, that these were debated actively and intensely in the 1930s. It constitutes an important part of the Arts Council's pre-history.

## The July 1938 Conference

Despite Hodgkinson's lame conference resolution, Christie was full of praise for him. He wrote to his friend Harry Colles, music editor of *The Times*:

> I think you will now have realised that the success of our operations was due to the wide, wise and strong element of the non-professional at our meeting. The vested interests did not know how strong we were. . . . The ball was definitely rolling to them when. . . they roused Hodgkinson, who, in a masterly speech at precisely the right time, won the day.[68]

Christie felt that his view on the issue of artistic excellence had prevailed. He wrote to another friend, the singer Roy Henderson: 'I am sure we are on the right track in concentrating on standard. I am sure that the standard is often impossibly low.'[69] Henderson was a strong ally. In an undated letter to Christie from this period he wrote: '... this is one hell of a life for anyone who feels that there is value in correct notes, correct time and rhythm and a dynamic range down to *ppp*.'[70] Christie confided to Colles one area of failure: '... there was one person with whom I entirely failed to make a contact – Miss Muriel Gough [the Old Vic/ Sadler's Wells nominee] – but I can only say that Rhona Byron [a friend and neighbour of Christie],[71] who is level-headed and sensible, thought Miss Gough as stupid as I did. She would not listen, but persisted in talking...';[72] a frequent Christie complaint.

The committee taking forward Hodgkinson's resolution consisted of Christie, Frank Eames, Secretary of the Incorporated Society of Musicians (ISM), which Christie had criticized so severely, Hodgkinson himself and Robert Mayer, the businessman and supporter of music for young people.[73] 'The profession' was in a minority of one. Each member approached the task differently. Christie used the committee to further his concept of musical standards. From now on the initiative was almost exclusively about music; he dropped his already very secondary focus on drama. Hodgkinson continued to try to keep the peace. Mayer worked behind the scenes, providing private advice to Christie. He argued, for instance, that it was unrealistic and damaging to distinguish between 'good music and "mere entertainment"',[74] since local councils would not accept this: 'Take a concrete case: Bournemouth subsidises an orchestra with a proviso that there are (x) concerts of classical music and (x) concerts of light music; you could not separate the two.... without the mixture they would not subsidise anything at all.' This was sound advice, on which Christie did not act.

The fourth member, Eames, wrote a paper setting out possible aims and terms of reference for the proposed national organization.[75] The paper managed the difficult trick of being simultaneously detailed and vague. The organization's primary purpose would be 'To promote the best interests of the Art of Music throughout the United Kingdom and any other countries'. The first proposed sub-purpose was 'To admit to representation on the Council such institutions, societies, committees or other bodies incorporated or unincorporated in such manner as may from time to time be determined'. Its functions would include: 'To watch over legislation affecting Music... and to oppose any legislation considered harmful to Music and generally to watch over, promote and safeguard the interests of Music'.

Given thinking and writing of this quality, it is no surprise that the committee's report, produced for Christie's conference in July 1938, lacked substance. It was mainly a list of organizations which might send representatives to constitute the 'Body who would gain the respect of the whole country', with few suggestions about what it might actually do, why and how.[76] By now it was called the National Council of Music (NCM). The committee envisaged there being twenty-one 'ordinary members' and a separate, subordinate group of 100 'representative members', drawn from organizations as diverse as the Welsh Education Board, the BBC, the ISM, the major music schools and the County Councils Association. Compiling the 'representative members' list was mainly Frank Eames' work. Christie and Robert Mayer showed more enthusiasm for the 'ordinary members', where they envisaged power residing.

Writing to Keynes, Christie explained that they would be '21... people of wide experience of life'; then 'music... will speak sensibly, because it will have to carry these 21 with it and this rules out pettiness, intrigues and feuds'.[77] The letter is further evidence that Christie thought well of Keynes at this stage. Christie had 'ventured to suggest your name as one of these 21', was 'delighted to hear' that Keynes would be attending the July conference, wondered whether Keynes' wife would be present, and hoped that he might arrive early so Christie could explain his proposals. (In fact Keynes withdrew from the conference two days later, again citing ill-health.)[78]

Robert Mayer produced his own list of possible 'ordinary members', his secretary noting that he had included women in his list, since in Mayer's view 'we can usefully imitate the U.S.A. where women take a much larger part in the administration of music....'[79] The women he suggested included the pacifist and social reformer Dame Elizabeth Cadbury and Baroness Ravensdale, daughter of Lord Curzon. Neither had much connection with music, though according to the Oxford Dictionary of National Biography Baroness Ravensdale began in 1917 a lifetime of voluntary work by singing at a boys' club in the East End of London.[80] Mayer's list also included Keynes, R H Tawney and Lord Macmillan, who became Minister of Information on the outbreak of war and was CEMA's first Chairman.

There was much overlap between attendance at the March and July conferences.[81] Jo Hodgkinson was again present, this time with his Toynbee Hall boss James Mallon, also active in the League of Audiences. As in March musicians were strongly represented, including, again, Ralph Vaughan Williams. And as in March the conference apparently saw little threat in the international situation. Indeed, Christie saw a positive side to turmoil in Europe: 'We have got a marvellous opportunity. The rest of the World is upside down and England is stable.' But he compared England unfavourably to Austria, where 'everyone seems to talk about music'. His opening remarks had two familiar themes: 'If you want people to respect music, I believe that you have got to concentrate on the standard of performance'; and 'If we could get the representation of music sufficiently authoritative, I believe that the Government and other people would pay attention'. For Christie, 'The existence of Entertainments Tax proves that there is no authority at the moment.' Frank Eames responded that 'it was entirely due to the work of the I.S.M. that the Entertainments Tax was removed from Music Societies'. This was not true.[82] Christie then illustrated the sort of person he had in mind to represent music:

> . . . I suggest a man such as Archibald Sinclair, Leader of the Liberal Party. He has got four million votes and is a power in the country. If people like that came to the conclusion that musicians were right. . . it would be difficult for the Government not to accept their opinion. . . . it would be a tremendous asset to Professional musical opinion if it could be backed by consultation with people such as Archie Sinclair.

Christie's paean to Sinclair then tailed off rather bizarrely: 'He has done nothing for music, and has achieved nothing, but it would, I believe, help in that way.'

When Eames introduced the committee's report, it became clear that his view of the proposed council differed fundamentally from Christie's. Eames expressed no interest in the distinguished 'ordinary members'; he supported the council's lobbying for state funding of music; but before that could happen, 'We want a complete statistical survey of music in this Country. Such a survey is necessary before the Council could approach the Government on any scheme for State Aid for Music'. This was a view Christie came round to several years later.[83] But the following exchange makes it difficult to understand why Eames had laboured so painstakingly on the council's membership and procedures – apparently he wished it to be powerless:

> **Dr.[James]Mallon** The words REFERENCE or ADVISORY do not sufficiently express the nature of the new body. . . I suggest 'Co-ordinating Body' or some word which suggests the power to initiate. . . .
>
> **Mr. Eames** I would like to suggest that it is most important that the initiative of this Council should be very severely restricted.

The July conference involved much discussion of this type, and still more about which organizations should be entitled to nominate 'representative members' to the national council (orchestras? music publishers? agents?). But the conference was more notable for Vaughan Williams championing the cause of amateur music-making. He argued that 'the backbone of music is the amateur. I am all for having ideals of high standards, but this must not discourage people.... Our object should be to raise the standard of music all over England.... What we want is a clause [in the statement of the council's functions] to encourage everyone to make their own music.' Christie's friend Harold Baker proposed that a clause drafted by Christie be added: 'To make a continuous effort to improve the standard of performance of music in England, with a view to raising the status of music in our lives.' This, he suggested, supported both amateur and professional music-making. Vaughan Williams agreed: '"To maintain a high standard" treads on nobody's toes.' But Robert Mayer, without explanation, described it as 'a dangerous clause'. With no further discussion it was rejected as one of the council's functions, instead being included in the preamble to its terms of reference.

The outcome of this conference too lacked substance: another committee to take forward the creation of the National Council of Music. Christie, Eames and Mayer were agreed as members of this committee as of the previous one; Robert Forbes and George Dyson (see below) were added; but Jo Hodgkinson had had enough: 'I think my work is finished with the work of the small interim Committee.' The minutes also record an enigmatic contribution by the concert promoter Harold Holt about the committee's membership: 'I suggest Sir Thomas Beecham. I withdraw that suggestion'; without intervening comments.

Then the participants adjourned for a performance of Verdi's *Macbeth*.

## Christie in the Approach to War

Robert Forbes, Principal of the Royal Manchester College of Music and now one of Christie's committee, was a strong ally. Following the July conference they reflected on the conference, musical standards and amateur music-making. Forbes believed that Christie's work at Glyndebourne had already 'done more for the prestige of English music than generations of choral societies, amateur orchestras, colleges..., schools of native composers, doctors of music and all the rest of the paraphernalia we look upon as our "National Musical Life"'.[84] Forbes 'was quite horrified at the outlook of people like Vaughan Williams, to whom standards of performance mean nothing.... This complacent contentment with mediocrity on the part of our so-called leaders of music in England has been a curse for many years.' Christie's reply was, for him, remarkably moderate: 'I agree with Vaughan Williams that we do not want a Nation of listeners, like America, and, in fact, neither my effort at standard nor Vaughan Williams' effort at public-house music [*sic*] is in itself complete. I think that Vaughan Williams is really coming round to see that both are necessary.'[85] But 'I can see so clearly that the prestige of music depends at this moment more on the standard of performance than on the number of people making music. The immediate purpose is to gain respect for music as such.'

Christie's next approach suggests a shift from this uncharacteristic moderation to something far less balanced. In October 1938 he wrote to Lady Reading,[86] who later founded and chaired the Women's Voluntary Service.[87] The letter was a distorted echo of discussion at the conferences, a remarkable communication from a man of high standing and achievement in the world of music, with substantial artistic, business and political contacts, to someone he scarcely knew. He chose Lady Reading as recipient 'because as you will remember I was so much impressed by your conversation with me at dinner'. He proceeded to offer alarming confidences and make still more alarming claims. He regarded Glyndebourne as 'only the first step' in his mission. With its prestige as 'an acknowledged and undisputed International achievement', he wanted to use it as 'the background of very much bigger and more important work… a National Council of Music, which shall be the sole and absolute Authority for music in the British Isles'. Concerning his credentials, Christie provided an account of the conferences at variance with their minutes: 'I summoned the leading musical people in England to two conferences at Glyndebourne with a view to the National Council of Music, and was told by them that, owing to the achievement of Glyndebourne, I was the one person in the country who had the right to summon them.' He suggested that 'a Committee is at work on what should be the final details'. He did not explain the purpose or methods of the 'sole and absolute Authority for music', and his account of the committee formed at the July conference was simply untrue. W E Edwards recorded in a memo (undated, but probably from early 1939) that 'There has up to the present time been no formal meeting of that Committee.… Mr Christie's desire is not to press for work through that Committee at the moment.'[88]

This was probably because Christie wanted no restriction on his power to run the show, as he explained with bizarre candour to Lady Reading: 'I hear on all sides that I have succeeded because I am an autocrat and not a Committee.' Alongside his national council he wished to form 'a Trust for music.… I want £1,000,000 and I want the Trust controlled by me, as an autocrat, with an Advisory and Consultative Committee which can only talk and not decide.…' As if writing of a third party, he 'believe[d] that this basis is the right basis and that it will receive the support of other people.... I cannot but believe that the Dictator of this Trust would act wisely....' The trust 'would be a force the Government would have to reckon with if the Government started interfering with music'. He was silent on what the trust would do, but continued baldly: 'I want to find some very rich person who will give the million....' Finally he explained what he sought from Lady Reading: 'Would you interest yourself as the link between me and such a benefactor?'

Unsurprisingly, Lady Reading's answer was 'No': '... I fear that I may have raised in your mind, hopes and expectations which, much as I would wish to do so, I am quite unable to implement.... frankly I have not amongst my acquaintances anyone who I think might possibly be prepared to offer £1,000,000 for your scheme.'[89] She did accept that 'there are people with money, and if one knew how to get hold of them they might put it up; people like Lady Yule, Lord Nuffield and very possibly extremely rich Welsh people who being such lovers of music might be prepared to act on its behalf'.

This correspondence showed Christie's delusional side. His dealings around this time with 10 Downing Street were more rational. He had several exchanges of letters with Neville Chamberlain and with Lord Dunglass, later Sir Alec Douglas-Home, Chamberlain's Parliamentary Private Secretary.[90] Writing to Dunglass in February 1939 Christie explained that he was addressing him rather than Chamberlain because 'I do not think it fair to ask him [Chamberlain] in these difficult times and when the Labour Party are behaving so badly, to give up his time to consider my problem'.[91] The problem was whom to appoint to the NCM. Christie's proposed categories of member suggested a nod towards Vaughan Williams' view of amateurs: '1. Leading musicians in England. 2. Most important – in fact more important than the leading musicians!... (a) Musical amateurs.... (b) Men of great distinction in England who would think it worth while to advise and support music, professional and non-professional.' He wished for Chamberlain's advice on this last category, explaining to Dunglass:

> I have already talked to Archie Sinclair about it and obtained his general approval. My own view is that Chamberlain would be almost the most suitable of all because he is a man who, of all the leading politicians, is almost alone in actually showing some interest in music. Sam Hoare has been to Glyndebourne, but I don't know him personally.

Christie displayed his less rational side in suggesting that professional musicians 'have been such fools and have done their work so badly that the politicians would be justified in turning round and giving them a damned good thrashing'.

And his lack of interest in the international situation perhaps showed in his noting, simply as an issue of timing, that 'I am going to Germany early next week'.

Dunglass replied the next day. While 'the P.M. is overwhelmed with work over the next week or so and I am doubtful whether, as P.M., he could be actively associated with such a body... he will I know be very much interested & I should like to talk the matter over with him'.[92] He seems to have done so: the archive contains a list of possible national council members which, according to W E Edwards' covering note, was 'a copy of the list of names given to you [Christie] by the Prime Minister'.[93] Elsewhere in the archive is what seems to be the original list (the names are identical), unsigned but on paper headed 'Prime Minister'.[94] There were nineteen names, including Tom Jones, who was to be the prime mover behind CEMA, and Lord Macmillan, its first Chairman; two Court of Appeal judges; several active or retired politicians, mainly Liberal or National Liberal, including Archibald Sinclair and Reginald McKenna, but also the Labour politician Hugh Dalton; Sir Montagu Norman, Governor of the Bank of England; Sir John Reith, recently retired as BBC Director-General; Lord Howard de Walden, who, among other links with the arts, had hosted the League of Audiences' first 'at home' in May 1935;[95] and J B Priestley.

The list is significant for showing that Chamberlain took Christie's initiative seriously rather than for its consequences: there is no evidence that Christie used it.

Christie's direct correspondence with Chamberlain was fairly frequent but mainly at a courtesy level – for instance, an invitation from Christie to Verdi's *Macbeth* at Glyndebourne in May 1939, and Chamberlain's reply that he had already arranged to see it in July: 'I am looking forward very much to the occasion, and hope that I may have the pleasure of seeing you and Mrs Christie then'.[96] *The Times* later reported[97] that Chamberlain and his wife 'were guests of John Christie... and sat in his private box. When the lights went up... the audience turned towards the box and stood cheering and clapping continuously for over a minute.' Their correspondence continued almost until Chamberlain's death in 1940. But in July 1939 Christie instead approached Dunglass again.[98]

This was in effect a begging letter on behalf of Glyndebourne, and apparently followed a meeting the previous day. Christie began by thanking Dunglass for his help and 'in case it may be of use to you... setting down one or two points that I made'. It, and Dunglass' reply, reveal Christie's inconsistent approach to the question of subsidy, and the government's view of it at the time. Christie wrote that Glyndebourne was 'self-supporting if people buy the tickets', but that he could not build up reserves to cover losses in 'a bad year Internationally, or perhaps from Labour troubles'. Accordingly, in order to maintain 'the prestige of the Festival in the eyes of the world, and so… the prestige of British music, which, as you know, is my essential concern, I am asking for £10,000 a year for a few years'. Christie bolstered this appeal with three arguments. First: 'So much money is taken by the Government out of music, it does not seem much to put back. If I had had £5,000 a year subsidy since I started, I should already have £30,000… to build up a reserve.' Second, 'Covent Garden has, after all, much more than this, and has only paid this subsidy to the foreign artists who arrive the day before and leave the day after with their fees.' Third, 'the National Council of Music should be formed after the holidays [that is, in autumn 1939], but it will be a little embarrassing for me immediately to ask their help as their first official duty.'

Dunglass replied on 18 August, two weeks before the outbreak of war: 'I find that the chances of a Treasury subsidy for Glyndebourne are, at present at least, not worth pursuing. I am met at every turn by the contention that a subsidy could not be justified… to something which caters to the comparatively wealthy.'[99] He recommended that Christie apply for funds to the Pilgrim Trust, a reasonable suggestion given that three months later the Pilgrim Trust provided the initial funding for what became CEMA. Christie seems not to have followed it up.

Christie's statement that the NCM was close to being set up was as false in July 1939 as in October 1938, when made to Lady Reading. But the prospect and then the declaration of war seemed temporarily to spur him on. In August 1939 he tried to organize yet another conference, to take place at his Devon home from 22 to 25 September: 'I am going to endeavour to get some special fares for the journey from the Southern Railway.'[100] He pursued the idea into September, writing to George Dyson, Director of the Royal College of Music, six days after war was declared: 'I believe that our Council should be formed now and that we should not wait for Peace.'[101] He proposed that the conference go ahead as planned: 'We have still got our servants and our house. The trains down here from London are at present not too full.' The conference was finally postponed at four days' notice, Christie hoping, as it turned out, in vain, that it would take place 'in two or three weeks' time'.[102] Even Robert Forbes, among Christie's most like-minded friends, wrote that while he 'had not heard… that the conference was postponed, I naturally assumed that it was bound to be for the present'.[103]

## Conclusion

John Christie had the qualities of a pioneer, including energy, vision and self-belief. These were evident in his creating the Glyndebourne Festival, from its earliest years recognized as providing the highest standard of opera performances available in Britain – for those with enough money and time. But as he said in a radio talk in July 1939, 'Glyndebourne… is the first step in our work. Our real purpose is to raise the status of music in England.'[104] This chapter has recorded his steps towards this larger goal up to the outbreak of war – determined, clumsy, sometimes deluded, always eccentric – and the debates which his work opened up.

Apart from Glyndebourne itself, Christie had little success by September 1939 in 'raising the status of music in England'. But his conferences and lobbying meant that artists, arts administrators and (to some extent) politicians were for the first time considering central issues of arts policy. He strengthened his efforts during the war. The following two chapters examine Christie's wartime attempts to create the National Council of Music, and suggest that they too have an importance in British cultural history which has been overlooked.

## Notes

1 See, for instance, John Maynard Keynes: 'The Arts Council: Its Policy and Hopes' (*The Listener*, 12/7/45).

2 Wilfred Blunt: *John Christie of Glyndebourne* (London: Geoffrey Bles, 1968); hereafter 'Blunt'.

3 London: Warner Books, 1998; hereafter 'Witts'.

4 Witts, p9.

5 Biographical material on Christie from Blunt and from Spike Hughes: *Glyndebourne: A History of the Festival Opera* (Newton Abbot: David and Charles, 1965), hereafter 'Hughes'.

6 Blunt, p12.

7 See Blunt, pp22–39.

8 Hughes, pp15–20, provides a history of the house and estate from 1300 to Christie's birth.

9 Blunt, p56.

10 Ibid., Chapters 6 and 7 *passim*.

11 Hughes, pp32–3.

12 Blunt, p161, quoting an article by Christie in the *Monthly Musical Record* for November 1933.

13 Ibid., pp172 and 180, respectively.

14 Isaiah Berlin: 'Mozart at Glyndebourne half a century ago', in John Higgins (ed): *Glyndebourne – A Celebration* (London: Jonathan Cape, 1984), p103.

15 Ibid., p104.

16 Blunt's book has the strengths and weaknesses of most authorized biographies, but does describe some of Christie's less attractive characteristics.
17 Glyndebourne archive: box 'John Christie correspondence 1934–37; misc correspondence July 1936-February 1940' (hereafter: 'Glyndebourne 1'), Christie-Herbert Read, 4/2/36.
18 Frank Prochaska, 'Lascelles, Sir Alan Frederick (1887–1981)', *Oxford Dictionary of National Biography*, Oxford University Press, 2004.
19 The Glyndebourne archive does not contain this letter; the date, and the following quotations, are taken from Lascelles' reply of 10/3/36, in Glyndebourne 1.
20 Letters in Glyndebourne 1.
21 Glyndebourne archive: box 'John Christie – letters re Glyndebourne Conference of Musicians 5&6/3/1938 and 2/7/1938' (hereafter 'Glyndebourne 2'), Christie-A P Herbert, 6/11/37, for all quotations in this and the following three paragraphs.
22 Blunt, p81.
23 Ibid., p79.
24 Ibid., p81.
25 Glyndebourne 2, Edwards-Christie, 29/12/37.
26 Ibid., Christie-Edwards, 30/12/37.
27 Ibid., Christie-Forbes, 29/12/37.
28 Ibid., Edwards-Christie, 14/1/38.
29 See, generally, Christopher Dyment: *Toscanini in Britain* (Woodbridge, Suffolk: Boydell Press, 2012).
30 Glyndebourne 2, Christie-Rudolf Bing (Glyndebourne General Manager), 28/1/38.
31 Ibid., Edwards-Christie, 26/1/38.
32 Ibid.
33 Ibid., Christie-Mase, 25/1/38.
34 See below and Chapter 7.
35 Glyndebourne 2, Christie-Lytton, 3/2/38.
36 Witts, p9.
37 Glyndebourne 1, Keynes-Christie 28/1/37.
38 Keynes-Tallents, 12/7/37, reprinted in Donald Moggridge (ed): *The Collected Writings of John Maynard Keynes Volume XXVIII: Social, Political and Literary Writings* (London: Macmillan/Cambridge University Press/Royal Economic Society, 1982), pp352–3.
39 Glyndebourne 2, file note by Edwards, 18/1/38.
40 Ibid., Keynes-Christie 22/1/38.
41 Glyndebourne archive: file 'Family correspondence, 1934–41', folder headed 'John Christie to Audrey Christie, 1938', Christie-Audrey Christie, 29[*sic*]/2/38 (presumably 28/2 or 1/3), for this and the following quotations.
42 Glyndebourne 2, document headed 'LIST OF GUESTS FOR WEEK-END, MARCH 5TH–6TH, 1938'.

43 Ibid., Christie's notes for conference of 5–6/3/38.

44 Ibid., Christie–Harry Colles, 24/1/38.

45 Ibid., file note by Edwards, 18/1/38.

46 Robert Armstrong, 'Mayer, Sir Robert (1879–1985)', *Oxford Dictionary of National Biography*, Oxford University Press, 2004.

47 Glyndebourne 2, Mayer-Christie, 19/1/38.

48 Ibid., Edwards-Christie, 26/1/38.

49 On Hodgkinson's and Baker's work for the League see, generally, Chapter 5; for Baker see also Chapter 3.

50 Glyndebourne 2, file note by Edwards, 18/1/38.

51 Ibid., Edwards-Christie, 26/1/38.

52 Baker's friendship with Christie is clear from correspondence in the Glyndebourne archive, not from published sources.

53 Glyndebourne 2, Christie-Baker, 4/2/38.

54 Ibid., manuscript document headed 'SUGGESTED SCHEMES', undated but from context February 1938, for quotations in this and the following paragraph.

55 Glyndebourne 2, Christie-Boult, 16/2/38.

56 Ibid., Boult-Christie, 19/2/38.

57 Ibid., unsigned note to Christie headed 'Time-table and information'.

58 Glyndebourne 2, minutes of conference of 5–6/3/38, for all quotations in this and the following eight paragraphs except where specified otherwise.

59 See Chapter 3, pp36–7.

60 Leventhal, p317, and see, generally, Chapter 8.

61 Leventhal, p297.

62 Reprinted in Ralph Vaughan Williams: *National Music and Other Essays* (London: Oxford University Press, 1963), p68; hereafter '*National Music*'.

63 Cecil Palmer: 'Music and Personal Interpretation', *The Musical Times*, Vol 78 No 1134, August 1937, p697.

64 Reprinted in *National Music*, pp1–82.

65 23/6/37, p12; see also Chapter 9, p207.

66 Glyndebourne 2, Resolution from conference of 5–6/3/38.

67 Witts, p33.

68 Glyndebourne 2, Christie-Colles, 8/3/38.

69 Ibid., Christie-Henderson, 16/3/38.

70 Ibid., Henderson-Christie, undated.

71 Blunt, p220.

72 Glyndebourne 2, Christie-Colles, 8/3/38.

73 Ibid., report of committee appointed at conference of 5–6/3/38.

74 Ibid., Mayer-Christie, 19/4/38.

75 Ibid., memo by Frank Eames, 28/4/38.

76 Ibid., report of committee appointed at conference of 5–6/3/38.
77 Ibid., Christie-Keynes, 18/6/38, and for the following quotations.
78 Ibid., postcard Keynes-Christie, 20/6/38.
79 Ibid., Robert Mayer's secretary-Christie, 23/6/38.
80 Anne de Courcy, 'Curzon, (Mary) Irene, suo jure Baroness Ravensdale, and Baroness Ravensdale of Kedleston (1896–1966)', *Oxford Dictionary of National Biography*, Oxford University Press, 2004.
81 Glyndebourne 2, minutes of conference of 2 July 1938, for attendance list and all quotations in this and the following three paragraphs.
82 See Chapter 9.
83 See Chapter 8.
84 Glyndebourne 2, Forbes-Christie, 6/7/38.
85 Glyndebourne 2, Christie-Forbes, 7/7/38.
86 Ibid., Christie-Lady Reading, 27/10/38, for all quotations in this and the following paragraph other than that by Edwards.
87 http://www.history.ac.uk/reviews/review/379 ; retrieved 15 April 2013.
88 Glyndebourne 2, undated memo by W E Edwards headed 'Steps Already Taken In The Formation Of The National Music Council'.
89 Glyndebourne 2, Reading-Christie, 11/11/38.
90 'Lord Dunglass' was a courtesy title which did not prevent his being an MP.
91 Glyndebourne 2, Christie-Dunglass, 1/2/39.
92 Ibid., Dunglass-Christie, 2/2/39.
93 Ibid., Edwards-Christie, 19/4/39, covering list of names headed by Lord Alness.
94 Glyndebourne archive: box entitled 'National Council of Music – Minutes and Correspondence 1940–1942' (hereafter 'Glyndebourne 3'), undated manuscript note.
95 Chapter 3, pp32–3.
96 Glyndebourne 3, Chamberlain-Christie, 27/5/39; Christie's invitation is not in the archive.
97 3/7/39.
98 Ibid., Christie-Dunglass, 18/7/39.
99 Ibid., Dunglass-Christie, 18/8/39.
100 Ibid., Christie-Sir Walford Davies (Master of the King's Music), 11/8/39; similar letters went to other leading musicians, including Ralph Vaughan Williams.
101 Ibid., Christie-Dyson, 9/9/39.
102 Ibid., Christie to the invitees, 18/9/39.
103 Ibid., Forbes-Christie, 22/9/39.
104 Ibid., text of interval talk in a BBC broadcast of Verdi's *Macbeth*, 7/7/39.

# 7

# 'CEMA is already broken down': John Christie and the National Council of Music 1939–41

## Introduction

Most of this book is about the 1930s. But there is such continuity between John Christie's pre-war and wartime efforts to create and lead a government-funded body to support music that it would be artificial to end the story in September 1939. There are several more specific reasons to consider Christie's work in wartime. It shows that CEMA was not, and at the time was not seen as, the only possible model of arts funding. Christie's discussions during the war with artists such as Ralph Vaughan Williams reveal the changing philosophy behind state funding of the arts. And he exerted an important but wholly unacknowledged influence on CEMA's evolution into the Arts Council.

This chapter examines Christie's work early in the war. Despite various missteps, this was mainly a tale of achievement in enlisting distinguished figures within and beyond British music to support the National Council of Music (NCM), a proposed organization whose only constant feature was Christie's central role. It also demonstrates how little CEMA figured in the NCM discussions. Chapter 8 discusses the period from 1941, and how Christie's hopes were dashed due in large part to Rab Butler and John Maynard Keynes.

## Preliminary Lobbying: To Summer 1940

Glyndebourne's prestige meant that in 1939 Christie could count on senior politicians treating his views with apparent respect, or at least politeness. Correspondence unrelated to state support of music provides a good illustration. On 9 September 1939 he wrote to the Liberal Party leader Archibald Sinclair, whom in 1938 he had named as an ideal member of the NCM, suggesting that his work at Glyndebourne could assist the war effort generally:

> I can bring my organisation with me, which contains accountants and men of constructive ability. The work… we are now doing at Glyndebourne, may well become the basis of new Social work on a large scale after the War. … I feel that one of the important problems of the day is a check on all the appalling extravagance all the little jacks in office are letting loose in every direction.[1]

This may have referred to Glyndebourne's receiving, on the outbreak of war, 260 child evacuees and sixty helpers,[2] though the letter itself failed to explain this. Nonetheless, rather than sending a bare acknowledgement Sinclair forwarded it to Lord Macmillan, Minister of Information. Macmillan thanked Sinclair for bringing to his attention Christie's 'very generous offer' and undertook to deal direct with Christie if ever 'in a position… to make practical use of it'.[3]

The same month Christie wrote to Neville Chamberlain about setting up an equally ill-defined 'Ministry of Economy'. Chamberlain replied that this 'would be impracticable in these present days when we are urgently engaged in bringing the war machine into operation', but undertook 'to have the proposal more fully examined as soon as the pressure under which we are now working is somewhat relaxed'.[4]

Given that he was dealt with so respectfully in areas where he lacked standing and expertise, it is not surprising that Christie was taken and took himself so seriously in his specialist area, music, despite his lapses from rationality. There were two reasons why such lapses were more common during than before the war. First, he did not have the opera festival to absorb his energies. Second, his wife, the soprano Audrey Mildmay, generally a restraining influence, was in Canada and the USA with their children from 1940 to 1944.[5] Some close friends, particularly Harry Colles, music editor of *The Times* from 1911 to his death in 1943,[6] tried to take on this role, but with limited success. From the research perspective, however, Audrey's wartime absence had a major benefit: Christie's frequent and lengthy letters to her[7] provide an invaluable insight into his activities, views and state of mind throughout this period.

Although Christie wrote to George Dyson in early September 1939 that the NCM should be formed immediately and 'we should not wait for peace',[8] he made little progress before summer 1940. Instead he engaged in combative but illuminating correspondence about CEMA and the NCM with Dyson and Sir Walford Davies, Master of the King's Music, and formed a surprisingly strong, and potentially highly valuable, bond with the newly appointed President of the Board of Education, Herwald Ramsbotham, the Minister responsible for supporting CEMA.

A brief outline of CEMA is necessary here, as its founding and development had crucial consequences for Christie's NCM. Initially CEMA (at that time the Committee, not Council, for the Encouragement of Music and the Arts) operated with only charitable funding, from the Pilgrim Trust. It was, however, always closely connected with the government. It was set up following an approach from the Board of Education in late 1939 suggesting that the Trust might support amateur artistic activity. From the start CEMA had government help in kind, being based in Board office space and having Mary Glasgow, a Board schools inspector, as its first staff member. It first applied for a Treasury grant in March 1940.

Fred Leventhal wrote in *The Best for the Most* that initially CEMA focused on 'amateur and educational activity in which professionals might play an auxiliary role'.[9] This is a reasonable summary of CEMA's early philosophy and practice, though in reality they were never so simple. From early on, for instance, George Dyson organized orchestral concerts in industrial areas for which CEMA provided guarantees against loss, with similar arrangements for tours by professional drama repertory companies.[10] Bidding for Treasury funds in March 1940 CEMA formulated broad and ambitious objectives:

> a. The preservation so far as possible of the highest standards in war-time of the arts of music, drama, and painting and design.
> b. The widespread provision of opportunities for hearing good music and for the enjoyment of the arts generally among people who, on account of war-time conditions, have been cut off from these things.
> c. The encouragement of music-making and play-acting by the people themselves.
> d. Through the above activities, the rendering of indirect assistance to professional singers and players who may be suffering from a war-time lack of demand for their work.[11]

Leventhal noted that maintaining high standards had not previously figured so prominently among CEMA's objectives, but that throughout its first year 'CEMA was nothing if not improvisational, shifting uneasily between encouraging amateur activity while supporting professional performances'.[12]

Christie's reaction to CEMA combined belief that it was of little significance with unshakeable confidence that the backing of the (unformed) NCM was essential to CEMA's success. At this period George Dyson, Director of the Royal College of Music, also had the title Hon Director, Pilgrim Trust Concerts. In February 1940[13] Christie suggested to him that CEMA would fail without the NCM behind it. If the government refused a grant, the Pilgrim Trust would have 'no authority with which to combat their refusal. This is exactly where the National Council of Music should come in.... the question of how much contribution the Government should make is, in my opinion, exactly the kind of point on which we should want advice from our Council.' (It is not clear who were the 'we' in this sentence.) Furthermore, work was needed on 'the kind of way in which the money is to be used... once more a matter for the Council'. Overall, 'the Government will feel much more secure with our Council behind it to back it. It is a vital necessity that the Government should be conscious that our Art is organised, and powerfully organised.' Perhaps wisely, Dyson's reply did not address Christie's claims for the NCM:

> ... the Pilgrim Trust Committee... includes members nominated by the Board of Education.... The President of the Board [of Education][14] is very interested, and it is from this side that a possibility of Government help may arise.... I am sure you will agree that all these steps are completely in keeping with the ideas that our National Council of Music would exist to further.[15]

Christie's other correspondent, Sir Walford Davies, also supported the NCM up to a point, and like Dyson was closely involved with CEMA.[16] Writing in March 1940[17] Davies questioned Christie's tactics: 'The more I think over it the more certain I am that we cannot ask the Government to invite "self and three friends" (so to speak) to form a National Council of Music *ad hoc*, least of all at this juncture.' He also opposed the idea of setting up the NCM without government support, though he did advise that 'an *ad hoc* Music Council with Dyson as Chairman would be practicable, and... might form the exactly right nucleus for a permanent National Council of Music after it had done efficient War Service and proved itself'. His letter also described CEMA's perceived purpose at this period: '... the "Committee for Encouragement" has, I gather, had specific orders to do what is a war-time job of limited extent.' This view, that CEMA's duration would be brief and its role restricted, persisted almost universally until late 1941.

While Christie took no further public steps to set up his National Council until June 1940, the archive contains a manuscript note by him from March, reporting: 'The present suggestion is that we four persons, Sir Walford Davies, Dr Colles, Dr Dyson and John Christie should receive an invitation from the President of the Board of Education to form this Council [the NCM].'[18] The note contains no context, and does not specify who had made the 'present suggestion'; probably Christie himself.

Around this time Christie also wrote, though circulated only several months later, a 'Memorandum on Music and Drama'.[19] Despite its title, and despite its argument that two councils should be established – 'Both bodies would be interested in the good stuff rather than in the rubbish' – music was his only real concern. Alfred Wareing's League of Audiences, while supported by many musicians, concentrated on drama. Neither Wareing nor Christie lobbied effectively on behalf of music and drama jointly, which reduced the effectiveness of both campaigns.

The memorandum's 2,000 words about the state and the arts contained no mention of CEMA. Christie dropped the relatively conciliatory approach of the 1938 Glyndebourne conferences. His focus was on musical standards alone, to the exclusion of broadening music's availability and encouraging amateur music-making. He suggested that there were two 'classes of thought': that represented by 'Vaughan Williams and Sir Hugh Allen, that the people should be making music and that then all will be well'; and that represented by Glyndebourne, that the highest standards of performance would cause people to 'think about music, write about it, talk about it and pay for it. . . . respect rather than familiarity is the keynote'. The future depended on the NCM, 'on which Glyndebourne has been working for two years and [which] is about to be formed', as it was, according to Christie, so often between 1938 and 1944.

Christie's vision of the future was rosy; his view of the present far less so: 'Almost the whole of the public funds devoted to music in the form of the Municipal Orchestras and the B.B.C. are devoted to offering rubbish with which an attempt is made to mix a small quantity of good stuff.' This theme of 'rubbish' versus 'good stuff' featured strongly: 'Woolworth's cannot sell Rolls Royces and. . . a tiny Municipal Orchestra, required to play rubbish on the pier, cannot once a week turn its hand to Beethoven and Mozart. . . the public taste is damaged by being continually offered rubbish.' His plea for organization was 'only for good music and good drama. The rubbish can look after itself. . . Charabanc trips are arranged. . . only for the rubbish. All forces conspire to assist the rubbish.' And in another nod towards subsidy: 'It may be that the Entertainment Tax should be increased on the rubbish and that the good stuff should be financially assisted.'

Christie circulated the memorandum in July 1940, following further correspondence with Walford Davies. Davies was forced to defend CEMA from what he saw as Christie's unfair attacks: 'Colles tells me of the impression that nothing is happening [ie that CEMA was doing nothing]. Are 1200 or so music-makings in needy places, however modest, nothing?. . . When the War is over, with hopes of a long-term peace. . . then long live the National Council of Music.'[20] Writing to Harry Colles about this letter, Christie suggested that CEMA's music organizers, Davies, George Dyson and Reginald Jacques, 'have got something like a student performance in their minds. None of these 3 men, as far as I know, have worked with great artists. . . .'[21] To Davies himself, Christie was patronizing and grand: 'I don't know much about C.E.M.A., but this work has been given to you, Dyson and Jacques & Co. to do and your position would be safer if you had the protection of my Council. . . . I am not at all proposing that our Council should dictate to you, more especially as you have been given the job and the money.'[22]

Also at this time Christie got to know Herwald Ramsbotham, who succeeded Earl De La Warr as President of the Board of Education in April 1940. Ramsbotham, heading the department responsible for funding CEMA, was potentially a huge catch for Christie. Christie first wrote to him in June 1940, proposing that Glyndebourne be funded to create an orchestra for regional touring during the war.[23] He followed this with a stage-managed dinner at Brooks's Club. Christie promised Ramsbotham that 'The incidents of British music are not without humour',[24] and asked his friend the singer Roy Henderson 'to give him [Ramsbotham] some idea of the actual nature of a musician's life. . . [then] you [Henderson] should retire home shortly after 9 p.m. so that I can go on with my stuff'.[25] Henderson, undismayed by his subsidiary role, wrote subsequently to Christie that Ramsbotham was 'an extremely nice fellow, and one who really had culture at heart'.[26] Ramsbotham failed to secure CEMA funding for the proposed Glyndebourne orchestra, though wrote to Christie that 'Council members were in full sympathy with all your points'.[27] The letter also set out the official view of CEMA in June 1940: '. . . [its] mandate from the Treasury is to bring the arts to people who do not normally get them and who may be feeling the strain of war. It is trying to do this quickly as a real emergency measure. . .' Their cordial relationship continued for several years, well beyond Ramsbotham's time at the Board of Education.

## 'The psychological moment has arrived': To December 1940

### Christie and the Musicians

Alongside Christie's view that music was a central element of life was his disregard of the war's relevance. Both characteristics were on full display in the next phase of his campaign for the NCM, from summer 1940 to spring 1941 – the period of the Battle of Britain and the Blitz. He exhibited an idiosyncratic, indeed eccentric, perspective on the Blitz: '. . . it's all nonsense about war nerves. The very idea!. . . It's children's fireworks. The children would enjoy the bangs; so would you & of course I do & always did.'[28]

During this period Christie invited a roster of distinguished musicians and others to discuss the non-existent Council, received ready acceptances from most, gathered many of them for several large meetings in smart London hotels, and gained their agreement that the NCM should be formed.

In July he wrote to Walford Davies to announce that 'The psychological moment has arrived' to set up the NCM.[29] Its first task should be to ensure the viability of the major British orchestras. Christie's one concession to the war was acknowledging that 'there is no question of asking for money for the next month or so until this invasion scare be overpassed'. In reply, Davies advised patience:

> ... I cannot refrain from counselling you to wait a little longer.... You speak of the 'psychological moment' as having arrived. This statement convinces me of nothing but your own delightful and admirable enthusiasm. I am afraid, dear man, this letter will seem stodgy and annoying, but I had to write it... seeing the danger of a premature Council, queering the pitch for the real thing after the war.[30]

Davies' comradely tone is notable, given his disagreement with Christie's strategy and tactics for the NCM, and Christie's disparaging comments about CEMA. Furthermore, in the same letter Davies expressed deeply uncomradely views of another key musical figure: 'I cannot but feel that the Nation's music will suffer as little if the L.P.O. [London Philharmonic Orchestra] dies as it would if Beecham died.' This is not the only example of Christie's bluntness and lack of discretion prompting a similar response in his correspondents.

Harry Colles saw this letter as a serious blow: 'It is just what I feared would happen when I advised you to let him [Davies] alone for a bit. Now he has dissociated himself definitely from your project and that means that if he is consulted about it as "Master of the King's Musick" he will say so, and that will crab it in "Royal" circles. However, it can't be helped now.'[31] Ten days later Colles was more sanguine: 'I am told that Walford has had a short holiday since he wrote to you. That may have done him good. However, better leave him to me for the present.'[32]

Most of Christie's correspondents around this time were more positive than Walford Davies. In August 1940 Christie wrote to Sir Adrian Boult that the NCM was 'At long last... being formed', and inviting Boult 'to join as one of the leading Professionals'.[33] CEMA was not mentioned: 'The proposal is to form a new Company not for profit, which can undertake any work for which the Government pays.... The contribution I have in mind... from the Government... is say, a million a year.' As ever gilding the lily, Christie claimed: 'I have got acceptances and extremely strong support... for this scheme, and I am advised also that it should be put in execution now.' But Christie admitted to Boult: 'For your private information... dear old Walford Davies is hanging fire, but I expect will come in presently.... I feel it is better to leave him alone at the moment. I hear he is bombed down in his cellar every night.' Boult took all this at face value: 'I shall have much pleasure in serving on your Committee. I must get formal permission, but am sure this will be granted as my Chief, Nicolls [Basil Nicolls, BBC Director of Programmes], whom you met the other day, knows all about it. I will not tackle Walford unless he talks to me about it.'[34]

Throughout his work on the NCM one constant was Christie's claims, sometimes with slight justification, more often with none, of its imminent formation. The surprise is not that he seemed to believe this but that so many of his correspondents did so.

Malcolm Sargent was as enthusiastic as Boult, writing, also in August 1940: 'I think your scheme is excellent, and am delighted to come in on your executive committee.'[35] Rare among Christie's correspondents at this time, Sargent saw CEMA as a possible competitor. He reported talking to Christie's friend Robert Forbes, who had been 'full of the work that the C.E.M.A. is doing at the moment and inferred that they would be carrying on after the war and would become the permanent organising body of England's music.... I think you should look into this, as it would cut across your plans.' Christie claimed to be unconcerned: 'I am quite happy about C.E.M.A. They are only temporary. They have no foundation, and they are doing some work I expect quite decently, only it is not the work which is of the more difficult kind....'[36]

Forbes himself expressed to Christie no doubts about the NCM, and did not mention CEMA: 'I should be very happy indeed to become a member of your proposed National Council of Music, and I take it as a compliment that you should ask me....'[37] As in 1938 his views were possibly more extreme than Christie's:

> I am in entire sympathy with your aims.... If we can all get together... something may happen, and possibly quite quickly. In my own view the great trouble in this country is that the Government and the great bulk of the population have always resolutely refused to recognise music as an Art; – it is mildly tolerated as a social amenity, as a harmless recreation, as an educational instrument... but as one of the Fine Arts – never!

Forbes complained about the Carnegie UK Trust funding 'assistance to amateur choral and orchestral societies, rural music schools, village choirs, and so on and so forth – possibly worthy enough objects in themselves, but none of them, to my mind, helping Music'. He concluded, surprisingly in August 1940: 'I agree with you that there could be no better time than the present to influence the official attitude towards music...' Replying to Forbes,[38] Christie himself mentioned CEMA, possibly prompted by Sargent's letter. Alongside his usual bluster ('I feel absolutely certain that we are on the right lines in this Council. We cannot be disputed or if we are we can win'), he wrote, apropos of nothing: 'I do not feel in the least concerned about C.E.M.A. It is already broken down.... It was altogether too small in purpose, in scope and in personnel.'

Roy Henderson helped feed Christie's over-confidence. A letter from him of August 1940[39] may explain Christie's reference to CEMA's having 'already broken down': 'I wish your Council was in being. There is such a lot of devilish work going on' – the twin villains being CEMA and ENSA.

The work of ENSA – the Entertainments National Service Organisation – is beyond the scope of this book. For Janet Minihan the distinction between CEMA and ENSA was that 'ENSA... had no goals beyond enlivening the tension and drudgery of war service with music, films, variety shows and drama. CEMA started with broader aims, which developed throughout the war and ended with the development of the Arts Council.'[40] This CEMA-centric description echoed Keynes': 'E.N.S.A. was charged with the entertainment of the Services... the duty of C.E.M.A. was to maintain the opportunities of artistic performance for the hard-pressed and often exiled civilians.'[41] Basil Dean, ENSA's founder and no fan of Keynes, resented this view: '... it was irksome to find ourselves regarded as the chain-store of the concert world, while CEMA dealt only with the custom-built trade. We had our exclusive counters, too... but we did not waste time preening ourselves so much.'[42]

Henderson was much concerned about the status of musicians, and thus of music, at wartime concerts. For those organized by ENSA, 'the conditions are dreadful, people eating and I daresay talking during the performance, with the possibility of hostile aircraft at any moment.'[43] Each singer was required to perform 'at not less than 14 concerts, sometimes over 20 in a week, half of them after midnight, for a maximum of £7 per week, less what he has to pay for board+lodging!!!... There is no thought of the long training+the professional status of musicians.' As for CEMA, Henderson had grave concerns about Reginald Jacques, its Music Director: 'Jacques seems to administer great chunks of this money. He knows nothing about the profession except a very few artists and his own orchestra [the Jacques String Orchestra]. The result is that his orchestra has been well looked after....' Even worse, Jacques had decided that concerts should have free admission: 'What a let-down for the artists to be the objects of a collection! What a status for the profession!' Henderson concluded: 'I am anxiously awaiting news of your Council.' In later letters[44] Henderson showed himself even more adamant than Christie that government funding for music should be channelled not through musicians but through what he called 'Patrons'.

## Successes and Excesses

Writing in July 1940 to Neville Chamberlain, at this point Lord President of the Council, Christie expanded on the suggestion that CEMA had 'already broken down'.[45] He began with the familiar, baseless, claim that 'At long last our National Council of Music is to be formed'. Concerning CEMA, not referred to by name anywhere in the letter, he wrote: 'I predicted that the Professionals leading this work would fall out with the rest of the Professionals and the Government would burn its fingers. So it has turned out. Now I am told by the Professional, Dyson of the College, that I had better get on with my own ideas.' It is unclear how much of this he believed; very little was true. Christie showed equal disregard for reality in setting out the NCM's plans, none of which, it seemed, required consultation with or decision by the NCM itself. Its priorities would be 'to deal with the Government in saving our four orchestras.... [and to] recommend that Glyndebourne should take over these four orchestras'. As for funding, 'the figure I have in mind to be allocated from the money collected by the P.O. for the B.B.C. [via the radio licence fee], but now pinched by the Treasury, is, let us say, a million' – a figure he often cited. Finally, Christie explained why he was writing: 'I want to start a similar organisation for Drama and I want to link up these... in one common Ministry of Fine Arts.... the ship would have to be steered through political waters, and... in my Council I have not so far included anybody who is able to do that. I should like to make a personal appeal... that you should join us.'

Even if the proposal had been more coherent, summer 1940 was the wrong time to put it to Chamberlain. His private secretary explained that he was seriously ill,[46] and subsequently wrote that 'His time and attention are already so completely occupied that he is quite unable to contemplate taking up any further responsibilities. Later on when the War is over and the burdens of office are not so heavy Mr. Chamberlain would be glad to reconsider the position....'[47] Chamberlain died that November.

What suggests that this response was a genuine expression of regret rather than an elaborate brush-off is the welcome given by so many others during summer and autumn 1940 to Christie's premature announcement of the NCM's creation. In July, for instance, Sir Kenneth Clark, Director of the National Gallery and a founder council member of CEMA, wrote to Christie: 'I am all in favour of a National Council of Music which should be concerned primarily with music and not with musicians and their employment.'[48] Writing to his wife on 25 July, Christie described how he had prepared the ground with Clark and with J B Priestley.[49] He had come to London:

> ... to see Sir Kenneth Clark & later in the afternoon I had a long talk with Priestley, both about the National Council of Music. Both are very much against all this amateur music & very strongly in favour of the highest standard. . . . I was well impressed by Kenneth Clark again by Priestley but in a different way. He is a splendid fighting man and is ready to take on the Government or anybody else.

He was concerned that Priestley 'has a bee in his bonnet about Lords & Ladies & the aristocracy... which may be dangerous if it breaks out in our Council. However I want the fight that is in him.' He also wanted Priestley's perceived influence on the Labour party, 'whom he will shame into giving their due support to music'.

Christie was clear whom he wanted and didn't want on the NCM. This letter contains the first mention of his recruiting 'Bongy – Sir Maurice Bonham Carter... who was Asquith's secretary & who feels very strongly about standard'. 'Bongy', a businessman and also Asquith's son-in-law, was to play a major role in the NCM. On the other hand, Tom Jones, Vice-Chairman of and the guiding force behind CEMA at this stage, 'is leading Walford Davies & the Pilgrim Trust in the direction of these amateurs, & he is now regarded... as unsuitable'. Among the 'suitables' Christie included 'Harry Colles, Kenneth Clark, Priestley, Bongy, N. Chamberlain, Finlay, Greene [two senior judges; Sir Wilfrid Greene, Master of the Rolls, became a major supporter], perhaps Mallon or Hodgkinson [from Toynbee Hall], perhaps A. P. Herbert'. Among possible musician members of the NCM he included Adrian Boult, Malcolm Sargent, Ralph Vaughan Williams, the heads of the major music colleges, 'when he returns to England, Beecham. Possibly Myra Hess.'

It says much for Christie's prestige that most of these were keen to be members. It says much for his lack of diplomatic skill that most of this support dribbled away over the following years. CEMA was hardly relevant: almost no one suggested that CEMA should do the job which Christie vaguely envisaged for the NCM. Kenneth Clark and Walford Davies, for instance, founder members of CEMA, saw no conflict between this and their potential role on the NCM.

Christie cast his net still wider during summer 1940, receiving acceptances from, among others, the mathematician and physicist Sir James Jeans, the architect Sir Edwin Lutyens, and John Spedan Lewis, founder of the John Lewis Partnership. Lewis hesitated due to pressure of business:

> I felt that not even my extreme desire to see this country moving towards abundance of real music and my gratitude for Glyndebourne and my very great regard for you and Audrey ought to induce me to allow myself the distinction and pleasure of being a member of your Council.... [But] the temptation was sore and... I will place myself at your disposal and serve on your Council if you wish.[50]

More effusive still was Ethel Snowden, widow of Ramsey MacDonald's Chancellor of the Exchequer Philip Snowden and, earlier in the century, an active feminist and suffragist:[51] 'I... offer you a thousand congratulations on having achieved a great piece of work.... I bless you for it.'[52] William Jowitt, Solicitor-General in the wartime coalition government and Lord Chancellor in the post-war Labour government, was 'tremendously in favour of making good music available for the people... [and] would gladly do what I can to help you in any way'.[53] He had some concern that joining the NCM might conflict with his government role: 'If in due course you made – as I hope you will – demands upon the Government for subvention, I might have to resist the "outrageous claim". It would be Pooh-Bah-ish of me to make and resist the claim.... [But] I think this largely theoretical... [and] subject to this... I'll readily do what I can.'

Alongside Christie's ability to enthuse his correspondents was a chronic tendency to overreach himself. Four days after reporting his meetings with Clark and Priestley, he wrote to Audrey: '... the first practical matter... is the saving of our four orchestras & I propose that the Council should recommend that Glyndebourne should be entrusted with it, the Government to pay. The next should be the control of the four antagonistic Opera Companies & again I propose that Glyndebourne should do it.'[54] The NCM was only the start: 'The next step will be the creation of a N. C. Drama.... Next we deal with the painters etc, & then with the architects. Lastly we combine all together in a Ministry of Fine Arts.'

Writing to Herwald Ramsbotham at the Board of Education (a manuscript letter beginning: 'Are you alive? I am & with ease. Here's progress!') in September 1940, Christie summarized his view of developments:

> My National Council of Music is nearly ready to be formed &, unless Hitler interferes, there is a reasonable chance of its first meeting being held in Buckingham Palace or Windsor by invitation of the K or Q. All the professionals have joined except Henry Wood who wants to be a free lance (carp not lance in my opinion) and Allen has not answered.... We have got it all cut and dried....[55]

As will be seen, Christie's references to royalty were groundless, and he overstated the enthusiasm in some quarters. Keynes refused membership of the NCM with apparent regret: 'I... wish the new project very well indeed. But I do feel that I must not take on a new activity.'[56] The music critic Ernest Newman refused because he thought the NCM could not work: 'I have had a very long and often close association with brave schemes for making this country musical and I have had the same melancholy experience with all of them.'[57] Christie persisted but Newman replied: 'I wish I could share your optimism, but alas, I can't. The intelligent musical public of this country I estimate at around 2/3,000 people all told.... As for a Ministry of Fine Arts... the very thought of it makes me laugh... and my own capacity for appreciating bad jokes is not what it used to be.'[58] Christie often copied to Harry Colles his correspondence about the NCM. Colles wrote of Newman's letter: '... frankly I do not think much of [it]. It is easy to be bitter and superior.'[59]

Christie suggested to Audrey that his failure to gain Sir Henry Wood's support was due to the influence of Lady Wood: 'A rather difficult lunch with Lady Wood, at which dear old Henry Wood was present.... Lady W I think intends to make mischief if she can.... Henry Wood visibly crumpled.... She is a tartar.... Harry [Colles] says there has not been a divorce, and she is not Lady Wood.'[60] (Wood was indeed not married to 'Lady Wood'. Wood's wife having refused a divorce, his partner, Jessie Linton, had changed her name by deed poll to Lady Jessie Wood. 'Lady' was thus not a title but a forename.)[61] Wood gave Christie a further opportunity to persuade him: while 'I never enter into any project unless I am certain it is of service to the work on which I have spent the greater part of my life',[62] he offered to delay a Promenade Concert rehearsal so that Christie could explain his plan in more detail over 'the stolid, solid fare at the Langham Hotel'. Colles' view was still 'that his [Wood's] woman will make him inimical. A pity!'[63]

But Wood was 'inimical' for other reasons. Apparently, at the lunch Christie argued that a key objective of the NCM should be to establish a new orchestra. Wood wrote afterwards that if Christie had, instead, made it a priority to stabilize the finances of the existing orchestras, 'I should have welcomed your proposed "National Council of Music"'.[64] This was capricious and ill-judged on Christie's part: in all his previous correspondence, he had made 'the saving of our four orchestras' an aim of the NCM, rather than creating a new orchestra. In his letter Wood also revealed an attitude to foreign musicians which Christie never shared:

> ... goodness knows where our fine orchestral musicians would find themselves eventually, since we are overrun with the foreign refugee, who will... be only too

> willing to allow his exploitation by managements. . . . we don't want the foreign conductors either – they must stay where they are after this war is over – and we have as good, and better here. . . .

Christie alienated other potential allies more directly. A key example was Sir Hugh Allen, ex-Director of the Royal College of Music and President of the Incorporated Society of Musicians (ISM). For the ISM Christie had contempt, for Allen himself, deep dislike. He wrote to Audrey following a meeting with Allen: 'He was silly & not constructive & not logical. . . . He has such strong bees in his bonnet & such prejudices that I just think he cannot be helpful. He won't learn and he won't understand';[65] criticisms from which Christie himself was not immune. Harry Colles, too, had little time for Allen and less for Frank Eames, the ISM's Secretary: 'I am still convinced that Eames... is the tail which wags the dog. Allen's bark comes out the other end.'[66] Christie wrote at length and disparagingly to others about Allen and the ISM. He lost William Jowitt's support by sending him a tirade whose only clear point was that he, Christie, found Allen's attitude 'ludicrously stupid'.[67] Jowitt's response was: '... I feel that the opposition of Allen should make me... reconsider my position. . . . Sir Hugh Allen is a great name in the world of music and I think I might incur the censure of my superiors if I lent my name to any controversial matter in which the Government have not taken sides.'[68] But Herwald Ramsbotham at the Board of Education read a similar letter 'with great interest combined with sympathy for you. . . . I am sure you are right in resisting the inclusion of what is in effect the trades union element in your organisation.'[69]

The archive also contains a draft letter to Allen,[70] not sent, in which Christie wondered 'What judgement will our Council make of you and your attitude to us?... I am afraid they will be likely to condemn you. Don't be a Hitler.' He warned that 'Our Council will judge you with cold steel', but concluded: 'Is there anything. . . I have expressed to which you take exception?' But this hostility may have been in Christie's mind alone. Allen accepted Christie's invitation to his January 1941 meeting on the NCM (see below) in positive and cordial terms: 'It's good news to know that you are bringing together the members of the National Council for Music. . . . I shall be very glad to come to the meeting.'[71]

The 'Hitler' letter to Allen may have remained unsent on the advice of Harry Colles in his role as restraining influence. Roy Henderson, on the other hand, egged Christie on, commenting that the letter was 'candid and fair and straight from the shoulder'.[72] Colles certainly dissuaded Christie from writing insultingly to Myra Hess, whose offence had been a polite refusal to join the NCM because she was too busy running the wartime National Gallery concerts. Christie's draft reply is not in the archive; Colles' response to it suggests its nature: '"O no John", etc! You know perfectly well, my dear John, that Audrey would never pass such a letter as this to Myra Hess. It is the sort of thing we all write, or think of writing, when we are annoyed, but before the ink is dry we know that its only possible destination is the waste paper basket!'[73] A week later Colles himself persuaded Hess to join the NCM.[74]

Sir Alan Lascelles, George VI's Private Secretary, had less success as an adviser, a role he had played also in Christie's pre-war conferences. His correspondence with Christie between August and October 1940 illustrates Christie's tendency to damage his case by overstatement and wish-fulfilment. Lascelles' position led him to hesitate to join the NCM: 'If I were just I, I should say "Yes" at once to your flattering offer. But since my only claim to sit on any Body of importance is based... on my right to use this [Buckingham Palace] note-paper, I have got to be ultra-careful of my virtue.'[75] A 'Yes' would depend on Christie's gaining sufficient support from 'the professionals – Allen, Dyson, Forbes, H.Wood, V.Williams, etc'. Christie's reply was cavalier: 'Dear old Walford Davies, he is backing out of the scheme at the moment and giving, fortunately, the most ridiculous reasons.... I should not be surprised to find that Allen, Vaughan Williams and Walford Davies, all seventy years old, perhaps back out. These three are not quite reliable and they are losing contact.'[76]

Despite this, Lascelles replied that 'you can certainly put me down as a provisional acceptor'.[77] Christie then enquired about holding the NCM's initial meeting at Buckingham Palace, and about royal involvement generally. In a manuscript note of September 1940[78] Lascelles was negative on both counts. Concerning royal support: 'Such expert opinion as I have taken is unanimous in saying that Walford Davies' co-operation is essential to any approach to R. [Royal] family. He may be tiresome, but for good or ill, he holds the appointment of Master of the Music....' As for using Buckingham Palace, 'Clearly no meetings can be held at B.P. at present – or anywhere else, I shld say, until life is less disorganized + people more inclined to gather together.'

So when, two days after Lascelles' note, Christie wrote to Herwald Ramsbotham that there was 'a reasonable chance' that the King or Queen would invite the NCM to hold its initial meeting at Buckingham Palace or Windsor Castle, not only was this claim baseless, it directly contradicted the explicit advice of the King's Private Secretary. Ramsbotham was not the only Minister whom Christie misled about this. On 2 October he wrote to Audrey that he had used a mention of royalty to overcome William Jowitt's doubts about the propriety of a Minister joining the NCM: 'A great day. I saw Jowitt, who I find a strong supporter.... Jowitt hesitated a little until he found there was a possibility of the K[ing] & Q[ueen] being interested and inviting us to Windsor. Then he said at once he would join. That perhaps also applies to Ramsbotham & to Bevin. . . . I like the idea of Windsor.'[79]

Lascelles was deeply unimpressed when Christie explained how he had secured Jowitt's support:

> 'The Buckingham Palace scheme', I imagine, means the suggestion that possibly a council meeting might be held here; that suggestion, as far as I know, has gone no further than private conversation between you and me. . . . Their Majesties' knowledge of the whole idea is limited to a conversational reference by myself, and I have certainly never mentioned to anybody that they had any views about it. . . .[80]

Lascelles became blunter still: '. . . as I have always said – I fear many times – the fundamental rule. . . is that The King and Queen can never be asked to associate themselves, directly or indirectly, with any public scheme until it is a going concern, de facto and de jure; and this scheme cannot be said to be that.' Lascelles had indeed made this point to Christie as early as 1936.[81] Now he hammered it home: 'Their Majesties must never be associated with a dud concern, and it is our business to safeguard them from such a possibility.' He set out the steps needed before Christie could ask to lead a deputation (including the Master of the King's Music and a representative of the Board of Education) to the Lord Chamberlain in order to seek Royal support: 'Till you have done that, let nobody whatever make any use at all of The King's name or The Queen's.' Lascelles concluded in a more conciliatory but no more hopeful tone: 'Are you sure that the man in the bomb-torn street is in the right frame of mind to take. . . as much interest in your scheme as he ought to? I am not.'

A letter to Audrey suggests that Christie did not ignore Lascelles' lecture:

> I dropped in this morning to the Lord Chamberlain's office. . . . He said he recognised me at once, so I supposed he had been at Glyndebourne. . . . It is satisfactory that Glyndebourne should be found to get this recognition. He thinks the K.&Q. should certainly be interested in this scheme, but we all agree now that this is not the right moment.[82]

And he made some effort to correct the false impression of royal support. Backtracking somewhat, on 29 October he wrote to Jowitt that 'at the right moment when warlike conditions are calmer and better, [we shall]. . . approach the King and Queen'.[83] This, however, was the same letter in which his attack on Sir Hugh Allen and the ISM caused Jowitt again to withdraw his support.

But Christie was not discouraged – quite the reverse.

## 'Let the flags be out. Let us drive in State': To Spring 1941

In all that Christie wrote about the NCM he rarely described it the same way twice, was often entirely vague in setting out its aims, and, when specific, often contradicted earlier statements. It would, variously, co-ordinate the main British orchestras and opera companies, fund them, put them under Glyndebourne's control, create a 'super-orchestra' to supplant them, bring over world-class foreign musicians to train British musicians, advise the government, or 'protect' CEMA in some unspecified way. The only constants were its exclusive focus on Christie's concept of 'standards', and Christie's and Glyndebourne's central role. Audrey Christie urged greater clarity. Writing from Canada, she quoted Hester Colles (Harry Colles' wife) reporting to her that 'you [Christie] have your stuff so clear in your own mind that you don't make it clear to others'.[84] She confessed that she herself needed help with this: '... apropos of Hester: Will you give me in concise a.b.c. form the fundamental reasons for N.C.M. I find if I try to explain it I don't really know what I am talking about.'

Christie did not respond to this challenge. There were two main elements to the confusion about the NCM: its shifting scope and purpose, and Christie's lack of clarity when describing it. It is remarkable that at this stage these drawbacks put off very few of those he sought to persuade. The nearest the NCM came to a clear statement of purpose was in its draft memorandum and articles of association. These appeared in summer 1941 and are discussed in the next chapter. They arose from four elaborate meetings at London hotels in early 1941, but owed more to detailed work by Christie, the Master of the Rolls Sir Wilfrid Greene and Sir Maurice Bonham Carter.

The first meeting was at the Dorchester Hotel in January 1941. Preparing for it, Christie wrote two memoranda. One was a rambling, elitist justification for the NCM and public funding of music.[85] The NCM should operate with:

> ... that freedom of thought and action in regard to music which is beyond the restrictions of individual and particular bodies and institutions.... While such a plan will rightly pursue the greatest good for the greatest number, it will not subscribe to the dissipation of the whole substance for the passing vanity of so-called popular or mass entertainment.

Concerning public funding, 'where the work is on a national basis from its inception, then it cannot be... voluntarily supported where the subject of that work is Art.... [Instead,] under the aegis of a properly constituted body, with men of repute in public affairs... the Nation should provide such sustenance as is required' – an obscure way of saying that good music needed subsidy distributed by people like him. The other memorandum[86] was about the NCM's potential to create more and better musicians. To ensure the conductors of the future, 'The musically talented child should be grabbed by the scruff of the neck at an early age. Starting somewhere about the age of 6. . . . by that means at the end of say 20 years we should probably have a star conductor.' Also from the age of around six, gifted instrumentalists should 'study at either of our Royal schools with perhaps the N.C.M. or the music school as the foster parent'.

Perhaps fortunately, neither memorandum was circulated. Christie's invitation to the Dorchester meeting was, by comparison, bland: '. . . a resolution will be moved that The National Council of Music be formed, and that a Committee be appointed to consider the Memorandum and Articles of Association, and also the formation of an operative company to carry out the work of the Council.'[87] But this was more controversial than it sounded: it soon became clear to some at least that the proposed structure – council plus operative company – was cover for Christie's intention to control the NCM.

On the invitation's reverse Christie listed 'the names of those who have accepted membership of our Council'. The forty-one names were impressive: musicians enthusiastic for the NCM such as Sir Adrian Boult and Malcolm Sargent, some qualified supporters such as Ralph Vaughan Williams and Sir Walford Davies, 'Patrons' including Sir Kenneth Clark, Sir James Jeans and Sir Edwin Lutyens, and 'Politicians and Public' including James Mallon, Sir Maurice Bonham Carter, Sir Wilfrid Greene and J B Priestley.

Priestley had in fact declined Christie's invitation due to pressure of work and because 'at the moment the mere use of my name might, with some sections of the government, do you more harm than good'.[88] This was the period of his weekly 'Postscript' radio talks, more popular with the public than with the government. But most of those listed had genuinely signed up. Christie expected good attendance but included among those who would not be there 'Lady Reading who cannot get away & Priestley who has an inferiority complex. . . . We look like being 40 at the meeting. . . . It's a very good response in these times.'[89] Among the few direct references to the war was Malcolm Sargent's acceptance – a postcard with the message: 'I have been very busy in the North both conducting + bomb-dodging.'[90] Christie's and Bonham Carter's plan for the meeting ran: 'Bongy calls on me to move the resolution. I make my address 15–20 minutes. Malcolm Sargent seconds it. Harry Colles says a few words. Then anyone else, including I suppose Allen. But Malcolm says that Allen swims with the tide & at the time will be quite tame. He has seen him like it before.'[91]

Attendance at the Dorchester meeting, though thirty-one against Christie's projected forty, was distinguished. In addition to most of those listed above, Myra Hess, Sir Alan Lascelles and Mary Glasgow, the Secretary of CEMA, attended.[92] Stanley Marchant, Principal of the Royal Academy of Music, wrote to Christie afterwards that he 'thought it very remarkable that you were able to collect such a galaxy of people, and I congratulate you on doing so'.[93] Christie's opening remarks, moving the motion to found the NCM, were separately printed.[94] The starting points were that 'When we win this war we shall have great prestige and we shall excite great jealousy. We must show ourselves worthy of that prestige'; that 'It is respect rather than familiarity which is important'; and that the NCM 'can give protection to the government'. Abandoning or concealing his wish for Glyndebourne to establish a 'super-orchestra' or run the whole British operatic and orchestral machinery, he claimed to want collaboration between the 'four famous orchestras: the L.S.O., the L.P.O., the Halle, and the Scottish' (the BBC Symphony Orchestra was not mentioned) and the 'four famous opera companies: Covent Garden, Sadler's Wells, the Carl Rosa, and an other' (*sic*; a coy reference to Glyndebourne). And 'the dignity of our personnel should guarantee protection to anyone who accepts our advice. . . . we can help to hold the prestige of our Empire, we can help and help in time to build a better world'.

Seconding the motion, Malcolm Sargent said that there was widespread and unsatisfied love of music in Britain and that the NCM 'should form the channel through which governmental provision could be made'.[95] No speaker suggested that this might be CEMA's role, and the meeting unanimously supported the NCM's creation. Sir Hugh Allen and others were more doubtful about the second part of the resolution, that a committee examine the NCM's setting up an operative company. But this too passed after Vaughan Williams amended the resolution so that the committee would have to report back to the full council. A committee of seventeen was appointed and 'The meeting then adjourned, after Sir Adrian Boult had proposed a vote of thanks to the Chairman'.

Writing to Audrey,[96] Christie described his own speech as 'intended to be referred to in later years, rather than for immediate consumption'. He summarized Vaughan Williams' intervention as 'All the performances abroad were bad. All in England were good.. . . . The speech was so divinely silly'. He was scathing about Sir Hugh Allen and his ally Lord Palmer, Vice-President of the Royal College of Music: 'Tommy [Lascelles] watched him [Palmer] at lunch, & said to me afterwards, I have always found, that any man who wears a diamond ring is a shit. Palmer drank my health at lunch. Allen had his head right in the trough. He is a ridiculous man.'

By contrast, Christie was positive about Malcolm Sargent. They 'had a long talk together & there is a simple, open and frank understanding between us'. The committee appointed at the Dorchester would meet on 23 January, 'I expect at the Ritz'. Overall, 'I can say that up to now it has been a triumph.... Harry [Colles] is indignant that it did not occur to any professional to say how much indebted we all are & should be to me.... I think he is right.'

Audrey Christie did what she could to guide him by correspondence. In the letter requesting 'in concise a.b.c. form the fundamental reasons for N.C.M', she also offered Christie tactical advice: 'Don't let Palmer's "smallness" sidetrack you.... I am sure you despise the means but when the job is worth something then it is worth a little juggling to smooth out stupid little kinks in personalities. He has given a good deal to music in his time I suppose & is rather proud of himself. A little recognition... & he will be utterly mollified.'[97] There is no evidence that Christie acted on this advice.

Eleven committee members, including Bonham Carter, Greene, George (now Sir George) Dyson, Myra Hess, Harry Colles and Christie himself, met at the Ritz on 23 January. The meeting almost foundered on two issues raised by Dyson. First, he 'thought that some existing musical Institutions were suspicious of the Council and its intentions',[98] suspicions fuelled by the NCM's wide terms of reference and particularly by the executive role of its operative company. Second (remarkably, this issue had not been raised before), Dyson 'asked... how the work of the Council would differ from such existing bodies as C.E.M.A.'. For some reason, Christie's response, that the NCM was a 'much larger scheme [than CEMA].... the whole intention of the Council should be to insist upon a very high standard of work', seemed to satisfy most of those present. As for the operative company, Bonham Carter, again chairing, commissioned Christie to produce a note in favour, and Dyson a note against, for the next meeting.

Christie wrote to Audrey[99] that he had chosen venues and personnel with care: NCM members 'must be conscious that they are having only the best.... The Dorchester, The Ritz, & obviously distinguished & leading & big men instead of the Covent Garden crowd'. But his account of the committee meeting suggests that it was a fraught occasion: '... half the time (2 hours) was spent blowing off steam'; and following Dyson's many interventions 'at last I went up in smoke'. For Christie the disagreement was about defining and achieving high artistic standards. He summarized Dyson's argument, and CEMA's approach, thus: '... every town must... have their own orchestra, & that rivalry would make them compete and that this would produce the right standard.' His view was that with so many orchestras, most 'would get a conductor who was a choirman who would appeal to the crowd and its vulgarity. The vulgarity would increase. You will get more vulgarity.' State aid required tight organization, close control (by Christie himself, via the NCM), and very few orchestras: '. . . the Govern't will demand and rightly demand that we do this.' According to Christie, 'Dyson's eyes started from his head at what I was saying or at the vehemence of it, he grew pale & he was out of breath.' As usual, Christie praised those 'professionals' who agreed with and flattered him: 'Theodore Holland [composer, and professor at the Royal Academy of Music] has written to me "We are all deeply indebted to you for your guidance". That's the sort of professional I like!'

The committee met to consider Christie's and Dyson's notes, again at the Ritz, in early February 1941. Christie's was a none-too-subtle attempt to make the council itself largely irrelevant, concentrating power in the 'operative company', which would be under his control: '. . . the members of the Council cannot reasonably be called upon to devote a great amount of time to routine work. . . . The Company is essential for this practical work. The Council remains the Advisory Body.'[100] Dyson's note was blunt: '(1) The proposal is not practicable. . . . (2) The Company may seriously impair the prestige and independence of the Council. . . . (3) The Company is unnecessary. The proper functions of a National Council can best be performed by its own Committee of Management.' The committee's report left the question to be decided at the next full meeting – a question apparently about structure but in fact reflecting Christie's determination to control the NCM and Dyson's suspicions about this.

By now Christie had a strong antipathy for Dyson. He wrote to the music publisher Leslie Boosey that artists like Myra Hess and Adrian Boult 'know what we are talking about, and the professors like Dyson. . . do not. Dyson has lived an isolated life. . . . He has not mixed with artists and the great musicians. . . . We appear to be fundamentally opposed.'[101] Straight after the committee meeting, Christie telegrammed Audrey to report 'OPEN SUPPORT EVERY INDIVIDUAL EXCEPT DYSON STRONG SUPPORT ASTOR JOWITT RAMSBOTHAM GENERAL FORMATION MEETING SOON POSSIBLE TRIUMPH VERY WELL HERE NO COLD CLOTHES'.[102] His following letter[103] included the usual exhaustive account of the meeting, designed to demonstrate that the committee 'seem to take entirely my conception of the scheme & believe it and say so'; that 'Dyson is a most peculiar man. He simply does not listen'; and that 'I have steered this ship astonishingly well & with unerring judgement'. But he was not absolutely blinded by self-love and by his practice of imputing his own faults to others: 'It seems almost incredible that I should have done all this without your being here. I expect Harry [Colles] saw that too & has kept a special watching brief.'

Attendees at the next meeting, in March 1941 at the Dorchester, included Edwin Lutyens, Malcolm Sargent, Ralph Vaughan Williams and John Spedan Lewis, as well as Hugh Allen and George Dyson.[104] Given the state of the war, Christie's opening remarks, again printed separately,[105] were extraordinary. He saw the NCM as a world-wide concept: '... this is a matter of supreme importance. If this scheme is right in this country, it is right in Canada, in Australia, in America, in Germany and Italy.... I look forward to the creation of National Councils of Music in all these countries... created by England, with its headquarters in London.... We can have the whole world looking to us....' The speech sagged into cliché: 'All is in the melting pot. It is now or never. I ask you to think big. We want a better world'; and its conclusion was massively overblown: 'Let the flags be out. Let us drive in State and let Victory find us in the first Coaches.'

No one sought to match Christie's rhetoric. Malcolm Sargent again seconded the motion.[106] Vaughan Williams said that 'It would help me, and I think others, to know that other points of view – other standards [of artistic excellence, apart from Christie's] – can be allowed for'. Christie reassured him, and the resolution passed unanimously. The meeting passed several other motions: that Bonham Carter, Wilfrid Greene and Christie should constitute the NCM's 'legal committee', consulting the Inland Revenue and Charity Commission to ensure the NCM's charitable status; that if there were no problems, the NCM should then be immediately incorporated; and that its first meeting should be held within four weeks of incorporation. Despite this apparent success, Christie's account of the meeting to Audrey displayed self-doubt unusual for him at this period: 'I did badly [as a correspondent] for three weeks. I was busy & worried about the N.C.M.... I was in an uncertain mood & not inclined to sit down & write letters.... But it turned out all right &... I don't think we have anything to fear at the moment.'[107]

This mood is the more surprising since in early 1941, alongside the successful hotel meetings, Christie was strengthening his relationship with Herwald Ramsbotham at the Board of Education. In January he reported to Audrey[108] that Ramsbotham had helped substantially both with Glyndebourne business (helping with the naturalization application by Rudolf Bing, Glyndebourne General Manager) and potentially with the NCM, 'offer[ing] to go with me to see Kingsley Wood [Chancellor of the Exchequer] at the Treasury. I expect we shall do it.' Less than two weeks later he wrote: 'Today I went to see Miss Glasgow [Secretary of CEMA] and Ramsbotham. They both regard Dyson as difficult.'[109] In reply to Ramsbotham's repeated offer to meet Sir Kingsley Wood with him, Christie said (according to his letter to Audrey) that there were two methods of dealing with the Treasury: '(1) W[ilfrid] Greene's gentle, clever persuasion backed by his known ability & importance & skill, (2) my overwhelming vehement keenness & determination when I know that I am right.' He listed for Audrey his supporters within the government: 'Jowitt, Bevin, Archie [Sinclair], Ramsbotham, Morton [Desmond Morton, an assistant to Winston Churchill and former pupil of Christie at Eton] & R. [Ramsbotham] says we must get Churchill in on this if necessary.' The list was exaggerated but Ramsbotham was a genuine enthusiast and a potentially crucial ally.

## Christie's Friends and Supporters in Spring 1941

In early 1941 Christie was an influential figure whose ill-defined NCM seemed on the point of being set up. This was despite his extreme views and equally extreme expression of them, volatility and arrogance, failure to think strategically on the subject, passion for overstatement, and tendency to insult those who disagreed with him. Considering Christie's friends and supporters alongside his personality helps explain why at this stage he seemed close to success with the NCM.

First, though he engaged in broadsides against professional musicians and 'the professors', he was inconsistent in this as in many other respects: both types of hate-figure were among his admirers and confidants. Robert Forbes and Ralph Vaughan Williams are considered below. Other musicians, too, respected him, his work and his views. Sir Adrian Boult temperamentally very different from Christie, wrote after the first Dorchester Hotel meeting to thank Christie for 'a most excellent lunch and delightful meeting.... you have certainly collected a first-class gathering of brain-power', adding in manuscript: '... if the Council is run by the Amateurs, it really should get things done!'[110]

Even with musicians with whom he often disagreed, such as Sir Walford Davies, Christie could demonstrate affection and openness, though this sometimes led him to displays of vanity. In his final letter to Davies, who died in March 1941, Christie wrote: 'I feel that I am miles ahead of the Continent, and that I can see the way to make England the great Centre of the World's music.... At this point I appear egotistical and shall do so as long as I am wanted. Then the Council must completely eclipse me.... Think big.'[111]

Other musicians, such as the violist Lionel Tertis, were simply fans. Tertis wrote to Christie that he had taken a house in Hereford to nurse his sick wife 'with a feeling of concern that its distance from Town may prevent me from giving to you and the fine project on which you have embarked, such help as I may be capable of. . . . In You. . . a Champion has at last arisen who has at heart the highest standard of musical art.'[112]

Second, alongside his ranting Christie was generous and could be discreet. One illustration of this was his anonymous financial support for Alfred Wareing when Wareing and the League of Audiences fell on hard times.[113] Third, he could on occasion inspire almost instant and deep respect. This, for instance, comes from a letter of May 1941 by George Evan Smith, an Australian on attachment to the BBC: 'I felt so stimulated by your ideas. . . that I felt impelled to drop you a line. . . . Meeting you has been an experience that I shan't lightly forget. . . . when I return to Australia I shall be able to say: "Here was a man."'[114]

Finally, while he was a 'big thinker' and good hater, he was more moderate than some of his allies. John Spedan Lewis, after the first Dorchester Hotel meeting, urged Christie to 'build up your organisation in such a way that the position in it of all professional musicians without exception is wholly and solely advisory'.[115] Recognizing that this 'requires some definition of a professional musician', Lewis proposed a handy rule-of-thumb: '. . . anyone, who cannot deny that he has made in any twelve months as much as a hundred pounds by making music or writing about it, should be disqualified for any but advisory functions.' Three months later Lewis suggested that 'so far as there is a real drive towards mediocrity, the true roots of that drive are not in the potential audience but in the present performers'.[116]

Robert Forbes, Principal of the Royal Manchester College of Music and an ally since the 1938 conferences, made these views seem tame. Writing to Christie in February 1941,[117] Forbes displayed contempt and spite towards his profession and colleagues. Unable to attend the 1941 meetings due to wartime disruption, he expressed his 'complete and absolute agreement' with Christie on two points: '. . . the first is that "the Musicians must depend on Music rather than Music on Musicians". . . . The second is your insistence on the raising of "standards".' Forbes elaborated on these themes: 'The plain and obvious truth is – but of course neither I nor anyone else dare say it where it ought to be said – that 90% of the members of the I.S.M. have no claim to be musicians in the real sense of the word.' The ISM was not the half of it:

> It is equally true – and Dyson knows it as well as I do – that not more than 10% of his students or Marchant's or mine have any real right to contemplate a musical career. But we are all caught in the monstrous machine that grinds out hundreds of mediocrities year in and year out, and incidentally grinds a

> good deal of the music out of those of us who have to spend our days teaching 'unteachables'. . . .

Forbes wrote at length of 'this wretched commerce of musical "education". . . the talented wasting their lives in teaching, or pretending to teach, those without any talent. . . . I can see no hope of getting out of this morass except by raising of "standards" and a ruthless squeezing out of mediocrity.' As for his antagonists, 'Why Dyson can't see this I can't imagine. . . . Vaughan Williams. . . seems to enjoy really bad amateur performances of his own works – I think a first class one would probably hurt him.' He included a self-pitying anecdote about 'what an appeal to the mob results in' – in this case, Forbes' ousting as conductor of the Halle Orchestra's 'Municipal Concerts' by 'a shocking little bounder – one of the monkey-on-a-stick type of Conductor – [appointed] to give "popular" concerts'. He concluded with further personal attacks: 'The trouble is that. . . [Sir Hugh] Allen can't conceive a musical enterprise being of National importance unless he is at the head of it, . . . [and] Dyson is always right and everybody else wrong.'

Harry Colles commented on this letter: '. . . much of it is true. But it is certainly bitter in tone + that does not make me put entire confidence in him as a colleague. However it is our fate to accept help from men on whom we cannot put unreserved reliance.'[118] Christie's reply to Forbes was less bitter and more self-confident than Forbes' letter. The answer lay in:

> Thinking big. . . . There are certain strong prejudices in the path, that of mere consumption and that of the anti-foreigner, anti-Jew, anti-whatnot. Thinking big we cannot be bothered with these prejudices. . . . I just think that we cannot fail for the simple reason that everything so far has shown that the scheme is right. . . . We are certain of success.[119]

Unlike Forbes, Christie was rarely misanthropic. His openness to debate and respect for some of those whose views he disagreed with are illustrated in his correspondence with Ralph Vaughan Williams. Christie and Vaughan Williams often disagreed and traded heavy verbal blows. Their relationship deteriorated later, but at this time their discussions were cordial. In June 1941, for instance, Christie wrote to Vaughan Williams seeking unsuccessfully to persuade him to accept the post of Master of the King's Music in succession to Walford Davies: 'Who else is there?. . . You are considering your own whim. . . . The interest of music urgently needs that you should accept.'[120]

And his honesty evoked honesty in return. Writing to Christie at this period, Vaughan Williams explored the issue of Englishness in art, using Glyndebourne itself as illustration:

> It provided a wonderful and beautiful entertainment for those who could afford it. But it has not built for the future. It has done nothing towards fertilizing the dormant seed of English opera.... The few English performers... merely became... bad imitations of continental singers.... [Glyndebourne] is like a bunch of flowers in a glass of water – very lovely while it lasts but having no roots in the soil.[121]

He generalized the point: 'What course are we to pursue? Are we to take the English standard of singing and mould it to opera or are we to force the continental style down English throats...? Perhaps... you really think that we in England have no musical tradition worth speaking of.... (The doctrine of "Herrenvolk" is not confined to the Nazis).' More generally still: 'Do you in fact wish to establish a little "Europe in England"... affecting among Englishmen only those snobs and prigs who... do not recognise the intimate connection between art and life?' Vaughan Williams used Roy Henderson as illustration: 'It was painful to me to hear great artists like Roy Henderson and Heddle Nash trying conscientiously to be funny in the Teutonic manner.' He supported his case in language as extreme as Christie's: 'If musical life in this country is merely to be a bad imitation of continental methods it is doomed. See the awful results at Sadler's Wells of smearing themselves with the droppings of the Russian Ballet.' He concluded with this plea: 'Your task, it seems to me, is to become musically an Englishman and to see music as we see it and then add to it your own unique experience and knowledge.'

## Conclusion

It is notable that in many cases Christie's professional relationships were both intense and relatively short-lived. He worked closely with Harold Baker and Robert Mayer during the 'Council of Power' period,[122] but they seem to have played no part in his work after 1939. His correspondence about the NCM with Sir Alan Lascelles, Sir Adrian Boult, Robert Forbes and John Spedan Lewis seems to have largely ceased in 1941. He later formed an alliance with Lord Esher, but that too was brief.[123] After summer 1941, Christie's confidants and colleagues on the NCM were few, primarily Harry Colles and Roy Henderson from the musical side and Maurice Bonham Carter and Wilfrid Greene as 'men of affairs'. Christie had the capacity to inspire enthusiasm, respect and affection; for whatever reason the resulting relationships often did not last long.

In spring 1941 the aims and methods of Christie's proposed National Council of Music remained shifting and obscure, and at least some members of the musical establishment distrusted him. But he was supported by many leading musicians and such other distinguished figures as Sir Edwin Lutyens, Sir James Jeans and Sir Kenneth Clark. He had a strong relationship with Herwald Ramsbotham, the Cabinet Minister most relevant to his cause. His London hotel meetings had concluded with the resolution to establish the NCM. He was closely advised by the music editor of *The Times*, the second most senior judge in England and Wales, and a businessman with strong political connections. All seemed set fair for the NCM. Artistic and policy issues could for now take second place to the administrative and legal challenges of setting it up. But while Christie continued to campaign energetically within and beyond government, and Harry Colles, Wilfrid Greene and Maurice Bonham Carter provided almost unquestioning support, the NCM was never established. The next chapter discusses how and why it failed, and considers Christie's 'shadow presence' in the creation of the Arts Council.

## Notes

1 Glyndebourne 2, Christie-Sinclair, 9/9/39.
2 Ibid., Christie letter of 18/9/39 to the invitees to the cancelled September 1939 conference.
3 Ibid., Macmillan-Sinclair, 25/9/39.
4 Ibid., Chamberlain-Christie, 19/9/39.
5 Blunt, Chapter 19.
6 Ivor Atkins, 'Colles, Henry Cope (1879–1943)', rev. Nigel Scaife, *Oxford Dictionary of National Biography*, Oxford University Press, 2004.
7 Hundreds of John Christie's letters, though few of Audrey Christie's/Mildmay's, are in the Glyndebourne archive. All quotations from these letters in this chapter are from a box of family correspondence, 1934–41 (hereafter 'Glyndebourne 4').
8 Glyndebourne 2, Christie-Dyson, 9/9/39.
9 Leventhal, p295.
10 Ibid., p296.
11 National Archives file ED136/188B, 'Memorandum in support of an Application to the Treasury for Financial Assistance', 6 March 1940.

12 Leventhal, p298.
13 Glyndebourne 2, Christie-Dyson, 1/2/40.
14 At this point the National Labour politician Earl De La Warr.
15 Ibid., Dyson-Christie 5/2/40.
16 Weingärtner, p58 et seq.
17 Glyndebourne 3, Davies-Christie, 31/3/40.
18 Glyndebourne 3, ms note by Christie; undated, but covering developments to March 1940.
19 Glyndebourne 2, undated memorandum by Christie (probably March 1940), for all quotations in this and the following two paragraphs.
20 Ibid., Davies-Christie, 5/6/40.
21 Ibid., Christie-Colles, 7/6/40.
22 Ibid., Christie-Davies, 7/6/40.
23 Glyndebourne 2, Ramsbotham-Christie, 8/6/40, replying to Christie-Ramsbotham, 4/6/40 (not on file).
24 Ibid., Christie-Ramsbotham, 10/6/40.
25 Ibid., Christie-Henderson, 13/6/40.
26 Ibid., Henderson-Christie, 23/6/40.
27 Glyndebourne 3, Ramsbotham-Christie, 27/6/40.
28 Glyndebourne 4, folder headed 'John Christie to Audrey Christie in Canada, 1940', hereafter 'Glyndebourne 4/1', JC-AC, 30/9/40.
29 Glyndebourne 3, Christie-Davies, 26/7/40.
30 Ibid., Davies-Christie, 2/8/40.
31 Ibid., Colles-Christie, 10/8/40.
32 Ibid., Colles-Christie, 20/8/40.
33 Ibid., Christie-Boult, 19/8/40.
34 Ibid., Boult-Christie, 21/8/40.
35 Ibid., Sargent-Christie, 29/8/40.
36 Ibid., Christie-Sargent, 2/9/40.
37 Ibid., Forbes-Christie, 27/8/40.
38 Ibid., Christie-Forbes, 2/9/40.
39 Ibid., Henderson-Christie, 17/8/40.
40 *The Nationalization of Culture* (London: Hamish Hamilton, 1977), p216.
41 'The Arts Council: Its Policy and Hopes' (*The Listener*, 12/7/45).
42 Basil Dean: *The Theatre at War* (London, George G Harrap, 1956), p135.
43 Glyndebourne 3, Henderson-Christie, 17/8/40.
44 Ibid., Henderson-Christie, 2/ and 13/11/40.
45 Ibid., Christie-Chamberlain, 26/7/40.
46 Ibid., Chamberlain's Private Secretary-Christie, 29/7/40.
47 Ibid., 26/8/40.

48 Ibid., Clark-Christie, 27/7/40.
49 Glyndebourne 4/1, JC-AC, 25/7/40, for all further quotations in this and the following paragraph.
50 Glyndebourne 3, Lewis-Christie, 8/8/40; correspondence with the others listed is also in this file.
51 June Hannam, 'Snowden, Ethel (1881–1951)', *Oxford Dictionary of National Biography*, Oxford University Press, 2004.
52 Glyndebourne 3, Snowden-Christie, 4/9/40.
53 Ibid., Jowitt-Christie, 6/9/40.
54 Glyndebourne 4/1, JC-AC, 29/7/40.
55 V&A Archive, CEMA papers, file EL2/4-A (hereafter 'V&A EL2/4-A'), Christie-Ramsbotham, 20/9/40.
56 Glyndebourne 3, Keynes-Christie, 30/9/40.
57 Ibid., Newman-Christie, 4/8/40.
58 Ibid., Newman-Christie, 13/9/40.
59 Ibid., Colles-Christie, 23/9/40.
60 Glyndebourne 4/1, JC-AC, 26/8/40.
61 Arthur Jacobs, 'Wood, Sir Henry Joseph (1869–1944)', *Oxford Dictionary of National Biography*, Oxford University Press, 2004.
62 Glyndebourne 3, Wood-Christie, 21/8/40.
63 Ibid., Colles-Christie, 7/9/40.
64 Ibid., Wood-Christie, 28/10/40.
65 Glyndebourne 4/1, JC-AC, 2/10/40.
66 Glyndebourne 3, Colles-Christie, 8/10/40.
67 Ibid., Christie-Jowitt, 29/10/40.
68 Ibid., Jowitt-Christie, 8/11/40.
69 V&A EL2/4-A, Ramsbotham-Christie, 31/10/40.
70 Glyndebourne 3, Christie-Allen, 6/11/40.
71 Ibid., Allen-Christie, 15/12/40.
72 Ibid., Henderson-Christie, 13/11/40.
73 Ibid., Colles-Christie, 15/10/40.
74 Ibid., Hess-Christie, 21/10/40.
75 Ibid., Lascelles-Christie, 13/8/40.
76 Ibid., Christie-Lascelles, 19/8/40.
77 Ibid., Lascelles-Christie, 22/8/40.
78 Ibid., Lascelles-Christie, 18/9/40.
79 Glyndebourne 4/1, JC-AC, 2/10/40.
80 Glyndebourne 3, Lascelles-Christie, 11/10/40.
81 See Chapter 6, pp95–6.
82 Glyndebourne 4/1, JC-AC, 21/10/40.

83 Glyndebourne 3, Christie-Jowitt, 29/10/40.
84 Glyndebourne 4, folder '1940–41 Audrey Christie (in Canada) to John Christie', hereafter 'Glyndebourne 4/2', AC-JC, 26/1/41.
85 Glyndebourne 3, undated memorandum 'N.C.M. Notes incidental to a number of points on the formation of a National plan'.
86 Ibid., undated and untitled memorandum, beginning 'I see four distinct lines'.
87 Ibid., invitation, undated apart from heading 'Christmas 1940'.
88 Ibid., Priestley-Christie, 20/12/40.
89 Glyndebourne 4/2, JC-AC, 2/1/41.
90 Glyndebourne 3, Sargent-Christie, 31/12/40.
91 Glyndebourne 4/2, JC-AC, 2/1/41.
92 Glyndebourne 3, minutes of 9/1/41 Dorchester Hotel meeting.
93 Ibid., Marchant-Christie, 11/1/41 (letter mistakenly dated 1940).
94 Ibid., printed note headed 'National Council of Music'.
95 Ibid., minutes of 9/1/41 Dorchester Hotel meeting.
96 Glyndebourne 4/2, JC-AC 11/1/41, for all quotations in this and the following paragraph.
97 Ibid., AC-JC, 26/1/41.
98 Glyndebourne 3, minutes of 23/1/41 Ritz Hotel committee meeting, for all quotations in this paragraph.
99 Glyndebourne 4/2, JC-AC 27/1/41, for all quotations in this paragraph.
100 Glyndebourne 3, quotations from undated notes by Christie and Dyson, circulated to attendees at 6/2/41 Ritz Hotel meeting.
101 Ibid., Christie-Boosey, 29/1/41.
102 Glyndebourne 4/2, telegram JC-AC, 7/2/41.
103 Ibid., JC-AC 7/2/41.
104 Glyndebourne 3, minutes of 3/3/41 Dorchester Hotel meeting.
105 Ibid., printed copy of Christie's opening remarks for 3/3/41 Dorchester Hotel meeting.
106 Ibid., minutes of 3/3/41 Dorchester Hotel meeting.
107 Glyndebourne 4/2, JC-AC, 19/3/41.
108 Ibid., JC-AC, 27/1/41.
109 Ibid., JC-AC, 7/2/41.
110 Glyndebourne 3, Boult-Christie, 16/1/41.
111 Ibid., Christie-Davies, 25/2/41.
112 Ibid., Tertis-Christie, (received) 26/3/41.
113 See Chapter 5.
114 Glyndebourne 3, Smith-Christie, 30/5/41.
115 Ibid., Lewis-Christie, 10/1/41.
116 Ibid., Lewis-Christie, 15/4/41.

117 Ibid., Forbes-Christie, 26/2/41.

118 Ibid., Colles-Christie, 9/3/41.

119 Ibid., Christie-Forbes, 18/3/41.

120 Ibid., Christie-Vaughan Williams, 10/6/41.

121 Ibid., Vaughan Williams-Christie, undated, probably June 1941.

122 See, generally, Chapter 6.

123 Chapter 8.

# 8

# Butler, Keynes and the End of Christie's National Council of Music: 1941–4

## Global Ambitions and Legal Minutiae: The NCM Spring to Autumn 1941

The story of John Christie's National Council of Music has a similar arc to that of Alfred Wareing's League of Audiences several years earlier – unexpected success and substantial credibility followed by decline, fall and obscurity. Both seemed on the verge of a breakthrough after major meetings, though with a stark contrast of venues: Wareing's at Toynbee Hall in May 1938 chaired by the Archbishop of Canterbury, Christie's at the Dorchester and Ritz Hotels in early 1941. For both, this proved deceptive: these meetings marked the high point of their campaigns. Both went downhill from then on, though this became apparent sooner in Wareing's case than in Christie's. Both influenced the design and focus of the Arts Council. Both failed to have this influence acknowledged by the Arts Council or later commentators. Both have been mainly invisible ever since.

Christie's NCM took a surprising route after his 'hotel meetings'. Until summer 1941 he corresponded widely about it. Then discussion about the NCM between him and the musical world dried to a trickle. Instead, Sir Maurice Bonham Carter and Sir Wilfrid (by now, Lord) Greene worked on the formalities of establishing it and Christie expanded his ill-defined ambitions worldwide, seeking to engage government Ministers and officials in his plans. He still saw CEMA as no challenge to the NCM, a mistake which was to prove costly. The major factor weakening the project at this period, however, was Christie's increasingly grandiose aims and his compulsion to keep all power in his own hands.

This became clear from the NCM's proposed structure. In July 1941 Bonham Carter wrote to the members of the still notional NCM,[1] reporting that he, Christie and Greene (the 'Legal Committee' established in March) had agreed its draft memorandum and articles of association. Musicians would have no positions of responsibility: '. . . your Committee was strongly of the opinion that it was inadvisable for professional musicians to be included on the Board of Management [where power would lie].' Indeed 'under the advice of learned Counsel' (not in the archive; it may have been a euphemism for Greene) any professional musician on the Board would be ineligible to take paid work with an institution benefitting from the NCM, and having a musician on the Board would endanger the NCM's charitable status. Instead musicians could sit on the council itself and on a 'Technical Advisory Committee'. Neither would have any authority. Bonham Carter claimed that in order to complete the articles of association it had been necessary to list in advance, thus without consultation, who would sit on the Board and Technical Advisory Committee. He, Christie and Greene had appointed themselves to the Board, plus three other 'men of affairs': John Spedan Lewis (more anti-musician than Christie himself), the judge Viscount Finlay and the Chairman of Barclay's Bank Edwin Fisher (neither of whom had been active in previous NCM discussions). Most of the nine members proposed for the Technical Advisory Committee were musicians more or less sympathetic to Christie, including Adrian Boult, Harry Colles, Myra Hess, Malcolm Sargent, Lionel Tertis and Ralph Vaughan Williams.

One name not included was Sir George Dyson, now wholly disenchanted with the project. He wrote to Christie that he did not want join a committee 'so lacking in effective authority',[2] and since 'I cannot belong to the Board of Management, apparently, on account of my professional position. . . [and] all the active functions of the Council are given to the Board of Management, membership of the Council is not really the place for those of us who already have wide responsibilities in other spheres'. By contrast, Lionel Tertis, for example, remained delighted to be part of Christie's plans, and could 'only hope that I may prove of real use to you. You know what I feel concerning this noble project. . . . I see in you a champion for our cause at long last.'[3]

The structure Dyson objected to was set out in the 22-page draft memorandum and articles of association, prepared by June 1941.[4] This is the closest Christie came to specifying the NCM's purposes and methods. But its fifteen 'Objects', running to more than three closely printed pages, provided no clarity. The first was that the NCM would be the 'central authority. . . on all matters connected with the art of music', the second that it would 'act as an advisory or consultative body to H.M. Government' on all matters connected with music. Most objects were equally general, such as co-ordinating 'the activities of companies and persons. . . [providing] musical, operatic, corybantic [*sic*] and other performances. . . connected with the musical life of the nation generally'. Money was not mentioned until object (E): 'To receive, administer, control and distribute, or determine the distribution of funds provided by H.M. Government. . . .' Later objects included setting-up and awarding music prizes, establishing music libraries, commissioning works of music, providing musical performances ('so far as may be considered necessary') and co-ordinating 'musical culture in England and other countries'.

In fact almost anything connected with music could be within the NCM's scope. Most of the objects, to be realized, would require existing organizations, including the British government, to cede power, money or both to the new organization, which none of them had agreed; and there was no indication of the source of the NCM's authority. What was clear was that power would lie with the Board of Management, responsible for 'the management of the affairs of the Council' including the appointment of its members, of whom there would be no more than fifty. The Technical Advisory Committee 'shall be advisory only'.

Meanwhile Christie attempted to woo Whitehall, sometimes to advance the NCM but more often to share increasingly grand and woolly visions. In May 1941 he wrote to Audrey: 'I see Ramsbotham fairly often on one thing or another. Yesterday afternoon I saw Horace Wilson head of the Treasury & then Alan Barlow (brother of Tommy) about £5,000 a year grant for the expenses of the N.C.M. It was an unofficial visit and Bongy is following it up.'[5] (Sir Alan Barlow was a senior Treasury official whose public spending responsibilities included the Board of Education.) While happy to exploit his contacts ('Of course, I used the link with Neville Chamberlain'), Christie was aware that this strategy had its limits: 'I am pleased that when I ring up (without writing) the head of the Treasury he at once sees me, but I shall be infuriated if the only result is to turn us down. I don't want the compliments. I want the substance.'

In June 1941 he wrote to Barlow with the draft memorandum and articles of association.[6] The letter was mainly a marketing pitch. Christie enclosed, and suggested that Barlow 'might add to our file', the letter in which George Evan Smith at the BBC had written of Christie 'when I return to Australia I shall be able to say: "Here was a man."' He reported, truthfully, that 'I am backed by the strong personal support of men such as Bongy, Wilfrid Greene. . . and others. . . . Wilfrid Greene has been giving up other work to help us. . . with the legal side.' He stated as if it were an established fact that 'There is to be an N.C.M. in every country – an international organisation with headquarters in London'. While remaining entirely vague on details, Christie 'would remind you that we stand for constructive policy as opposed to the mere consumption of money'. But his main selling point was that 'For the first time, Music will be in the hands of wise men of affairs as well as of musicians. I assume that the Government will welcome this step forward.' The use of Bonham Carter's nickname suggests that he, Barlow and Christie were acquainted, as does the letter's postscript: 'I have 12,000 bottles of German wine buried in the Downs – enough for three [Glyndebourne] Festivals.' But the archive contains no reply, and later events suggest that Barlow was unpersuaded by Christie's letter.[7]

Setting up the NCM remained slow work. Christie, inclined to mark the slightest advance by sending Audrey self-congratulatory telegrams and detailed letters, wrote to her in early August 1941: 'I have been a bad correspondent. I have no news. I am waiting to finish the N.C.M. & days pass & practically nothing happens.'[8] But even in the course of this letter his mood lifted: 'We shall gather a fighting force. Some of us want to take our coats off. . . . a new world is in the air. . . . In the Council & in my leading of it lies progress.'

In summer and autumn 1941 Christie made few attempts to gain new allies. Among these few were discussions with the theatre director Tyrone Guthrie, and, on Adrian Boult's advice, with the composer Arthur Bliss.[9] He described Bliss to Audrey as 'a splendid man outspoken and vehemently declaiming against the bad standard in England. . . . I want a bit more of this kind of thing from the British Musician.' More often Christie dealt with his frustration at the NCM's slow progress by large, vapid ideas of 'an N.C.M. in every country'. A July 1941 telegram to Audrey read: 'AM ASKING SUPPORT BRITISH COUNCIL CHURCHILL SOME HOPE SENT CANADA AMERICA. . . .'[10] In the August letter chiding himself for being a bad correspondent he anticipated the NCM's being established and its first meeting being held the following month. Then 'I think I could arrange for my passage to Canada for a few days afterwards, assuming the British Council approves.'[11] He considered this likely since 'I have the strong support of the Chairman. . . for the N.C.M. in Canada & the States'. Later in August: 'I have a new idea which is revolving in my mind. I think you must create the N.C.M. in Canada. I will come over and start it with you. . . .'[12] In his next letter he reported that he 'saw Vincent Massey [the Canadian High Commissioner to the UK] yesterday & he approved of your being the driving force in Canada as I am here. He also wants me to get Churchill to send me to Mackenzie King [the Canadian Prime Minister].'[13] According to Christie, many in the British Embassy in Washington thought that 'the Americans only want guns & blood & thunder'; he himself believed that 'the N.C.M. is just what Roosevelt will want. It is above dollars & trade unions. It is a matter of right & wrong & not of politics.'

The archive contains no evidence of much reality behind any of this.

With the NCM proceeding so slowly Christie passed the second half of 1941 lecturing Audrey on the political condition of England. One theme was the dead hand of civil service control: 'For years we have been strangling the Francis Drakes & now we reap the reward. Men of action are rare & when you do get them you get brutes like Beaverbrook who use the situation to get power (it used to be money) at the expense of others who are not so self seeking and are of good principles.'[14] Another theme was more extreme still: 'I feel that all cultured people... must organize and let their organization work for them and insist on the support of the higher things of life in the new world. Let us give tangible shape to the new World now. Let the organization be called the Glyndebourne Society.'[15] Christie's syntax became mangled, the concept woozily prophetic:

> Let it be the central organization of all the arts, of Learning, Literature, Science. Let all these form (through you & me) their N.C.M's. N.C. Architecture, N.C. Science, etc., which will advise and protect us, the Glyndebourne Society. We want the support of all the Press, of all organizations.... We should have power.... we don't beg but lead.

He spent several pages expounding these ideas, sometimes obscurely ('We stand once more for right and wrong as we do in Music'), sometimes mundanely ('The fee for joining the organization should be 1/-'), before reporting that 'I have no news of the N.C.M.'.

Christie wrote several times to Audrey about the Glyndebourne Society, showing little regard for logic: 'I think it is the only way of beating the Politicians & the Civil Service.... I want the Cabinet to join first of all',[16] and at times toppling into megalomania: 'I want it supported by all the press, by all professional organizations, Clergy, Lawyers, Scientists, Accountants & learned Societies.... all of which will deal with Glyndebourne.' He had 'discussed it shortly with Barrington-Ward, the new Editor of The Times & he thought I should get the scheme backed by all the groups, societies etc first & then go to the P.M. and the Cabinet with it'.[17] As often with Christie, it is unclear whether this accurately reflected the discussion or was a projection onto others of his own views. He acknowledged that his pursuit of wilder dreams was due in part to lack of other occupation: '... here life is so dull & one never sees anyone. The only thing for me is to have an intense interest such as the N.C.M.'

He continued to write about NCMs in Canada and the USA, repeating to Sir Ronald Campbell, Minister in the British Embassy in Washington, that he 'expect[ed] to be sent to Canada... with a personal recommendation from Churchill to Mackenzie King',[18] and that the NCM 'is just what Roosevelt will want'. He suggested that 'The other Arts will settle round Music because we are first in the field', and concluded: 'You can see in this scheme a fiery star leading the New World.' It is doubtful whether, in September 1941, Christie had any reason to expect that Churchill would send him to Canada or the USA. It was only in October that he approached two members of the Cabinet about this: the Foreign Secretary Anthony Eden and the Minister of Information Brendan Bracken. To Eden he elaborated on the theme of NCMs throughout the world in a letter headed 'Reconstruction and the New World'.[19] He began (as usual): 'We are just about to incorporate the National Council of Music.' Suggesting, with no further explanation, that the NCM's aim was 'to advise the Government and to protect it in taking our advice', he continued: 'But the next step concerns you. I want to be sent officially to America and to Canada to Roosevelt and Mackenzie King to get the scheme started there as well. After the war in all Countries.... This scheme gives Roosevelt and the Federal Government just what they want.' The Glyndebourne archive contains no reply.

Christie approached Brendan Bracken less directly, as part of a complex scheme to get to Winston Churchill. He explained, confusingly, to Audrey: 'I have written to Morton [in Churchill's office] telling him that I want with the assistance of Bongy to approach Churchill through Mrs. Churchill with a view to his sending me direct to Roosevelt and Mackenzie King, and Morton has sent my letter to Brendan Bracken.... Probably it depends on him.'[20] This approach too went nowhere.

But Christie's relationship with another Cabinet Minister was far more important than those with Eden and Bracken, and had much to do with his ultimate failure.

## 'We are at last unofficially accepted & wanted': Christie Misunderstands – Autumn 1941 to Spring 1942

In July 1941 Rab Butler replaced Herwald Ramsbotham as President of the Board of Education. It took Christie a long while to realize how damaging this development would prove to his plans.

He was optimistic at the start. Although on Butler's appointment he wrote to Audrey: 'The [NCM] plans have been put out of joint by the change from Ramsbotham to Butler at the B of Education',[21] his first meeting, a month later, filled him with enthusiasm. He reported this 'splendid interview' to Audrey in the letter[22] where described the complex manoeuvrings intended to enlist Churchill's support: '[Butler] told me... that the B[oard] of E[ducation] were very much interested. It is clear that Ramsbotham has left a very good recommendation. . . .' This was not all: '. . . almost the best thing was that he said – quite rightly – that he did not wish to prejudge the matter [of the NCM] but would like to talk it over with a friend of his whose opinion he very much valued & that if I liked I could be there too. Whom do you think – Wilfrid Greene! It just could not be better.'

Following the meeting he also wrote an upbeat letter to Butler.[23] Its terms make clear that Christie had shared with Butler his vision of the Glyndebourne Society; this is unlikely to have raised Butler's opinion of him. Later in October 1941 Christie wrote to Audrey that Butler had indeed discussed the NCM with Greene.[24] He believed that Butler and his officials 'are realising that the Government has to do this and other things [presumably a vague reference to long-term government support for the arts], but we are first in the field with the right people and the right scheme and I am accepted as a result of Glyndebourne'.

He also believed he was working well with Mary Glasgow, CEMA's Secretary. In November he reported to Audrey a meeting with Glasgow at which he found 'intense indignation there [at CEMA] against E.N.S.A. and particularly Basil Dean [ENSA's Director]. They would like to cooperate with me. So all that is sweet.'[25] The apparently good relationship continued: later in November Glasgow was a guest at Glyndebourne, where (this seems to have been written during the visit) 'we have been talking about C.E.M.A. N.C.M. Carnegie & all. It seems that Dyson was turned off C.E.M.A. by Macmillan [Chairman of CEMA; this was not so]. . . . They don't think well of him there. . . . I think I stand well with all except Dyson. . . . I have got a good deal of information from Miss Glasgow.'[26] He was clearly exhilarated by the visit, writing two days later to Audrey that 'We talked of C.E.M.A., N.C.M., New World etc. until she must have been exhausted. Our [the NCM's] Memorandum & Articles had been sent to the Board of Education. . . & had been sent to her to deal with!. . . The Government departments are, I think, supporting us.'[27]

These meetings led to a short-lived but marked rise in his opinion of CEMA. Previously he had nothing good to say for it. Now he suggested that CEMA might be central to his dream of extending the NCM model to other subjects – now including 'Religion, Cruelty to Animals & Children' alongside the arts, architecture and science:

> Then an enlargement of C.E.M.A. . . . into a central body to coordinate all these interests, perhaps on the basis of my idea of 1/- a head from a million of the people to show their interest. . . . It may be that Glyndebourne should become the headquarters of this organization. . . . Our family being the host but all paid for by the Government. Will you let me know your views. . .?

Audrey's response, if any, has not survived, though Christie persisted for a while in the view that 'the whole lot [of National Councils] should be collected under some Committee such as an extension of C.E.M.A.'[28]

But Christie was fundamentally mistaken. The more positive he became about Butler and Mary Glasgow, the more comprehensively his hopes were to be dashed. It is true that the government was, in late 1941 and 1942, thinking seriously about the need to continue arts subsidy after the war, that Butler was an enthusiast for this, that discussion within and between CEMA and the Board of Education about this longer-term support was along lines which Christie would have approved, and that Christie and the NCM even featured in this discussion. But in practice all of these points harmed rather than furthered Christie's hopes.

The obviously crucial development was Butler's appointing John Maynard Keynes as Chairman of CEMA in early 1942. This is considered below. But Christie's problems with the Board of Education and CEMA began before this. While commentators agree that Keynes' arrival led to a change in CEMA's approach, from amateur to professional and from spreading resources widely to raising standards, these changes owe much to earlier work by Mary Glasgow, Robert Wood (Deputy Secretary at the Board of Education) and Butler.

Glasgow's central role in CEMA and the Arts Council has received relatively little attention. Far more has been given to the dominant but contrasting figures of Keynes, CEMA's second Chairman, and Tom Jones, its first Vice-Chairman and initial guiding force. But a frank note of August 1941 from Glasgow to Robert Wood[29] made what may have been the earliest references to two matters which would prove crucial to CEMA's history and Christie's failure. The first was the suggestion that Keynes should have a role on CEMA's council. The Pilgrim Trust had announced that it would soon cease co-funding CEMA. Since CEMA's Chairman (Macmillan) and Vice-Chairman (Jones) were there by virtue of being on the Pilgrim Trust Board, their future on CEMA was uncertain. Glasgow made her sympathies clear: 'Lord Macmillan is... quite useless as a Chairman.... he writes periodic letters of appreciation, but gives us no direction of any kind.... Would it be possible to make the Vice-Chairman, who has done all the work, Chairman?' Beyond this, 'There should be some distinguished [generalist] names on Council: e.g. Mr. J.M. Keynes.' The latter suggestion probably owed more to Keynes' connections within and beyond the arts than to his reputation as an economist – there is no indication that such skills were thought relevant.

Glasgow's second theme was that CEMA needed more expertise in the areas it funded, drama, music and visual art. A Council member should chair an

'Executive Committee' for each of them. This is the first mention of the expert panels for music, drama and visual art which Keynes introduced in late 1942 and which led Christie to believe that his ideas had been stolen – see below. Finally, although Glasgow backed Tom Jones for Chairman and Jones was a keen advocate of amateur arts, she did not share this enthusiasm: 'I would also like to add a recommendation that Mr. du Garde Peach [CEMA's head of amateur drama] & Amateur Drama should be totally abandoned.'

Robert (later Sir Robert) Wood, best known as one of the architects of the 1944 Education Act,[30] was also central to CEMA's evolution into the Arts Council. A letter from him to Tom Jones of September 1941,[31] cited by several commentators,[32] was the earliest official attempt to consider public funding of the arts 'from the point of view of permanent planning as opposed to present emergency arrangements'. Wood considered that while CEMA was 'a war emergency organisation... the Exchequer will, in fact, have to continue to support this sort of effort to bring the best to the most in Music, Drama and Art'. Four years before the Arts Council came into being, the letter accurately sketched out this more permanent body. Concerning its form, 'there is, I think, much to be said for putting it a bit outside the purely Departmental machine.... This Council... should, I believe, quite definitely be related to the Board of Education, although... the fact that it has a separate entity... might be recognised by some form of incorporation or Charter.'

Given Jones' support of amateur arts, Wood stepped carefully when considering the new organization's priorities. It was important 'to clear our minds between what is emergency and what is permanent'. In the beginning, 'C.E.M.A. directed its attention to the amateur field to prevent things being blacked out by the war.... [but recently] we have been concentrating more and more on the professional side'. Wood suggested that while this 'duality of purpose' was acceptable in wartime, a permanent peace-time body 'ought to concentrate on and confine itself to the maintaining of the highest standards; on the fostering of the very best in Music, Drama and Art....' Wood ended by noting that he had discussed this with Butler, who 'would probably not be unsympathetic to the considerations I have put down'.

Thus Glasgow had proposed the creation of specialist committees in CEMA for music, drama and art, and Wood envisaged CEMA's becoming a permanent body operating under charter at arm's length from the Board of Education and supporting only high quality professional work. Much of this might be seen as the realization of Christie's dreams. But a reference at the start of Wood's letter, unremarked by commentators, suggests a different view: '... as you will know, there are various stirrings of the waters, e.g. John Christie with his proposed National Council of Music, but I am not at all sure that these stirrings will always produce waters of healing, and it behoves us, perhaps, to be thinking ahead a bit'. It seems that while the Arts Council's founding principles were similar to Christie's, among the early motivations for setting it up was Wood's wish to pre-empt Christie. The reasons for this are considered below, with other examples of the same phenomenon.

Jones replied to Wood that 'our moving away from the amateur field is against the original understanding with the Treasury who all along have stressed "making by the people themselves"'.[33] This did not appeal to Wood or Butler: it is not surprising that they favoured Keynes over Jones for Chairman. Butler approached Keynes in December 1941, suggesting that chairing CEMA 'would not demand too much from you in actual time… [but] your guidance at this stage of its development would be invaluable'.[34] As to the future, 'while the Council's work will remain emergency war work, it does, I think, point the way to something that might occupy a more permanent place in our social organisation'. Keynes required some coaxing. Not only was he hugely busy, but 'I have been in only limited sympathy with the principles on which it [CEMA] has been carried on hitherto'.[35] At a meeting in January 1942, Butler apparently overcame Keynes' doubts: a few days later he accepted the chairmanship.[36]

Keynes had long been a formidable advocate of high standards and professionalism in the arts. Fred Leventhal, citing a letter from Christie to Glasgow and a meeting between Keynes and Glasgow, both in July 1940, described Keynes as an 'even more trenchant critic' than Christie of CEMA's initial focus.[37] (This was Leventhal's only reference to Christie; he did not mention the NCM.) Soon after agreeing to become CEMA's Chairman, Keynes made his, and apparently Glasgow's, approach to arts funding clear in a letter to Ifor Evans, a CEMA member:

> I was worried lest what one may call the welfare side was to be developed at the expense of the artistic side and of standards generally. Before agreeing to act as Chairman, I expressed this view very clearly to [Butler].… He told me that I need have no anxiety on that head, that he shared this view himself and that, with the disappearance of the Pilgrim Trust from the management (combined with Miss Glasgow's bias in the right direction) all ought to be well on this score.[38]

Butler was not the ally Christie thought him, and the combination of Butler and Keynes ultimately proved fatal to the NCM. But Christie's later conflicts with

Keynes, as with Butler, were not over issues of principle: they had similar views on the arts and on the role of state support. There clearly came to be a clash of personalities, though this was not apparent during their cordial exchanges in 1938.[39] The root of the problem, however, was that both felt the need to be in charge, that Keynes was in fact in charge, and that Keynes became increasingly frustrated by Christie's failure to explain with any clarity what the NCM was about.

Butler's note of the meeting at which he persuaded Keynes to accept the chairmanship[40] is significant in these and other respects. First, it confirmed that Keynes was 'keen that C.E.M.A. should concentrate on standard and not on mere dissipation [*sic*] of any form of music and art. . . . He objected to C.E.M.A. being a welfare organisation'. Second, Keynes 'responded well to the suggestion that we should organise a Council outside a Government office, which should encourage in general music, drama, and the arts, and act as a channel for the granting of Government money'. Thus even before Keynes became CEMA's Chairman, he and Butler had agreed the essential structure of the post-war Arts Council. Third, Keynes 'agrees with me that Mr. Christie's organisation will have to play in with us in any ultimate scheme'. This final point confirms that Christie was in the minds of, and influenced, those planning CEMA's future, Butler and Keynes as well as Wood. Wood wished to outflank Christie's NCM. Butler and Keynes required the NCM to co-operate with and subordinate itself to any new permanent organization (if this is what 'play in with us' meant). For all of them, Christie and his plans were both highly relevant and an object of suspicion.

Two further examples, respectively from within and outside Whitehall, illustrate negative attitudes towards Christie and his plans during early planning for what became the Arts Council. First, in December 1941 Butler noted a discussion about CEMA with Sir Alan Barlow of the Treasury. He prefaced this, apropos of nothing else in the meeting, by recording that 'the Treasury were not disposed to give Mr. Christie any money'.[41]

Second, in March 1942 Lord Esher, President of the British Drama League, wrote to congratulate Keynes on becoming CEMA's Chairman.[42] Esher noted that 'the patronage system has been at last destroyed by the war. . . [so that] music, drama & painting [have] no alternative but to throw themselves into the arms of Socialism'. Despite or because of this lack of alternatives:

> London. . . is alive with people devising schemes for state subsidy & avoiding state control. Mr. Basil Dean has plans for the control of E.N.S.A. over drama after the war. Mr. John Christie has a Committee ready to take over the control

> of subsidised music after the war. Now I am against both of these unpopular 'strong' men, & I am convinced that in C.E.M.A. we have the embryo of the required organisation.[43]

Esher argued that expert advisers be added to CEMA, to increase its credibility in the artistic world, protect it from direct government control and diminish the influence of such 'strong men'. Keynes may have been flattered by Esher's letter. He noted to Mary Glasgow: 'I think it very likely that Lord Esher himself might be a suitable person for a reconstructed Council, when the time comes for that.'[44]

The suspicion which Christie aroused, and his unawareness of it, are graphically illustrated by Christie's and Butler's widely differing accounts of a meeting between them in February 1942, soon after Keynes agreed to become CEMA's Chairman. Christie's was in a letter to Audrey, Butler's in a minute for his officials.[45] Christie introduced his with: 'Now I have good news. I went to see Butler this morning & had a splendid interview.' His letter was mainly in the form of a reconstructed dialogue between him and Butler but with arbitrary and confusing switches between direct and reported speech:

> I began by telling him that if the Government create their own music council, if it goes wrong they get blamed & they have no protection. If our show goes wrong, that is our funeral & the Government escape.... They don't want to create their own show. When do you want to start? Now; for one thing if we don't you never know but something else may crop up. I think you are right.

On this point, Butler's note simply recorded Christie saying that plans for the NCM were far advanced and that Lord Greene had 'run circles around the Board of Trade's legal adviser', and Butler responding, 'I was quite in favour of the idea of his Council remaining as independent as possible.'

Concerning the possibility of the NCM and CEMA co-operating, Christie wrote (in Butler's voice):

> I [Butler] have asked Keynes to become Chairman & he has accepted. I think C.E.M.A. is to become later the central body which will coordinate Music, Drama & Painting. I have talked to Keynes about it and he talked about you [Christie]. I want you to go and see him in the near future. Make your own appointment with him. Go alone, not with Wilfrid Greene. You are the fons et origo of the whole thing.

In Butler's account, he asked Christie 'whether he was averse from linking up with C.E.M.A. now. He did not give me a negative answer, but rather implied, at my suggestion, that he might have a talk with Mr. Maynard Keynes. I am accordingly warning Mr. Keynes that he may be favoured by a visit from Mr. Christie.' This strange, convoluted form of words suggests that Butler originated the idea that Christie and Keynes should meet.

The two records diverge startlingly on the issue of funding the NCM. Butler wrote: 'Mr. Christie... said that all he now wanted was £5,000 for secretarial expenses. He told me that he had had a most unsatisfactory interview with Sir Alan Barlow. He did not give me any indication as to how he now expected to receive the subsidy which his Council needs.' In Christie's account, Butler asked 'What are you doing about expenses? Well I [Christie] have asked for £5000 a year.... Yes I [Butler] think you are quite right to begin small.' After exchanges about George Dyson being a 'difficult man', Butler said (according to Christie): 'Well I will see Alan Barlow at the Treasury about it.' Christie's conclusion to Audrey was: 'So there we are. We are at last unofficially accepted & wanted. The Treasury are realising that they will have to carry the Burdens. You see Butler's wife was a Courtauld & they cannot or won't go on paying for art. So Butler is well able to bring the position home to Barlow.' Both accounts mentioned a sum of £5000. They had nothing else in common. This alone suggests that Christie's plans were facing problems.

Butler's note reveals a further complicating factor: ambivalence towards Christie as an individual. Butler took him and the NCM seriously: 'Christie has a strong Council and, as is known, great energy. It would be a pity to dismiss his efforts; on the other hand, these will be apt to stray and will want careful watching.' He was not keen 'to hurry on the final marriage between C.E.M.A. and this Council. What would be best would be to find some device whereby the Council could justify its existence for a short period, and, if it proves its worth, eventually be associated in some way with the post-war C.E.M.A....' But Butler also found Christie rather ridiculous. He reported that Christie 'appeared to me to be dressed in evening dress' and 'told me in passing that he had sold all his wine for some £20,000, which had given him considerable satisfaction. He told me that in future people would drink beer at Glyndebourne....' A figure of fun is at a disadvantage, particularly one like Christie, too insensitive to spot it and anyway too maladroit to remedy it. He reported to Audrey that 'Butler was delighted at our wine sale & thought we deserved it'. He was still seen as a serious player rather than as buffoon or nuisance, but Butler's mixed attitude was a sign of things to come. With Keynes as CEMA's Chairman the balance shifted decisively against Christie. His mistaken belief that Butler would attempt, and probably succeed, to persuade the Treasury to provide a grant, his own fruitless efforts to gain funding, and his increasingly bitter relationship with Keynes together proved fatal to the NCM.

## 'Damn the machine': Keynes Blocks the NCM – Spring and Summer 1942

In his biography of Keynes, Robert Skidelsky commented that arts policy at CEMA under Keynes's chairmanship 'was closely bound up with his own personal philosophy. He brought to his new job a worshipful attitude to the arts, decided views on how they should be financed, and a strong but limited range of sympathies.'[46] The description could be applied equally to Christie. But these similarities, coupled with temperamental differences, led not to a meeting of minds but to mutual mistrust, scorn on Keynes' part and rage on Christie's.

A letter of March 1942 from Christie to Audrey[47] set the scene for his attempts to work with Keynes, a lengthy, digressive statement of his views on England finally working round to the NCM, CEMA and Keynes. He suggested that lack of imagination rather than bravery had got Britain through the Blitz. Churchill's leadership had helped, but 'I don't like him and am shy of him. I suspect that he is dangerous.' The problem was 'the machine' – the system created and sustained by cowardly politicians and civil servants. Christie regarded himself as 'just the kind of man they [the creators of 'the machine'] wish to destroy'; he put Sir John Reith and J B Priestley in the same category. Only bullies like Churchill and Beaverbrook ('I hate Beaverbrook & regard him as being totally evil') could successfully fight the machine. Christie wondered whether Keynes was a Beaverbrook, a Reith, or a small-minded coward: '. . . he comes from the Treasury. Will he play big or just fiddle? I don't know.' Never reticent about emphasizing his own qualities – 'I have the vision, the experience, the contacts, the abilities & the credentials' – he believed that he and Keynes could do much together, provided that Keynes would 'see big. . . [and] see his opportunity as well as mine'.

He was to be disappointed. His initial approach to Keynes is not in the Glyndebourne archive, but Keynes' reply is:

> If you will let me have a clear statement of just what it is you want and put it forward with the approval of your Council, I will then ask my CEMA officials if they think it has any relevant bearing on our activities. . . . I have not in fact the foggiest idea of just what you want and should not have the foggiest idea what to reply to you.[48]

Christie's response to this[49] was sadly incoherent. The points that emerged clearly were that the NCM did not yet exist (the legal formalities were still being settled) but that there would by some unexplained route be similar councils for drama and 'painting'. Apart from that (the fractured syntax seems to indicate confused thought), he understood that CEMA 'is likely to develop from an organisation for providing music and consuming money into say five just men who will co-ordinate the needs of music, drama and painting after receiving the advice of the National Council's music, drama and painting and so advise the Board of Education'. Yet more obscurely, he suggested, in relation to these three councils, that 'some settling of their claims will be desired by the President of the Board of Education. I hope C.E.M.A. will do this.'

Keynes was unimpressed: 'I am still quite in the dark as to the meaning of your letter. . . . I must, I am afraid, beg. . . that you must first of all tell me in plain terms what it is all about, and that the proposal is an official one from your Council.'[50] Christie drafted a long reply which, without answering Keynes' concerns, attempted to describe how the NCM and CEMA might work together. But this remained unsent. Meanwhile he confessed to Audrey that 'I have been disturbed. Keynes, the new Chairman of C.E.M.A. practically refuses to see me.'[51] He reported Lord Greene's telling him that Butler should not have appointed Keynes, and wondered 'whether there is a suspicious hostility between G[reene]. & K[eynes]. . . . . They are perhaps Brains Nos. 1&2 in England.' He was concerned that Keynes would simply pass him on to more junior members of CEMA, which would be 'obviously nonsense'.

He waited several weeks before, on Greene's advice,[52] sending a modest response to Keynes admitting that Keynes' letter 'has embarrassed me' and that 'I cannot give you the official view of my Council' as it was not yet incorporated.[53] He still sought a meeting, but with less bluster than before. At this point, as Christie predicted and presumably in order to avoid further correspondence, Keynes suggested that Christie deal not with him but with CEMA's Music Director, Reginald Jacques, since 'I [Keynes] would be quite out of my depth'.[54] Never one to take a hint, Christie replied enclosing a new memorandum about the NCM. He half apologized for troubling Keynes again, but 'I cannot escape the conclusion that you and I are thrown together in this matter'.[55] He suggested that the memorandum 'should not be discussed with the musical members of C.E.M.A. . . . when you have read [it]. . . you may perhaps agree'.

The memorandum[56] contained few new thoughts. The key themes were the low status and poor condition of music in England, the need for the NCM 'to represent the art of Music with the necessary authority to plan for music and to support the Government', for 'respect rather than familiarity', and for 'State Aid', which Christie tried and failed to distinguish from subsidy. The one concrete proposal was that an unspecified public body should 'pay the cost of [the NCM's]… investigation of Musical conditions and results and needs in this country, and also to pay the cost of the Council's formation'. The memorandum proposed a sum of £5,000 a year, with the NCM's office and staff based at Glyndebourne. Concerning the investigation, 'We are not prepared to accept someone else's analysis of the present position.'

Keynes checked with Mary Glasgow that CEMA could not grant the NCM £5,000 even if he wanted to.[57] Glasgow advised that the Treasury would not 'look kindly upon our using money to finance somebody else's investigations in our own field of operations'.[58] Keynes was thus highly discouraging to Christie on this point and on the memorandum generally: 'This is still too nebulous. I cannot see what proposal I could possibly bring before my Council [nor]… how you could reasonably expect CEMA to express any opinion on the matter with only the foggiest ideas of what the body would do.'[59]

Christie tried another route to influence the government, with a rambling letter to Sir Stafford Cripps, Leader of the House of Commons and Lord Privy Seal.[60] Alongside dreams of a new Glyndebourne in Ontario and obscure passages about his wish 'to crystallize the National Conscience by giving it a constitution and a home (Glyndebourne)', he sought to interest Cripps in the NCM. This went to CEMA for advice. It indicates CEMA's low opinion of Christie by this stage, or its sniffy attitude to a potential rival, that Glasgow reported to Sir Robert Wood: 'The Christie persecution has extended to Sir Stafford Cripps.'[61] On Glasgow's advice, Cripps brushed off the approach.

Writing to Audrey in early June,[62] Christie suggested that CEMA 'are trying to dig themselves in & to prevent the N.C.M. from working.… Chairman Keynes… refuses to see me. Jacques a second class musician & Miss Glasgow a civil servant and school inspector. All they do is spread mediocrity.… It is depressing.' For Christie, Sir Kenneth Clark, also on CEMA's council, was its one saving grace. After meeting Clark, he wrote several days later but in the same letter: 'I said [to Clark] the N.C.M. news was good only because of Clarke's [*sic*] enthusiasm. I sent on the memorandum to Keynes with express instructions that it was not to be sent on to his musicians – Vaughan-Williams [*sic*] and Jacques. Clarke said we should have a good deal of trouble with V-W & that he thought him very silly'. Christie indulged in increasing and unfair criticism of Vaughan Williams at this period, in contrast to their previous mutual respect.

As Keynes and Glasgow became more dismissive of Christie, his closest associates, Harry Colles, Lord Greene and Sir Maurice Bonham Carter, rallied to him. Colles reported to Christie: 'I have written to Keynes, simply and a little bluntly, to tell him that he is wrong in thinking the N.C.M. to be solely your scheme backed by "paper" names. . . . we who have been attending conferences & meetings about it for the past four years are also busy people who may reasonably expect him to spend one hour in hearing about it from you.'[63] Colles also offered Christie tactical advice should he meet Keynes:

> . . . you had better confine it simply to the need for the N.C.M. itself. . . . It will be necessary to convince him that we have our feet planted on certain ground, because he evidently thinks that you are standing on your head! So don't, my dear man, talk about founding N.C.M's all over the place, about Glyndebourne in Canada or National Conscience at Glyndebourne, or the cause may be lost from the first.

The aim of meeting Keynes should be simply to 'make him realise that we are out to straighten out the confusions of musical life in post-war Britain. . . [and] that we already see ways of beginning. . . . I want to get past this stage of suspicions in the mind of Keynes and of others.' Colles' blunt but sympathetic tone, and his evident expectation that Christie would not take offence at it, help explain how Christie could inspire such affection in his friends. Colles even parodied Christie's own style: 'My ideas are not "always right", but I <u>know</u> that this one is.'

But there was no meeting. Keynes' reply to Colles was terse and grand. He did not object to Christie's meeting anyone at CEMA, but 'as Chairman of CEMA, it is not my business to discuss proposals in their early stages. I am mainly occupied in quite different matters.'[64] Colles wrote to Christie: 'I fear I can do no more. I think the idea of your being granted permission by his Lordship to see Jacques or V[aughan].W[illiams]. about it is rather funny! Nevertheless as you know I'm sorry rather than amused.'[65]

Bonham Carter too approached Keynes, using his own involvement in the NCM as evidence that Christie was no crank: 'My excuse for adding to the correspondence. . . is that I have taken part in the discussions. . . in the drafting of the [NCM] constitution, and in the present approach to the Government.'[66] This attempt fared no better than Colles'.

Christie's secretary W E Edwards wrote to Lord Greene that Keynes' stonewalling and barely disguised insults had created 'a strong sense of disappointment in Mr. Christie's mind at this dull culmination of his informal but encouraging conversations with Mr. Ramsbotham and later with Mr. Butler. . . . Mr. Christie thinks now that... the only important question is whether or not it is worth attempting to go on in the face of the now seeming discouragement in official quarters.'[67] Greene shared this frustration, writing to Christie: 'I fear that Butler is just playing with you and that there is nothing to be done in that direction.'[68]

Christie pithily summed up to Audrey his state of mind in June 1942: 'Damn the machine.'[69]

Nonetheless he had not lost all credit. Lord Esher, critical of Christie in March 1942 (see above), invited him to stay just two months later. Christie reported to Audrey: 'I liked him very much. Very easy to work with and no trace of selfishness.... We talked about ideals and planning and he is considering the National Council of Drama. He is inclined to join up with the N.C.M. I am inclined to agree.'[70] This was accurate, rather than a Christie delusion. In July 1942, Butler reported to Keynes Esher's proposal that 'Drama would be organised on much the same lines as... Christie had organised his Council of Music'.[71] Butler hoped that Esher 'did not think the Christie model was ideal', but Esher stuck to his point: 'Christie had collected an interesting set of people together', whereas CEMA 'included too many people too close to the job and not independent enough'. In December 1942, Keynes proposed and Butler agreed that Esher should join CEMA's council.[72] This suggests once again that Keynes and Butler objected to Christie personally rather than to his views; though clearly they, unlike the NCM's supporters, found his proposals infuriatingly vague.

Meanwhile Christie remained uncharacteristically polite to Keynes, as if Keynes were offering advice rather than brush-offs. The nearest he came to a reproach was to suggest that 'Your [Keynes'] theory seems to be "start and we'll tell you if you're wrong", but surely discussion leading to a "right start" would be a good deal better.'[73] Keynes himself remained determined not to meet Christie, while CEMA council minutes suggest that disdain and impatience towards Christie was now official policy:

> The Secretary reported that the Chairman, the President of the Board of Education, and the Lord Privy Seal [Cripps] had all received a number of letters from Mr. John Christie in connection with his National Council of Music. It was not clear to any of them exactly what Mr. Christie was asking for and none of them felt that he had any spare time to go into the matter until further details were known.[74]

CEMA's council agreed that Christie should instead meet CEMA's music specialists. Christie accepted this with fairly good grace.[75]

The minutes of this meeting, in July 1942,[76] suggest that Christie left most of the talking to Bonham Carter and Colles. CEMA was represented by two Council members, Stanley Marchant, Principal of the Royal Academy of Music, and Vaughan Williams, plus Reginald Jacques and Mary Glasgow. Bonham Carter set out, more clearly than Christie generally managed, three possible ways forward for CEMA and the NCM:

> (1) that C.E.M.A. might be regarded as a special organisation set up to deal with wartime conditions; (2) that C.E.M.A. might go on after the war and itself assume the functions of a N.C.M; (3) that C.E.M.A. might become the general instrument to advise the Government on the allocation of funds for the Arts, working though the N.C.M. in matters concerning music.

Colles added that the NCM's members needed to know the government's attitude and whether CEMA might find £5,000 for the proposed survey of music in England. Neither point was addressed. The meeting's limited conclusion was that the NCM would put a more detailed proposal to CEMA and that meanwhile this meeting with the NCM would be reported to CEMA's council.

The NCM representatives did not see the meeting for the window dressing it was. Christie wrote to Lord Greene that 'apart from mild obstruction by old Vaughan Williams, [it] was quite happy.'[77] So Colles worked on the proposed national survey, Christie repeatedly sought news of CEMA's discussion about the NCM (which in any case would be no more than CEMA's taking note of the July meeting), and CEMA itself largely ignored the topic. On 1 September 1942 Christie suggested that the NCM and CEMA collaborate on the proposed national survey[78]– a major change from his earlier insistence on the NCM's independence. On 2 September CEMA's council decided 'it was impossible to give any adequate answer to Mr. Christie's request before seeing the details of the proposed investigation.'[79] On 3 September Christie wrote to Audrey: 'No telephone message this morning from Miss Glasgow. The C.E.M.A. meeting was last night at 5. I think that if they had readily cooperated, Miss Glasgow would have written. It looks bad.'[80]

It was worse than that: CEMA saw nothing with which to co-operate. Glasgow wrote to Keynes two days after the CEMA council meeting: 'You will… be interested to know that he [Christie] has rung up three times today (I was out each time) to find out what the Council's "decision" was. Which doesn't make sense because the N.C.M. are supposed to be preparing an outline of the "investigation" for the Council's consideration.'[81]

Within six months of Keynes' becoming Chairman of CEMA, Christie had become for him and Glasgow a combination of persistent nuisance and shared joke. Despite the best efforts of Colles, Bonham Carter, Greene and Christie himself, there was no way back to serious acceptance. These efforts included a massive scaling down of ambitions, from major pots of government money to spend and National Councils of Music around the world to the modest proposed joint CEMA/NCM survey of music in England. None of this impressed CEMA, which under Keynes' chairmanship increasingly saw itself as an organization focused on raising professional standards in the performing arts – the task Christie had envisaged for himself and the NCM.

## 'I see nothing but hate & envy': Late 1942 to Spring 1943

From autumn 1942 Christie saw his dream of a National Council of Music slipping away. On Colles' and Audrey's advice he remained on best behaviour when dealing with CEMA, but anger and depression were close to the surface. Anger showed in his reaction to Thomas Russell's book *Philharmonic*,[82] an account of the world of classical orchestras by the business manager of the London Philharmonic Orchestra. It contained a (slightly) veiled attack on the NCM: '… the convenor of one council of the dilettante type, patrons with other people's money, gathered a great deal of data from experienced orchestral organizers – but failed to invite any one of them on to his council.'[83] Christie wrote to Audrey: 'It has… completely misrepresented me & our N.C.M.… The man must be a cad.'[84] And later: 'I gather that Russell is a little man, very red, & thwarted.'[85] He aimed at external targets too: 'This war separates people… I think Churchill is responsible for that. He seems to me to base his attitude on the hate of the Germans. Hate is intolerable.'[86] He revealed his depression to Audrey: 'I am so lonely.… I can not tell you how bored I am. All the sense of development of achievement of inspiration has gone. I see nothing but hate & envy & irritation & blame of others.'

But he spent much of September 1942 working with Harry Colles on the proposed CEMA/NCM survey of music in England, and several days in October with Bonham Carter at Glyndebourne planning the final touches. In her letter of thanks, Violet Bonham Carter described Glyndebourne, with its resident evacuee children,[87] as 'perfect in conception & execution.… Plato's Republic & Utopia are left far behind.'[88] Christie hoped to persuade Butler to appoint Lord Greene chairman of the survey;[89] he failed even to secure a meeting with Butler.

The proposal was submitted in October.[90] Ignoring the NCM's pre-war origins, Harry Colles' introductory note began: 'Post-war music will be the consequence of war-time music, not the restitution of pre-war music. That, in a word, is the justification of the formation of a National Council of Music now.' Colles argued that before the war classical music had depended on private enterprise, but 'The principle that when private enterprise is insufficient, the Government may wisely step in has been admitted, first, in the case of the B.B.C, more recently in the creation of C.E.M.A. as a war-time expedient. Can it go further? It seems inevitable that it will be forced to do so by circumstance.' Colles used the increase in public demand for music as a slightly strained, and wholly elitist, argument for the NCM:

> [The demand is] now mainly from what may be called the smaller tax-playing class, and it is a class to which Governments are wont to incline their ears. . . . But some of us view this prospect with apprehension. The benefit of the taxpayer and the welfare of music. . . are two entirely different things, and it is with the benefit of music that we are concerned.

The answer was to create an independent council 'with an Executive of men of affairs, conversant with the Arts, but not claiming personal musicianship', helping the government to resist claims which 'might be disastrous to the art'. Colles' note was silent on why CEMA could not fulfil this role, on the relationship between this council and CEMA, and indeed on CEMA generally.

The bulk of the document, equally silent about CEMA, was the proposal for a survey of music in England. It would cover 'agencies by which music is provided', including orchestras, festivals, choral societies, and ballet and opera companies. The section on opera did not attempt impartiality: 'Glyndebourne is in a class by itself, as setting a standard of superlative work on international lines.' The survey's purpose was described only towards the end:

> . . . the practice and enjoyment of music is an important if not even an essential element in the cultural wellbeing of a civilised community. . . . [but] private patronage must restrict music to the few, is casual and often wasteful. . . . [The survey would] set up a policy which would justify State aid for music on a permanent basis.

This state aid was 'not to be confused with subsidies', though as so often the document failed to distinguish the two convincingly. Equally, '[for] the application of State aid, the art of music is not to be confused with "entertainment"'.

The document ended with the survey's proposed terms of reference, modest given Christie's grandiose utterances since 1938:

> To consider the conditions prevailing in normal times in regard to the Art of Music . . . .

> To prepare a survey of the principal fields of Music. . . .
> To consider the development of Music up to the present time and the use of State Aid to extend it. . . .
> To consider the problem of suitable buildings for musical work.

Keynes showed as little respect for this step-by-step, detailed approach to the NCM as for Christie's earlier vague and grand pronouncements. In effect he killed it by neglect. He took a month to write to Christie, then informed him that CEMA would probably not discuss the survey proposal for another two months.[91] In fact (see below) CEMA's council never discussed it. But it was the letter's other announcement which finally ended Christie's patient politeness in his dealings with Keynes. It reported a development which was to be central to CEMA's, and later the Arts Council's, way of working:[92] '. . . the addition to the Council of three Panels to give the other members of the Council the finest expert advice in the three branches of music, art and drama' – the proposal originated by Mary Glasgow more than a year earlier. The music panel's members would be Arthur Bliss, Myra Hess, the composer, conductor and critic Constant Lambert, and the frankly obscure composer Thomas Wood. Keynes explained that he and Butler intended this approach to supplement CEMA's expertise without adding to council numbers. Keynes would chair all three panels, and the council's specialists in each area (for music, Vaughan Williams and Stanley Marchant) would attend the meetings of their respective panel.

CEMA's panels were not the first of their kind. ENSA had Music and Drama Advisory Councils.[93] ENSA's antagonistic relationship with CEMA is beyond the scope of this book, but it suggests how Keynes and Christie viewed ENSA that in this correspondence neither even mentioned its music council, set up in 1941 and larger than and at least as distinguished as CEMA's proposed music panel.[94] It included the composers Sir Arnold Bax (Master of the King's Music), William Walton, and CEMA's recruit Constant Lambert; Malcolm Sargent, a strong supporter of Christie from 1938 to 1941; and two of his antagonists, Sir Hugh Allen and Sir George Dyson.

Mary Glasgow had prompted Keynes' letter to Christie about the music panel: 'I was wondering whether, on your principle of "doing anything you like, provided you tell enough people about it", it would be good to write (a) to Lord Esher and (b) to Christie giving them an idea of the Panel plans.'[95]

Christie and Keynes were at one in believing that state support for the arts should focus on raising standards rather than widening availability. But the development of expert panels suggests an area of difference: Christie, unlike

Keynes, saw no significant role for professional musicians. This did not prevent him from drafting a reply to Keynes[96] which suggested that 'it is the intention of C.E.M.A. to enlarge itself to do the work that the N.C.M. set out to do, and for this reason I propose to withdraw my efforts to help by creating the N.C.M.' – efforts Keynes had neither invited nor welcomed. He challenged Keynes' view that with these four advisers, CEMA would have access to the finest expert advice ('overstatement won't do in Art' – a dictum he rarely followed himself), and demanded that the NCM music survey proposal be returned and any copies destroyed. He ended: 'I am writing to Butler.' His draft letter to Butler[97] was a mixture of tale-telling about Keynes and warnings of disaster. It began: 'Months ago you told me personally that you wished me to see Keynes, and that as soon as possible. Throughout this period Keynes has refused to see me.' It continued, presumably referring to the proposed music panel, though the letter did not specify this: 'It seems clear that the Government intends to develop C.E.M.A. and not to use the N.C.M.... As Art is so essentially different from, say, tanks, will you allow me to ask you whether this is going to result in a catastrophic error?'

But the drafts remained drafts. Christie first consulted his three closest advisers. He wrote to Maurice Bonham Carter: 'I want to make Keynes show his hand. I think he will show his hand against us. Then I want to have Butler's sanction that I should address a full meeting of C.E.M.A. and I believe that I could win the day, and discomfit Keynes.'[98] He wrote to Wilfrid Greene that 'Keynes knows nothing about it.... I expect Butler understands these matters better than Keynes does.'[99] Greene had previously suggested to Christie that 'Butler is just playing with you.'[100] He now advised caution: '... your proposed letters... bang, bolt and bar the door. They also read (what is quite natural) as though you are piqued. If you send them it is the end of your efforts. Is this wise?'[101] Harry Colles disagreed: 'I think that the withdrawal of your memorandum from C.E.M.A. was the only course open to you.... the Government has made up its mind beforehand not to accept the N.C.M.... it is no good battling against a judgement which has been delivered before evidence has been taken!'[102] But Greene's view prevailed, the letters were not sent, and the initiative limped on.

Colles was, however, largely correct. After a brief and formal mention in October 1942,[103] CEMA's council never discussed the proposed music survey. Instead it was delegated to the first meeting of the music panel, in January 1943. Keynes reported the outcome in a letter to Bonham Carter.[104] His tone was less chilly than in his letters to Christie. The letter began with encouraging words: '... we shall be much interested in its [the survey's] conclusions and will hope to profit by them.... We and you are embarking on a new field of organisation, and the more we know about it the better.' But it was empty of substance: 'How much more, if anything, you want us to say at this stage, I am not quite clear. It is not within the terms of our Treasury grant to make a contribution to the expenses of an outside enquiry. . . .' Christie's response was to draft letters to Keynes and Butler[105] in which anger was mixed with icy formality. A typical passage in the letter to Butler reads: 'I have the honour to submit that Lord Keynes's letter of 22nd January is a most unsatisfactory culmination of twelve months' endeavour to fulfil your request that I should see him on this matter.' But these letters too appear to have remained unsent.

There seems to have been no more correspondence between Christie and Keynes about the NCM. They briefly encountered one another in Brooks's Club in February 1943, when, according to Christie, Keynes 'was civil for a moment and both of us avoided any mention of our contention & Keynes left.'[106]

While Keynes and Butler, the two people he most needed to influence, would have nothing to do with him, Christie retained not only his closest advisers Colles, Bonham Carter and Greene, but also, sporadically, other influential supporters. Some did not understand Christie's unhappiness about CEMA. Myra Hess wrote: '. . . it may not be necessary to take such a gloomy view of the current musical situation. In every plan C.E.M.A. discusses, the question of standard is considered with the greatest seriousness; and the aim of everybody, Keynes included, is that the artistic standard should be raised.'[107] But some appreciated Christie's hurt pride. One such was Herwald Ramsbotham, who on being replaced at the Board of Education by Butler had become, as Lord Soulbury, Chairman of the Assistance Board. Soulbury sought to approach Butler on Christie's behalf,[108] but when, after several months, he finally managed to do so, he reported that Butler's response had taken matters no further.[109] Their correspondence demonstrates that even a government and party colleague was unable to influence Butler in this respect.

Christie had more revealing discussions with Lord Esher, now on CEMA's council. Esher was in some respects a less pugnacious and more pragmatic version of Christie himself. Their relationship was good despite Christie's slight private doubts: 'We stand well together. But it is queer how unsuitably these new peers behave (his father was made a peer). Every piece of notepaper with a coronet and E under it.'[110] As noted above, Esher now supported Christie and wished to create a drama organization analogous to the NCM. He provided confidential, clear-sighted views about CEMA's attitude towards Christie's and his own plans.

Esher's 'drama NCM', the Civic Theatre Scheme, aimed to enable towns to open repertory theatres 'by a combination of Local and State subsidy, fifty per cent of the necessary funds being guaranteed by the Government and fifty per cent raised from Rates or from voluntary subscriptions'.[111] The plan was submitted to the government in late 1942 by a bewildering range of signatories including George Bernard Shaw, Malcolm Sargent, the playwright James Bridie, the Archbishop of Canterbury (William Temple, previously Archbishop of York), J B Priestley and T S Eliot.[112] The list thus included, in Bridie and Temple, two of the strongest pre-war supporters of arts subsidy (and the League of Audiences in particular) and, in Eliot, one of its strongest opponents.

Esher told Christie that CEMA's treatment of this proposal had been similar to its treatment of the NCM: 'The Civic Theatre Scheme has had considerable support.... But the crux of the matter is that C.E.M.A., who are as essential to our finances as they are to yours, fight shy of it & have postponed consideration of it for three months.'[113] Esher believed that:

> ...the real stumbling-block in the scheme is the suggested creation of a Civic Theatre Council with large powers & authority, which would inevitably be a rival to C.E.M.A., and which I am sure C.E.M.A. will never accept. The same applies to your proposed Council of Music, & I am convinced that both these Councils will either have to disappear or to be so modified that they are entirely subordinate to C.E.M.A.

Esher suggested that it be made clear 'these Councils are not there to rival C.E.M.A. but to assist and support C.E.M.A. in its inevitable fight with the Treasury'. Assuming, wrongly, that the NCM was a collaboration with, maybe even led by, music professionals, he wondered 'whether there is any chance of the music people modifying their plan', which Esher hoped to persuade the 'drama people' to do.

Christie's reply[114] partly accepted Esher's diagnosis but differed fundamentally as to prescription. CEMA had been set up as a wartime expedient, but now 'CEMA and Keynes are digging themselves in to do the work of the future.... [CEMA] has done nothing but mediocrity, which it has persistently described as "being the finest possible etc.".... ' High standards could come only from a body like the NCM, with similar independent bodies for drama and the visual arts. CEMA 'should be developed into... a small intermediary body to deal on behalf of the President [of the Board of Education] with our three Councils'. Instead 'Keynes is making a copy of our N.C.M., and, being a copy, perhaps a bad copy'.

Esher attempted to explain to Christie why the moment for the NCM had passed, probably for ever.[115] He understood Christie's criticisms of CEMA, but 'disagree[d] with your handling of the political situation.... Keynes' [music] panel can only be improved if those who want to improve it are not really out to supplant it' (which Christie wished to do). CEMA, as a quasi-public body seeking to raise artistic standards, had to fight on two fronts, against the Treasury and against the public – inevitably a slow and difficult business: 'Of all public departments, the Treasury is the most difficult to rush. Sapping and mining is the only hope.' As for the public, Esher used an elitist argument similar to that used by Harry Colles to support the NCM: 'Mediocrity is the eternal danger of democracy. . . . In a democracy, the public must be persuaded out of its instinct for mediocrity.' Christie had been 'able to avoid it [mediocrity] at Glyndebourne because A. You were an autocrat. B. You were an artist. C. You were rich – a most unusual combination.'

Esher's letter became more direct:

> I am sure C.E.M.A. are determined. . . to carry on after the War, and I am sure they will fight to the death any Council that tries to do the work they consider to be their function. They would never be content to be an intermediary body between the Board of Education and these Councils for the Arts. . . and the Board of Education will certainly support them.

Hence Esher now sought to 'persuade the theatre people to withdraw their suggested Council'. He suggested that 'C.E.M.A's Panels <u>may</u> be converted very slowly into something very similar to your National Council of Music. . .', a thought which may have pleased Christie less than Esher realized. And he sympathized with Christie's 'natural impatience with these fumbling steps in democratic progress. Successful autocrats are rare and you have been one. It must be painful to descend to the slow pace of democracy. . . . But you are now working in a field where these are the rules.'

The Glyndebourne archive contains no further letters between Christie and Esher. But some 'shadow-correspondence' in May 1943 seems to show Christie trying to resolve the tension between his own direct, guileless and tactically inept approach and Esher's extreme pragmatism in dealing with Keynes and CEMA. Christie had a letter critical of CEMA published in *The Times*.[116] Mary Glasgow assumed that Keynes would wish to reply to it, and drafted a letter for his signature. Keynes disagreed: '. . . my instinct very strongly is to make no answer whatever. . . . One cannot be appearing in public or writing in <u>The Times</u> too often. One must choose one's seasons carefully. . . .'[117] Christie, however, followed his *Times* letter with two draft letters to Keynes, neither of which seems to have been sent. One was emollient, in Esher's style: 'Would it now be a sensible thing for us to meet and talk over our respective points of view?. . . There will of course be honest differences of opinion between us, but that should not preclude reasonable discussion.'[118] The other, dated the following day, was far more 'Christie': 'With some abruptness you as Chairman of C.E.M.A. have refused to see me. . . . Is this intentional and is this extreme discourtesy a personal matter between you and me?'[119] The drafts suggest a troubled state of mind, as does a letter to Audrey from this time: 'Mentally I am rather shattered by my treatment over the N.C.M. . . .'[120]

There may have been a further reason for this. On 6 March 1943 he had written to Audrey: 'I enclose a cutting from today's Times at which I opened the paper & at first thought it must be the article [about]. . . which Harry [Colles] had telephoned. . . . Then I saw his name at the head of the article, and wondered why there should be this publicity. It did not dawn on me that it could be an obituary notice.'[121] Harry Colles, Christie's most constant friend and adviser during Audrey's absence, had died suddenly two days earlier.[122] Christie continued, with unusual simplicity: 'I am very sorry indeed. In your absence he had always done what you did so well [to] check and guide me and I was conscious of it. He gave me great strength in the background as it appeared to be but actually in leading me. There was always that happy smile.'

## The End of the NCM: Spring 1943 to Autumn 1944

Christie's work on the NCM did not end at this point. But his later efforts lacked sustained energy, showing flashes of wild optimism alternating with gloom and inactivity, and demonstrated even less realism than previously. His vision of the NCM became grander and more nebulous, then disappeared.

In spring 1943 he again sought official support to visit Canada and the USA to discuss 'the status which Art must have in the new World',[123] but the initiative was without conviction. He thought it likely that Richard Law, the Foreign Office Minister to whom he wrote, would consult Butler who in turn would probably 'be very glad to get me out of the Country so that I could not interfere with C.E.M.A. as many politicians would be glad to get Beveridge out! I don't for a moment expect that anything will come of it. Anyhow, I have tried it.'[124] As he expected, nothing came of it.

In June he wrote to Audrey: 'I personally think that the NCM is dead, though I expect that Keynes will bag most of the ideas for C.E.M.A. He has behaved like a cad.'[125] Two weeks later he reported that Bonham Carter and Roy Henderson both wanted the NCM initiative to continue, and that 'the better musicians don't like C.E.M.A. (which they think means the Council for the Encouragement of mediocre artists)'.[126] But 'the present position is that C.E.M.A. has the money which it spends on mediocrity & is actually doing things. The N.C.M. has no money. . . .'

In an optimistic phase, in July 1943, he organized an NCM meeting at the Ritz attended by Roy Henderson, Maurice Bonham Carter and Malcolm Sargent among others. He wrote to Audrey: 'I think in the future we may find that we carry the Public with us & the leading artists. . . . We may well find that C.E.M.A. gets into trouble and that Keynes is backing the wrong horse. The tea at the Ritz is excellent. The bill was £2.14 + 10/- tip.'[127] But his spirits sank again. In early September he wrote: 'This morning I got a letter from Myra Hess resigning from the N.C.M. I suspect that Marchant will follow suit and perhaps Vaughan Williams. Keynes's carrot of Treasury money will be too much for them.'[128]

Christie's most sustained later burst of activity on the NCM came in late 1943 and early 1944. The Glyndebourne archive contains a flimsy copy of a letter (so presumably it was sent) from him to the Chancellor of the Exchequer, Sir John Anderson, undated except for '? about Dec.'43' in manuscript. It was a further bid for government recognition and funding for the NCM. It did not make a convincing case, beginning in self-aggrandizing style, and growing wilder: 'I feel that I cannot avoid or delay in taking up the matter of Music with you personally. I regard the current position as almost wholly unsatisfactory. . . . The Government has got to act. It is necessary to back one man. I believe that man must be I.'[129] It continued:

> At present all are wrong:- Conductors. Orchestras, Soloists and Composers. . . . They are wrong because the conditions are wrong, but much more because they are smugly self satisfied, and their audiences are doped with mediocrity. The professionals must be under a new control which must never be satisfied. I can provide this control. . . . We are thwarted by the Treasury, by Keynes and by C.E.M.A.

The final sentence was unlikely to appeal to the Chancellor of the Exchequer. Equally ill-judged were Christie's view that 'the body controlling art must be independent of the Politicians and the Civil Service', his bald request for £1 million a year, and his summary of music abroad in such terms as 'France has counted but little. American musicians are controlled by gangsters.' The archive contains no reply.

But Christie began 1944 in unrealistically positive mood. Apparently unaffected by Keynes' refusal, over nearly two years, to see him, he wrote to Audrey of potential meetings in Buckingham Palace, national councils for a bewildering range of subjects, and the creation of a 'Ministry of the Mind' under the aegis of the Lord President of the Council.[130] Ignoring his consistent failure to gain a penny of public funding for the NCM, he proposed that all these councils be 'absolutely & entirely independent of the civil service and the Politicians but perhaps financed to some extent by the Treasury'. The letter does not show Christie at his most balanced: 'No-one in the Government is interested & nothing gets done. In other words, there is no channel. I create that channel.... I have a feeling that these things may begin to move. I have the advantage of age combined with youth:- I see in the dark like young people.'

There was little foundation for any of this, though in early 1944 Christie briefly and surprisingly managed to interest the Cabinet Secretary, Sir Edward Bridges, in his ideas. He told Audrey: 'I had an excellent talk with Bridges. I hear he is a very good man.... Bridges thinks he can help on the N.C.M. I think I have made the right contact....'[131] Ten days later: 'Bridges came to lunch & is a splendid collaborator. He thinks my plans for culture etc. are a splendid scheme.'[132] The NCM's articles of association were still in draft after three years; but once in final form, Bridges would 'start the ball rolling at his end.... When it comes off, the scheme will have full publicity. The forces of good will become vocal.... The Heavens are opening at long last.' He acknowledged short-term difficulties, but during this brief period his confidence was undented:

> Here on the one side I am planning National & International Work and likely to bring it off and on the other hand struggling for months over a petty cash sum.... It's too silly for words.... I think we can now get our N.C.M. through quite quickly and get a start made on the other subjects Architecture, Drama, Art, Letters, Prevention of Cruelty, perhaps Religion, Idealism and National Culture.

He did not explain what the National Councils of Religion, Idealism and the rest would actually do, but wrote about them often and repetitiously in this period.

Around this time he also wrote three memoranda with the general heading 'Art in Reconstruction'.[133] The intended audience was Robert Foot, briefly Director-General of the BBC.[134] Christie continued these efforts with Foot's successor, William Haley. The memoranda dealt not only with the NCM but also, at length, with the BBC's role as the main provider of music in Britain and the potential of the Royal Opera House Covent Garden to be the exemplar of artistic standards, a larger and geographically more accessible Glyndebourne. These memoranda were part of Christie's planning for a campaign to take over Covent Garden. Concerning the NCM they said little new. The history of Covent

Garden is beyond the scope of this book, but CEMA's discussion of it in the second half of 1944, considered briefly below, reveals CEMA's continuing negative attitude towards Christie.

Christie's somewhat manic optimism of early 1944 alternated with deep pessimism. He wrote to Audrey in February that at a meeting at the BBC 'I suddenly fizzed. I just let fly. . . . I have rarely created such an effect';[135] but in the same letter: 'The machine yawns. . . . The machine has won. . . . the machine is in control everywhere.' Temporarily at least, his view of Sir Thomas Beecham had altered from his pre-war suspicion:[136] 'I would gladly collaborate with Beecham. . . . We two could get on very well together. It was the little men who kept us apart.' Around this time he also corresponded with the Foreign Secretary, Anthony Eden. Eden responded non-committally to Christie's request that the Foreign Office provide £1000 to assist Audrey to pursue his plans in New York.[137] The archive contains no reply from Eden to a subsequent letter which somehow linked this with a 'proposal. . . to run permanent Opera, Operetta, Ballet, Drama and Chamber Music at Covent Garden and at two other theatres and at two or three concert halls in London, at a level of performance unknown in the past'.[138] This would 'light at the centre of things in the Capital of the Empire. . . a fire of such artistic intensity that the whole World gazes at it with open eyes and open ears'.

This period reached a climax in a letter to Audrey shortly before her return from America. The NCM formed a minor part of a far grander vision:

> My idea is to collect a large sum of money for a National Glyndebourne Trust to control a Corporation which shall run Covent Garden, The Haymarket. . ., the New Queen's Hall. . . all to be on superb lines and to link these up with the National Gallery & the National Portrait Gallery & the other Galleries. . . . I want the Treasury to collaborate. . . . We might get one of the Royal Houses in St. James's Palace as our Headquarters.[139]

There was more in the same vein, but nothing then or subsequently about the NCM's practical realization. During the rest of 1944 he concentrated on attempts to involve himself in the future of the Royal Opera House and to interest the Director-General of the BBC in his more obscure plans. The NCM project was effectively over.

As an epilogue, it is worth recording Keynes' continuing refusal to engage seriously with Christie during this later period, not only about the NCM but even about opera, Christie's area of expertise and success. Christie was a shadowy presence in discussions about Covent Garden's future at all three CEMA council meetings in the second half of 1944. Keynes was absent in America, and all were chaired by Sir Kenneth Clark. In July Clark reported on an agreement reached for the music publisher Boosey and Hawkes to take on the lease of Covent Garden from January 1945.[140] A committee to oversee this had been established comprising himself, Sir Stanley Marchant, Leslie Boosey and Ralph Hawkes. The committee had met once and had invited William Walton to join. Responding to a question from Lord Esher, Clark reported that the committee had also considered inviting Christie, that he, Clark, had been in favour, but that the committee had decided against this. Esher's response is revealing: '. . . he was glad to know that it was not the C.E.M.A. representatives who had opposed Mr. Christie's election.'

In September Clark reported that three further members had joined the committee, including Samuel Courtauld (Rab Butler's father-in-law) and, as Chairman, Keynes. Clark, apparently unprompted, 'was able to reassure the Council that Mr. John Christie had been brought into consultation by Mr. Leslie Boosey and had agreed with Mr. Boosey that he would not be a suitable member of the Committee'.[141] The reference was not explained further. But in November, the committee 'was still in touch with Mr. John Christie and it had now been suggested that Mr. Christie should join it. This proposal was awaiting Lord Keynes' approval.'[142] Keynes withheld approval. Christie remained excluded. Keynes was now Chairman of both CEMA and, in effect, the Royal Opera House. In every year since 1945, CEMA's successor the Arts Council has given a larger grant to the Royal Opera House than to any other organization.

## Conclusion

This chapter began by noting parallels between John Christie's National Council of Music and Alfred Wareing's League of Audiences. But in some respects they were fundamentally different.

The League sought and received public attention and aimed to influence public as well as government opinion. It gained considerable publicity for most of its existence. Before the lengthy period of extreme neglect set in, Wareing was in some quarters celebrated, sometimes in extreme terms, as a, indeed the, pioneer whose work led to the establishment of the Arts Council.

Christie was far better known than Wareing, and the 'Council of Power'/NCM had real importance in the history of arts funding. But despite Christie's central place as a provider of 'high culture', his powerful friends and associates, and six years of intense if erratic effort, this work has at no time, then or since, received public, or much academic, recognition.

There are obvious reasons for this, including his failure to produce a clear plan, rather than vague rhetoric, for how the NCM would work, and the determination of CEMA and of Keynes in particular not to deal with him. Christie's attitude to 'the mob', his tendency to alienate key individuals, his sometimes delusional flights of fancy and his unshakeable belief in his own rightness are also relevant. But these factors do not undermine the importance of the NCM initiative. Indeed, they may make it of greater rather than less interest. These three chapters have revealed important debates opened up by Christie from 1938; his relationship and dealings with key cultural figures of the time; his influence, in practice negative rather than positive, on planning for the Arts Council; the credit he had and often wasted due to the prestige of opera at Glyndebourne; his access to 10 Downing Street when Chamberlain was Prime Minister and the Board of Education when Ramsbotham was its President; and the misfortunes of timing, compounded by tactical ineptitude, which caused him to lose access when it mattered most. They have also illustrated the many contradictions of Christie's character.

John Christie's work on the National Council of Music played an important part in the history of arts funding in Britain. These chapters have sought to rescue it from almost total neglect – a neglect relieved only by the silliness of Richard Witts' statement that 'John Christie enjoyed the company of Nazis, while Maynard Keynes preferred the fellowship of boys. That is precisely why we have an Arts Council and not a Council for Music and the Arts.'[143]

## Notes

1 Glyndebourne 3, Bonham Carter-NCM members, July 1941 (no specific date).
2 Ibid., Dyson-Christie, 2/7/41.
3 Ibid., Tertis-Christie, 6/8/41.
4 Ibid., 'Memorandum and Articles of Association of The National Council of Music' for all quotations in this and the following paragraph.
5 Glyndebourne 4/2, JC-AC, 30/5/41, for all quotations in this paragraph.
6 Glyndebourne 3, Christie-Barlow, 4/6/41.
7 See the note of Barlow's December 1941 meeting with Rab Butler, below.
8 Glyndebourne 4/2, JC-AC, 5/8/41.
9 Ibid., 2/10/41, and for the following quotation.
10 Ibid., telegram JC-AC, 7/7/41.
11 Ibid., JC-AC, 5/8/41.

12 Ibid., JC-AC, 23/8/41.
13 Ibid., JC-AC, 30/8–2/9/41.
14 Ibid., JC-AC, 5/12/41.
15 Ibid., JC-AC, 2/9/41, and for later quotations in this paragraph.
16 Ibid., JC-AC, 28/9/41, for this and the following quotation.
17 Ibid., JC-AC, 11/10/41, for this and the following quotation.
18 Glyndebourne 3, Christie-Campbell, 8/9/41, for this and the three following quotations.
19 Ibid., Christie- Eden, 31/10/41.
20 Glyndebourne 4/2, JC-AC, 2/10/41.
21 Ibid., JC-AC, 30/8–2/9/41.
22 Ibid., JC-AC, 2/10/41.
23 Glyndebourne 3, Christie-Butler, 3/10/41.
24 Glyndebourne 4/2, JC-AC, 19/10/41.
25 Glyndebourne 4/2, JC-AC, 5/11/41.
26 Ibid., JC-AC, 22/11/41.
27 Ibid., JC-AC, 24/11/41, for this and the following two quotations.
28 Ibid., JC-AC 26/11/41.
29 NA ED136/188B, Glasgow-Wood, 6/8/41.
30 David Crook, 'Wood, Sir Robert Stanford (1886–1963)', *Oxford Dictionary of National Biography*, Oxford University Press, 2004.
31 V&A/EL2/4, Wood-Jones, 27/9/41, for all quotations in this and the following two paragraphs.
32 For instance Leventhal, p304, and Weingärtner, p86.
33 V&A/EL2/4, Jones-Wood, 29/9/41.
34 V&A/EL2/11, Butler-Keynes, 17/12/41.
35 Ibid., Keynes-Butler, 24/12/41.
36 Ibid., Keynes-Butler, 14/1/42.
37 Leventhal, pp301–2.
38 Keynes-Evans 28/1/42, cited in Anna Upchurch: 'Keynes's legacy: an intellectual's influence reflected in arts policy', *International Journal of Cultural Policy*, January 2011, Vol. 17 Issue 1, p77.
39 See Chapter 6.
40 V&A/EL2/11, untitled file note by Butler, 7/1/42.
41 V&A/EL2/4, file note by Butler, 4/12/41.
42 CEMA file 'Esher, The Viscount (Senior)', V&A/EL2/14, Esher-Keynes, 4/3/42.
43 Esher soon developed a more positive view of Christie – see below.
44 V&A/EL2/14, Keynes-Glasgow, undated, covering Keynes-Esher, 25/3/42.
45 Christie's account: Glyndebourne box titled 'Christie Correspondence JC-AC 1942–1943, 1945–51 etc' (hereafter 'Glyndebourne 5'), folder headed 'John

Christie-Audrey Christie (Jan to April)' (hereafter 'Glyndebourne 5/1'), JC-AC, 9/2/42. Butler's account: V&A/EL2/4, file note by Butler, 10/2/42. All quotations in the following four paragraphs are from these sources.

46 Robert Skidelsky: *John Maynard Keynes, Volume Three – Fighting for Britain 1937–46* (London: Macmillan, 2000), p287.
47 Glyndebourne 5/1, JC-AC, 17/3/42.
48 Glyndebourne 3, Keynes-Christie, 27/3/42.
49 Ibid., Christie-Keynes, 15/4/42.
50 Ibid., Keynes-Christie, 21/4/42.
51 Glyndebourne 5/1, JC-AC, 27/4/42, for this and later quotations in this paragraph.
52 Ibid., JC-AC, 30/4/42.
53 Glyndebourne 3, Christie-Keynes, 19/5/42.
54 Ibid., Keynes-Christie, 22/5/42.
55 Ibid., Christie-Keynes, 4/6/42.
56 Ibid., memorandum enclosed with Christie-Keynes, 4/6/42.
57 CEMA file 'Lord Keynes Correspondence 1942', V&A/EL2/37, Keynes-Glasgow, 5/6/42.
58 Ibid., Glasgow-Keynes, 6/6/42.
59 Glyndebourne 3, Keynes-Christie, 11/6/42.
60 Ibid., Christie-Cripps, 6/6/42.
61 NA ED136/188B, Glasgow-Wood, 20/6/42.
62 Glyndebourne 5, folder titled 'John Christie- Audrey Christie (May-Dec 1942) (hereafter 'Glyndebourne 5/2'), JC-AC, 1/6/42.
63 Glyndebourne 3, Colles-Christie, 15/6/42.
64 Ibid., Keynes-Colles, 16/6/42.
65 Ibid., Colles-Christie, 19/6/42.
66 Ibid., Bonham Carter-Keynes, 14/7/42.
67 Ibid., Edwards-Greene, 24/6/42.
68 Ibid., Greene-Christie, 2/7/42.
69 Glyndebourne 5/2, JC-AC, 29/6/42.
70 Ibid., JC-AC, 11/5/42.
71 ED136/188B, Butler-Keynes, 22/7/42.
72 Ibid., Keynes-Butler, 27/12/42.
73 Glyndebourne 3, Christie-Keynes, 4/7/42.
74 V&A/EL1/6, Minutes of CEMA's 16th meeting, 1/7/42.
75 Glyndebourne 3, Keynes-Christie, 3/7/42, and Christie-Keynes, 4/7/42.
76 Ibid., 'C.E.M.A. Paper 141 – Minutes of a meeting between representatives of the National Council of Music and music representatives of C.E.M.A. held at Alexandra House on July 22nd 1942'.
77 Ibid., Christie-Greene, 19/8/42.

78 Ibid., Christie-Glasgow, 1/9/42.
79 V&A/EL1/6, Minutes of CEMA's 17th meeting, 2/9/42.
80 Glyndebourne 5/2, JC-AC, 3/9/42.
81 V&A/EL2/37, Glasgow-Keynes, 4/9/42.
82 London: Hutchinson & Co, 1942.
83 Ibid., p154.
84 Glyndebourne 5/2, JC-AC, 28/8/42.
85 Ibid., JC-AC, 2/9/42.
86 Ibid., JC-AC, 25/8/42, for this and the following quotation.
87 See Chapter 7.
88 Glyndebourne 5/2, Violet Bonham Carter-JC, 13/10/42.
89 Ibid., JC-AC, 10/ and 13/9/42.
90 Copy in Glyndebourne Box 3.
91 Glyndebourne 3, Keynes-Christie, 19/11/42.
92 http://www.artscouncil.org.uk/media/uploads/pdf/Norgrove_governance_review_2013.pdf, p7 (accessed 24 September 2015).
93 Basil Dean: *The Theatre at War* (London: George G Harrap, 1956), pp470–1.
94 Ibid., pp214–5, 470–1 and 548.
95 V&A/EL2/37, Glasgow-Keynes, 13/11/42.
96 Glyndebourne 3, Christie-Keynes, 21/11/42 (not sent?).
97 Ibid., Christie-Butler, 21/11/42 (not sent?).
98 Ibid., Christie-Bonham Carter, 21/11/42.
99 Ibid., Christie-Greene, 21/11/42.
100 Ibid., Greene-Christie, 2/7/42.
101 Ibid., Greene-Christie, 24/11/42.
102 Ibid., Colles-Christie, 24/11/42.
103 V&A/EL1/6, Minutes of CEMA's 19th meeting, 20/10/42.
104 NA ED136/189, Keynes-Bonham Carter, 22/1/43.
105 Glyndebourne 3, Christie-Keynes and Christie-Butler, both 15/2/43 and both probably not sent.
106 Glyndebourne 5, folder titled '1943 John Christie to Audrey Christie (Jan to July)' (hereafter 'Glyndebourne 5/3'), JC-AC, 6/2/43.
107 Glyndebourne 3, Hess-Christie, 27/6/43.
108 Ibid., Soulbury-Christie, 9/, 15/ and 16/2/43.
109 Ibid., Soulbury-Christie, 1/6/43.
110 Glyndebourne 5/3, JC-AC, 26/1/43.
111 Norman Marshall: *The Other Theatre* (London: John Lehmann, 1947), p206.
112 Ibid., p205.
113 Glyndebourne 3, Esher-Christie, 21/1/43.
114 Ibid., Christie-Esher, 1/2/43.

115 Ibid., Esher-Christie, 16/2/43.
116 20/5/43, p5.
117 V&A/EL2/38, Keynes-Glasgow, 20/5/43.
118 Glyndebourne 3, Christie-Keynes, 24/5/43, labelled 'Draft'.
119 Ibid., Christie-Keynes, 25/5/43, with pencil note: 'Probably not sent'.
120 Glyndebourne 5/3, JC-AC, 4/6/43.
121 Ibid., JC-AC, 6/3/43, for this and the following quotation.
122 *The Times*, 6/3/43, p7.
123 Glyndebourne 5/3, Christie-Richard Law, 23/3/43.
124 Ibid., JC-AC, 29/3/43.
125 Ibid., JC-AC, 29/6/43.
126 Ibid., JC-AC, 10/7/43.
127 Ibid., JC-AC, 29/7/43.
128 Glyndebourne 5, folder titled '1943 John Christie to Audrey Christie (Aug to Dec, Canada and N.Y.)' (hereafter 'Glyndebourne 5/4'), JC-AC, 3/9/43.
129 Ibid., Christie-Anderson, probably December 1943.
130 Ibid., JC-AC, 18/1/44.
131 Ibid., JC-AC, 6/ and 9/1/44.
132 Ibid., JC-AC, 19/1/44, for all later quotations in this paragraph.
133 Ibid., undated.
134 Ibid., JC-AC, 14/2/44.
135 Ibid., JC-AC, 27/2/44, and for the following two quotations.
136 See Chapter 6, pp100–1.
137 Glyndebourne 5/4, Eden-Christie, 17/3/44.
138 Ibid., Christie-Eden, 20/3/44.
139 Ibid., JC-AC, 29/3/44.
140 V&A/EL1/6, Minutes of CEMA's 29th meeting, 25/7/44, for all material in this paragraph.
141 Ibid., Minutes of CEMA's 30th meeting, 26/09/44.
142 Ibid., Minutes of CEMA's 31st meeting, 28/11/44.
143 Witts, p9.

# 9

# 'No Levy on Laughter – and No Fine on Fun!': The Campaign against Entertainments Duty

## Introduction

Alfred Wareing's League of Audiences and John Christie's 'Council of Power'/ National Council of Music played an important part in the history of government support for the arts, and the stories of the League and the NCM cast new light on aspects of 1930s and early 1940s British cultural history. But neither achieved its aim of gaining state funding for theatre and live music. By contrast the campaign against Entertainments Duty, discussed in this chapter, was highly successful. Entertainments Duty was a tax on tickets for exhibitions, films, sports events and theatre and live music. Its history shows that government ministers in the 1930s were not only sympathetic to the financial plight of those putting on live performances, but were prepared to provide, and did provide, substantial assistance to mitigate that plight.

Historians have neglected this campaign even more than they have neglected Wareing's and Christie's. There are at least three reasons for rediscovering it. First, those who campaigned against Entertainments Duty succeeded in gaining government financial support for live music and theatre at a time when, according to the usual view, there was little campaigning and no success.

Second, the campaign against Entertainments Duty was deeply damaging to the League of Audiences. Alfred Wareing was prepared to work only with those whose purpose was identical with his own. This exclusivity – his focus on subsidy alone – limited the League's appeal, created powerful opposition within the theatre profession and contributed much to the League's decline. Entertainments Duty was the crucial area of disagreement. Many individual actors and playwrights supported Wareing. But the commercial theatre establishment saw abolishing the duty as a higher priority than gaining subsidy, and considered Wareing's 'subsidy first and only' approach to be a damaging diversion. The theatre establishment's alliance against Entertainments Duty became in practice an alliance against the League.

On the other hand, many general supporters of the arts saw the campaigns for subsidy and against Entertainments Duty as broadly interchangeable. *The Sunday Times* was typical, arguing in 1935 that 'The remission of a tax is, of course, a form of subsidy, and... is given on aesthetic grounds'.[1] This view was also held within parts of the government, which leads to the third reason for writing about Entertainments Duty. Since the subject involves tax revenue, politicians and civil servants discussed it at length. Treasury, Customs and Excise and Board of Education papers on the subject provide a unique insight into government attitudes to the arts between the wars.

This chapter sketches the history of Entertainments Duty from its introduction during World War I, then considers in more detail the two main elements of the 1930s campaign against it. The first was led by the Old Vic and Sadler's Wells, two not-for-profit theatres governed as one, seeking to have their work exempted from the tax as 'partly educational'. When the government conceded this in 1934, other not-for-profit arts organizations were able to take advantage. The second was the successful lobbying for all theatre and live music to be taxed at a lower rate, and in particular to be taxed less than cinema. The chapter ends by considering the importance of these episodes in the history of arts funding.

## Origin and History of Entertainments Duty to 1933

Entertainments Duty was a tax on admission prices for entertainment provided by others: '... payments for admission to watch other persons dancing or playing games are liable to the duty, but payments for the right to dance or play games are not'.[2] It was a literally visible tax, in the form of a stamp on tickets, a point considered below.

The duty was introduced by the Finance (New Duties) Act 1916 as a wartime measure. It stayed in force until 1960. The main published source of information on it is A P Herbert's *'No Fine on Fun'* (1957),[3] subtitled *The Comical History of the Entertainments Duty*. As title and subtitle suggest, this was not an objective account. Herbert campaigned against the duty as a writer for the theatre and musical stage and as Independent MP for Oxford University. It was, indeed, part of his platform as candidate in the 1935 election, when he said: 'I regard it as a tax upon knowledge and enlightenment and the free communication of minds. I shall therefore press for its abolition, at least, where it is imposed upon music and the living theatre.'[4] He put it more snappily in a 1953 speech, when no longer an MP: 'I offer to all parties this battle-cry: "No Tax on Thought – No Duty on Beauty – No Levy on Laughter – and No Fine on Fun!"'[5]

Herbert assumed that the duty's original purpose had been to raise revenue.[6] The earliest substantial Customs and Excise briefing paper, of December 1915,[7] suggests otherwise:

> We have been asked [by the Treasury] to report on the possibility of taxing amusements. As it is understood that the object in view is rather to reduce expenditure than to raise revenue, it is proposed to consider the methods by which such a duty might be levied, as well as its economic incidence and general effects, but to make no attempt at estimating its yield. . . .

Reinforcing the point, '[since] the object is to reduce expenditure on amusements, or by raising cost to reduce the amount of money which those who frequent them have to spend on other "luxuries," it appears preferable to arrange that the tax shall be paid directly and knowingly by the public. . . .' Thus the tax would be indicated by a government stamp affixed to admission tickets. While the tax should be 'comprehensive and heavy', this was not in order to maximize revenue but 'to effect a drastic reduction in the expenditure of the public on amusements generally'. The anonymous author seems to have been a true believer in the evils of entertainment:

> The Government will no doubt be subjected to sentimental appeals about 'amusements for wounded soldiers,' ... and about the numbers of those connected with theatres, &c., who would be thrown out of employment, but such appeals should not be difficult to resist. One great object of any such duty... would be to throw people out of such employments and into employments... more useful to the community.

The government made no such statement publicly, but *The Times* reported the Chancellor of the Exchequer, Reginald McKenna, justifying the duty to Parliament on other quasi-moral grounds: its purpose was 'to distribute the burden of taxation over the whole community, including the class which did not pay income tax at present, but still has money enough to spend on amusements. (Hear, hear.)'[8] To meet this aim, during the duty's first few years the government sought 'to tax the patrons of the lower-priced seats proportionately higher than the patrons of the higher-priced seats'.[9]

Attaching a government stamp to admission tickets involved the creation of several offences and classes of potential offender. Audience members without stamps on their tickets, box office staff issuing tickets without stamps or with forged stamps, ticket collectors permitting entry without a stamped ticket, and managers allowing any of this to happen would all commit criminal offences, though Customs and Excise believed that initially 'it is not desirable that penalties against members of the audience should be enforced. (Cautions will suffice.)'[10]

From the start, rates of duty were often amended. Customs and Excise first proposed a duty of 50 per cent at all ticket price levels.[11] But the rates in the Bill were far lower and, as noted, were weighted towards cheaper tickets, ranging from '1/2d on payments not exceeding 2d to 1s on payments between 7s.6d and 12s.6d'.[12] Rates were altered six times, both up and down, by 1935. By then, at most ticket prices, they were above their 1916 levels.

Also from the start, definitions posed problems and exemptions required complex casework.[13] Even during the Bill's passage the government had to table several amendments about exempted types of entertainment. There were exemptions for entertainments 'of a wholly educational character' and for those deemed partly educational if organized by a not-for-profit organization or by one 'founded with the object of reviving national pastimes'.[14] Oddly, while it was the job of the Board of Education to decide whether entertainments were wholly educational, decisions on partly educational cases were for Customs and Excise.[15] In the long term the 'partly educational' exemption for not-for-profit organizations proved highly problematic – see below. In the short term, even before the duty came into effect, the provision about reviving national pastimes caused controversy in Parliament and on *The Times*' letters page. The Gaelic Athletic Association, which prohibited British armed services personnel from taking part in its activities, sought and received tax exemption for football and hurling fixtures – an action a *Times* correspondent described as 'a sop to disloyalty'.[16] Concerning the detailed rules, even at the Bill's Report stage the Solicitor-General was unclear whether duty would be payable on, among other examples suggested by MPs, admission to botanical gardens or to entertainments put on by the Jockey Club.[17]

*The Times* welcomed the duty as 'perhaps the most popular in the [1916] Budget'.[18] It did not specify with whom it was popular; probably not audiences or spectators, and certainly not the entertainment industry. In a speech on the 1938 Finance Bill, A P Herbert summarized the theatrical profession's financial rather than cultural arguments against the duty:

> . . . managers, authors, designers and musicians spend. . . many months preparing the show. . . . The actors are drawing pretty good wages and salaries, and paying Income Tax, and rightly; the authors are drawing good royalties, and paying Income Tax, and rightly. . . . But the manager, who is taking the risks, is not

receiving a penny of profit. . . . and all that time the State is putting its hands into the till and grabbing 15 to 20 per cent. on the basic prices. Is there a single industry in the world where the same thing would be done or suffered?[19]

The campaign for abolition or reduction began almost immediately. It took several forms: opposing the principle of the tax, seeking a lower rate, advocating a wider range of exemptions, and arguing for a tax on profits rather than on gross takings.

Initially most protests came from cinema owners, perhaps because their ticket prices were low and thus they were worst hit. It was claimed in Parliament as early as 1917 that the tax had caused more than 700 cinemas to close.[20] Debating a provision in the 1917 Finance Bill to raise rates of duty, not a single backbencher spoke in support of the government's proposals. They nonetheless passed with only minor changes.[21] The Chancellor of the Exchequer, Andrew Bonar Law, resisted particularly concessions on cheaper tickets, pointing out that 80 per cent of tax revenue came from tickets priced sixpence or less.[22] Sir Edward Carson, Minister without Portfolio in the War Cabinet, wrote to Bonar Law that many cinema owners, incensed by the duty, planned 'to boycott all Government films and propaganda and further to use the screen to provoke a public agitation for the abolition of the entertainments tax'.[23] He considered it vital that they be offered relief: 'The whole attitude of the working classes to the War may be affected by the steps which are taken in this matter.'[24] The Treasury was unimpressed.

By 1923 the duty had outlived its wartime emergency origins but was considered no less necessary for that. Customs and Excise briefing for that year's budget shows that revenue was now the issue: 'It may be urged. . . that cheap entertainment is necessary to the contentment of the people. . . [but] all such arguments fail to recognise that the primary consideration at present is one of finance.'[25] Repeal would lose the Treasury £9.5 million a year, while the case for reducing the duty was weak because the industry's problems were due less to the tax and more to 'the general depression of industry. . . [and] unbusinesslike finance and methods'.[26]

By the mid-1920s a pre-Budget ritual had been established. The Chairman of Customs and Excise would pre-emptively argue against repeal or reduction. The Chancellor would receive delegations representing theatre and film interests. They would present a case sometimes for reduction but usually for repeal, because repeal was 'the only proposal on which it is possible for the various sections of the trade. . . to find complete agreement'.[27] Officials would calculate the potential loss of revenue, the Chancellor would express general sympathy, and the regretful conclusion was that current economic conditions prevented any change. Sympathetic MPs would table a flurry of amendments supporting the industry during Finance Bill debates, but usually the provisions would pass with amendments withdrawn and only minor government concessions.

Degrees of regret for being unable to meet the profession's demands varied between Chancellors and parties. The most sympathetic in the 1920s was Philip Snowden when Chancellor in the 1924 Labour government. He told that year's delegation 'that he had always opposed the duty, and would like to abolish it if the money were available. But if reduction only were possible, he would be inclined to begin at the bottom, and so make it more of a luxury tax',[28] a departure from previous principles. The 1924 Budget removed the duty on the cheapest tickets and reduced it on those slightly more expensive.[29] In 1925 the new Conservative Chancellor, Winston Churchill, initially requested the reverse: a reduction to benefit the buyers of higher-priced tickets.[30] This did not happen, Churchill instead following the usual pattern: sympathy with the aims of an amendment to abolish the duty, understanding of the hardships faced by the theatrical profession, and the conclusion that 'I am unable to find the money which would enable the tax to be reduced again this year'.[31]

Entertainments Duty could, it seems, sometimes be fatal for theatre companies. The Board of Education's Adult Education Committee produced a report in 1926 entitled *The Drama in Adult Education*.[32] It devoted several pages to the work of the Lena Ashwell Players,[33] praising Ashwell for continuing in peacetime in London boroughs her wartime theatre work in France and elsewhere for the troops. But in her memoir *Myself a Player* (1936)[34] Ashwell reported that the duty led to the Players' demise the very year the report was published:

> Without the Entertainment Tax we should certainly have survived but during the season 1926–27 for entertaining 174,000 people we were taxed £2,683.6.8. This charge was imposed before the running expenses were met and involved extra staff work for stamping the tickets. . . . We could not cut down expenses, the patrons could not afford to pay more, and so the tax was a dead loss to an enterprise. . . carried on only as a national service.[35]

By 1929 Customs and Excise staff were deeply attached to the duty. An internal minute to 'Mr Grylls' (not otherwise identified) and Sir Francis Floud, its Chairman, three weeks after the 1929 Labour government took office, began: 'I think we should be well advised to occupy some of our present leisure in preparing powder and shot in defence of the maintenance of the Entertainments Tax. Regard must be had to Labour utterances on the subject both in and out of office...'[36] Grylls commented, 'I am in complete agreement. Personally... I have very little sympathy with the squeals of the "movie kings".' Floud also agreed.[37] They need not have worried. The campaign for reduction or abolition continued, but government policy did not change. A *Times* editorial of December 1930 noted, perhaps sarcastically: 'While the Government remained unrepentantly philistine in its attitude towards the arts... there could be little hope of obtaining relief for hard cases.... But now we have a Government which professes enlightenment.'[38] In fact, in his second spell as Chancellor, amid a major financial crisis, Philip Snowden re-imposed the duty on the cheapest seats which he had removed in 1924.[39]

There were, however, two pointers to the future during the second Labour government. First, in some quarters exemption from Entertainments Duty came to be seen as a form of government support for music and drama – in effect, equivalent to subsidy. The 1930 Treasury grant to the Covent Garden Opera Syndicate via the BBC was noted briefly in Chapter 2. It led to this exchange in Parliament in December 1930:

> **Mr D G SOMERVILLE** asked the Chancellor of the Exchequer whether, in view of his assistance to grand opera, he will consider giving equal assistance to the drama by the reduction of the Entertainments Duty?
>
> **Mr P SNOWDEN** No, Sir.
>
> **Mr SOMERVILLE** In view of the fact that far more people attend the theatre and the Cinema than the opera, why should they not be treated with equal justice?[40]

The Speaker ruled this supplementary question out of order.

Second, a distinction began to appear in official attitudes about the duty: sympathy towards live music and theatre (and to some extent sport), but none towards the 'movie kings'. While it took several years for this to be reflected in government policy, the campaigns soon became wholly separate and then mutually hostile: those lobbying for tax reductions for theatre and live music actively campaigned against similar treatment for cinema.

Some MPs, for instance, noted with approval a provision in the 1931 Irish Free State Finance Act 'which exempts from Entertainments Duty all entertainments in which the performers are personally present',[41] and sought a similar provision in Britain. Theatre campaigners used arguments applying to live performance but not to film, with the economic case sometimes bolstered by xenophobia. Walter Payne, a leader of the campaign (see below), writing before the 1932 budget to the Chancellor of the Exchequer, Neville Chamberlain, distinguished between 'places of entertainment... at which living artists, the enormous majority of whom are British subjects, are employed, and... places where Cinematograph films, largely of alien origin, and the profits of which are sent abroad, are exhibited'.[42] Two weeks later Payne sought a meeting with Chamberlain to argue against reduced duty on cheap tickets. This would mainly benefit cinemas and 'would be tantamount to giving a subsidy for competitive forms of entertainment and would bring many legitimate theatres in the Country to ruin'.[43]

Chamberlain delegated the meeting to a junior Minister, the Financial Secretary – Walter Elliot, Alfred Wareing's loyal friend.[44] The meeting achieved little for Payne: the Customs and Excise view was that 'It would be impossible to justify taxing a person when he goes to a cinema but not when he goes to a music hall'.[45] This line was maintained in the lead-up to the 1933 budget, despite several MPs attempting to justify such a distinction. One of these was the very actorly ex-actor Alfred Denville, who wrote to Chamberlain in December 1932 to ask:

> In the goodness of your heart, will you fix a day on which such artistes as:-
> Dame Madge Kendal
> Sir Gerald Du Maurier
> Sir Johnston Forbes Robertson [etc, etc] ...
> can wait upon you with the object of pointing out the hardships suffered by the Theatres due to the Entertainment Tax, as different to the Kinemas [*sic*].[46]

Chamberlain refused this opportunity to mingle with the stars, responding that the duty was 'a tax on the entertainment-going public, and, therefore,... I could not... agree to make a differentiation in the duty as between different kinds of entertainment'.[47] He chose to omit a passage in the draft reply prepared for him pointing out that 'some of the artistes mentioned in your [Denville's] letter appear to find an outlet for some part of their energies in film production'.[48]

Campaigning intensified as budget day approached. The *Evening News* ran a feature in March 1933 about the damaging effects of Entertainments Duty on live theatre.[49] The same month, solicitors 'instructed by the Society of West End Theatre Managers, the Theatrical Managers' Association and the Entertainments Protection Association, who between them represent practically every Theatre and Variety Theatre in the West End and Suburbs of London and in the Provinces'[50] requested a meeting between Chamberlain and their clients; they wrote that live theatre could continue to exist only if taxed less than the mass-production industry of cinema. Alfred Denville attempted to involve himself in the subsequent delegation. Customs and Excise briefed Chamberlain that the delegation did not want this, that Denville's approach was 'a nuisance but... [it] will make for peace if you will give him and his two or three Artists ten minutes'.[51] The briefing argued, as usual, that tax rates should be uniform because it was a tax on consumers, not producers, of entertainment.[52] But it also contained the argument, novel for official circles, that granting 'special relief from the entertainments duty in respect of theatres and music halls would be tantamount to giving them a State subsidy in a disguised form'.[53]

These arguments prevailed. The lobbying continued. In July 1933 Walter Payne again wrote to Chamberlain. The letter's contents (the usual plea for tax relief on live performance) are of less interest than its list of other signatories: not only a bewildering array of representative theatre bodies but also individual theatres – Covent Garden, the Old Vic and Sadler's Wells, and the Shakespeare Memorial Theatre; the Musicians' Union and Actors' Equity; and spokespeople for 'ordinary taxpayers', in the form of the National Union of Ratepayers' Associations and the very right-wing National Citizens Union.[54]

Customs and Excise officials used several arguments to bat this away:[55] it was wrong in principle to benefit theatre at the expense of cinema; if theatre was facing hard times, this was due to changing tastes rather than the tax; it was inequitable to advantage (generally better off) theatre patrons at the expense of (generally worse off) cinema patrons; and it would be immensely complicated to distinguish between recorded entertainment and entertainment where 'the human element predominated'. But this apparently fixed policy continued for only two years more. Meanwhile the theatre and music world looked with interest at the attempt by the Old Vic and Sadler's Wells to have their performances classified by the government as 'partly educational'.

## 1933–4 – The Old Vic and Sadler's Wells: Music, Drama and Education

As noted above, performances were free from Entertainments Duty if they were wholly educational or if they were partly educational and were put on by a not-for-profit organization. Until the 1930s these exemptions were applied narrowly. The approach originated in a 1917 memorandum by Sir William Graham-Harrison, Second Parliamentary Counsel:[56]

> ... education is clearly capable of being used in a wider or narrower sense. In the wider sense it means, speaking generally, the enlargement or development of a

> person's knowledge, intelligence or taste; in the narrower, the training up of children or students by means of some definite or systematic course of instruction.... it is reasonably clear that the vague wide reading must be discarded.... any interpretation more favourable to the taxpayer would undermine the yield of the duty.

This style of argument is not unusual in government – working backwards from a desired outcome in order to justify a particular (not always the most natural) interpretation of the law.

This interpretation and reasoning were maintained for more than fifteen years, despite creating occasional absurdities. During the passage of the 1937 Finance Bill, A P Herbert provided an illustration,[57] by that time historical, of 'the strange idea that anything which is at all entertaining is something in the nature of an offence on which a fine ought to be imposed'. His lectures to not-for-profit literary societies had been considered partly educational, and thus tax-exempt, until Customs and Excise heard of one entitled 'On Being Funny', which was 'of a rather high-brow character. It set out to explain the Bergsonian theory of laughter and the essence of humour....' Herbert provided a precis:

> ... in order to assure the Custom House, first, that it was educational, and secondly, that it was not at all amusing. To my astonishment, knowing how little entertainment that lecture appeared to afford to the public, I was unable to convince them of the second part of the proposition. The unhappy society had to pay tax upon the lecture, and I was never invited to lecture there again.

There were a few, apparently arbitrary, exceptions: as early as May 1917, for example, the government Law Officers decided that the Royal Academy Summer Exhibition was partly educational and that tickets for it should be tax-free.[58] But generally the word 'educational', according to an internal 1920s Customs and Excise document, 'must be read in the strict sense of tuitional.... the entertainment must be given by persons whose relation to the audience is that of teacher to taught.... [To accept that] performances of "classical" music, drama, etc., were educational, as they tended to direct and elevate public taste... would lead to wholesale exemption.'[59]

While the government refused to regard music and drama as educational, the connection between the arts and education was in the air. Although *The Times* described the 1926 report *The Drama in Adult Education*, referred to above, as 'cautious almost to the point of sterility',[60] the report did reach one conclusion: that drama is 'a powerful instrument for the conveyance of ideas... [and] under the right conditions can be a most potent instrument of moral, artistic, and intellectual progress. . . .'[61] This finding was largely ignored until it was used to support a reversal of government policy in 1934.

In 1933 the Old Vic and Sadler's Wells (often known jointly as the Vic-Wells) applied for 'partly educational' tax exemption. This was a formidable test of government policy: the theatres' not-for-profit status, the range of their work and their roots in some of London's poorest communities made them strong candidates for exemption. Under Lilian Baylis's leadership the theatres performed opera, ballet and drama. Her work led indirectly to the foundation of the Royal National Theatre, and more directly to that of English National Opera and the Royal Ballet.[62] *The Drama in Adult Education* was fulsome: 'We cannot speak in too high terms of the great work done by Miss Baylis at the "Old Vic." It will always be an example to those who believe that the art of the theatre has a power and influence over the minds of men. . . .'[63] But this was not reflected in the theatres' tax status. In 1916 (before Sadler's Wells joined with the Old Vic) Baylis had sought tax exemption for the Old Vic and been refused.[64] But she had not argued, and Customs and Excise and the Board of Education had not pointed out, that while commercial theatres would be tax-exempt only if their work was wholly educational, the Old Vic, as a not-for-profit theatre, needed only to demonstrate that its work was partly educational.

The 1933 campaign began with a letter from the Vic-Wells Chairman, Lord Lytton, to Customs and Excise.[65] This focused on the dictionary definition of 'educational' (wide), on the word's construction by the courts (also wide), on the theatres' charitable objectives, which included providing performances for 'the recreation and instruction of the poorer classes', and on the London County Council's financial support for schools' attendance at their performances. Lytton wrote that he was seeking not special treatment nor a change in the law but the proper application of the current law. Customs and Excise officials proposed a flat refusal,[66] maintaining this position despite a question from the Prime Minister, Ramsay MacDonald, 'Can anything be done?', written on a copy of Lytton's letter sent to him by Lytton.[67]

Customs and Excise were also unmoved by a letter from the Vic-Wells Treasurer, Sir Reginald Rowe, to Neville Chamberlain.[68] They maintained their narrow interpretation of 'educational' – 'implying some definite form of tuition persisting throughout the entertainment. . . . Whilst the performances at the Old Vic and Sadlers [*sic*] Wells theatre are undoubtedly educational in the broad sense of the term they are clearly not educational in the strict meaning. . . .'[69] Chamberlain's private secretary commented: 'I am afraid this is only an outstanding case of a very common claim which has always had to be resisted in order to preserve the revenue from this tax.'[70] Chamberlain rebuffed Rowe.

But this ignored the distinction between the 'wholly educational' requirement for commercial companies and the 'partly educational' requirement applying to not-for-profit companies. Lytton, unlike Baylis in 1916, was alert to this. Having waited two months for a brief and dismissive reply from Customs and Excise,[71] he wrote to Chamberlain[72] arguing that since the Charity Commission accepted the theatres' not-for-profit status and partly educational purposes, so should Customs and Excise: '. . . it is difficult to for us conceive of any case to which these words [s1(5)(d) of the 1916 Act] could apply, if they do not apply to ours.' Customs and Excise officials continued to resist. They argued and Chamberlain agreed, though the files record no legal advice sought at this point, that as 'educational' meant 'tuitional' then 'partly educational' must mean 'partly tuitional': 'Some definite form of tuition must. . . be present' for the exemption to apply.[73]

Lytton let the issue lie until March 1934, then wrote to Chamberlain again.[74] He argued that for Customs and Excise to decide both individual cases for exemption and the meaning of 'educational' in the 1916 Act against which these cases were assessed 'puts an unusual and inequitable power in the hands of a tax collecting body'; and that the definition used by Customs and Excise was 'contrary to the meaning of the English language as interpreted by English dictionaries and to pronouncements on the subject by English judges'. He suggested that Chamberlain meet a Vic-Wells delegation: 'I have found by experience that half an hour's discussion brings one much nearer than months of correspondence and saves trouble in the long run.' Lytton distanced the Vic-Wells from the regular pre-budget lobbying on Entertainments Duty: 'I mean, of course, quite a private and informal [meeting]. . ., not the kind of deputation which you received from the theatre people on the 15th March.' This was disingenuous and perhaps disloyal. The 15 March delegation had been from the Stage and Allied Arts Defence League (discussed below). It had been led by the League's President, Lytton himself.

Chamberlain suggested that Lytton meet instead Sir Evelyn Murray, Chairman of the Board of Customs and Excise.[75] The briefing for Murray[76] used a further dubious argument to justify the narrow definition of 'educational': 'That the line of policy laid down by the Board has consistently been maintained with ministerial approval suggests that the policy is inherently sound.' It provided examples of the rare cases of performances declared exempt, including lecture concerts, where before 1923 'the criterion was that the illustrations, e.g., music, should not occupy more than about one-quarter of the time',[77] the Eisteddfod, and music competitions, provided that the competition was 'accompanied by a reasoned oral adjudication'.[78] It discussed applications which had been refused, including for concerts put on by the Oxford University Musical Club. This had failed when the club admitted that while music students attended for the purpose of study, 'the majority of the members went to the concerts for the purpose of enjoyment'.[79] The briefing assumed that Customs' interpretation was correct and would prevail.

At the meeting, in May 1934,[80] Lytton and Lilian Baylis argued that their theatres were unique, so exempting them would create no damaging precedent. Their charitable aims allowed them to receive grants from charitable trusts 'because it was recognised that the theatres were providing benefits for the people from motives of philanthropy'. And their approach to education was unique. Classes were held before productions, with participants then seeing at public performances the practical demonstration of what they had studied, and in some cases understudying minor parts. To that extent performances were 'tuitional'. If Customs and Excise still believed that this was not partly educational, then the law should be amended to exempt the two theatres specifically.

Sir Evelyn Murray disagreed that the Vic-Wells theatres were unique in ways relevant to the duty. If they were granted exemption, 'it could not be refused to a large number of other high class entertainments of cultural value... provided by non-profit-making syndicates'. He also reported that 'the [government] Law Officers were disposed to agree that the word "educational" was rightly construed' by Customs and Excise.

But this apparently secure position quickly fell apart. Following the meeting, the Vic-Wells asked for a judicial interpretation of 'partly educational'.[81] Murray wrote to Chamberlain[82] that since the Vic-Wells planned to take the issue to court, he would seek the Law Officers' opinion on the meaning of the phrase – an opinion which at the meeting he had claimed to possess already. The Law Officers' response made it clear that Murray had misrepresented them:

> ...the Commissioners have construed the words of section 1(5)(d) of the Finance (New Duties) Act, 1916, too narrowly. An element of tuition... is not, in our view, a necessary element.... the object of improving or educating taste in music or drama, just as much as in pictorial art or in literature, is an educational purpose within the section.... the proper construction of the word 'educational' is a wide one.[83]

Murray reported to Chamberlain: 'The result of this opinion is that we shall have to abandon the doctrine... that "partly educational" connotes some element of tuition as distinct from culture, and the administrative difficulties of deciding what is and what is not within the scope of the exemption will certainly be aggravated.'[84] Lytton quickly sought to exploit his victory, asking Murray whether, 'As I am also interested in the Shakespeare Memorial Theatre', the exemption would apply there also.[85] He still attempted to reassure Murray: 'I do not think that the exemption in their [Shakespeare Memorial Theatre and Vic-Wells] case will serve as a precedent for any other institutions.'

Customs and Excise saw such reassurance as hollow. Within days of receiving the Law Officers' opinion, its Board apparently embraced the doctrine that music and drama were often partly educational. It drew on the 1926 report *The Drama in Adult Education*, which had previously been ignored and whose conclusions would, until a week earlier, have been anathema:

> . . . the Board's feeling [was] that. . . it would be expedient to tend towards liberality rather than rigidity. Any other attitude would seem to conflict with the views expressed in the Report. . . by the Adult Education Committee of the Board of Education. That Committee gave cordial endorsement to the claim that drama produced with what may be called serious purposes. . . is a valuable educational factor.[86]

The Board did not explain why it suddenly accorded the report such authority, beyond noting that 'it seems to contain some useful indications for the practical working of the "partly educational" exemption'.

It was a substantial project for Customs and Excise to create guidance for its staff and to process the casework following the policy change. An early, somewhat ramshackle, attempt was made by a Customs and Excise lawyer to classify plays of educational value under headings including 'Greek play', 'Shakespeare', 'Other old plays' and '"The play of ideas"' (all *sic*), and to provide an equivalent system for classifying theatrical producers operating for public benefit. Admission even to a production of doubtful educational value might be tax-exempt if the producer was of the right kind: 'It would obviously be inexpedient to haggle with the Old Vic over "The Importance of Being Earnest". . . . [The 1926 report] may be treated as evidence of particular weight in the case of any particular organisation which it mentions.'[87] Within a few weeks, things became more systematic. Once it was clear that the producing organization was not run for profit, its objects and work were examined: it must be 'genuinely working to spread knowledge of the theatre or of music. . ., [and] the individual play or music must have some claim to be regarded as respectable – a mere farce or musical comedy is not good enough'.[88] The Solicitor to Customs and Excise acknowledged that 'difficult borderline cases are bound to occur from time to time',[89] but did not suggest that the volume would be great or that the department's staff were unqualified to make such judgements.

The Vic-Wells decision received a fair amount of press coverage,[90] leading to many new applications for tax exemption.[91] The casework was on occasion intricate. The Crompton Stage Society in Lancashire, for instance, produced both plays by members for private audiences of members, which were declared tax-exempt, and productions designed to reduce the resulting financial loss. The latter were taxable because 'the purpose of these and other "big productions" is to raise money by inducing the general public to pay for entertainment pure and simple'. Some cases were arcane, such as the Southport Society of Practical Psychology, all of whose public activities were declared tax-exempt, including a lecture 'to deal with such matters as… "Pythagoras' message to all peoples regarding the end of the world, which is fast approaching"…. interspersed with "Colour-music", which consists of ordinary light music and dance music of inferior quality'. The Board of Customs and Excise was clear that there were no short cuts: '… the actual programme of every individual entertainment must be inspected.'[92] But it sought to minimise extra work (and loss of revenue) by not publicizing the change of policy: '… if the Society, etc, had never at any time made a claim to exemption on "partly educational" grounds the question should not be raised by the Department.' There were also some cases of Customs misleading by omission or worse. For example, the Town Clerk of Bideford, Devon, sought tax exemption for admission to a schoolchildren's pageant celebrating the 1937 coronation. Rather than assessing this as a partly educational entertainment by not-for-profit organizations (the council and local schools), Customs advised him to apply to the Board of Education for a 'wholly educational' exemption; the Board of Education turned him down.[93]

On the other hand, the government could be surprisingly flexible if the applicant was grand enough. In 1939 the Royal Opera House applied for tax exemption for a Royal Command performance to be attended by the President of the French Republic.[94] Customs concluded that there was no legal basis for exemption, and asked the Treasury to sort it out. The Treasury obliged: '… in the special circumstances of the case, They [*sic*, the Lords Commissioners of the Treasury] are prepared to authorise an extra-statutory exemption.'[95] No attempt was made to specify the 'extra-statutory' powers concerned.

Apart from such outlying examples a formal system was soon established for seeking and granting 'partly educational' exemptions. Customs and Excise files of applications by the London Philharmonic Orchestra,[96] for instance, contain template exemption certificates granted:

> . . . on the understanding that the musical programmes would be of a character similar to those previously exempted. A programme of each of these concerts should be furnished as early as possible. . . . [Customs and Excise] reserve the right to call for duty in any case where they are not satisfied that the programme submitted is of such a standard as will contribute to the musical education of the audience.

But leaving decisions to Customs officials provided an easy target for the system's critics. The November 1936 editorial in *Drama* (the British Drama League's magazine) reported the experience of one not-for-profit theatre: '. . . plays by Shakespeare and Milton were granted exemption, [but] relief was refused for a public performance of Jonson's "The Mask of Cupid."'[97] And John Christie complained to the Treasury about the (as it seemed to him) arbitrary and unfair operation of the tax.[98] He claimed that Customs had a 'definite and monstrous hostility' against him because he had pointed out anomalies in the tax, and that 'having exempted us from Entertainment Tax in our second [Glyndebourne] Festival, [Customs] told us that we were not exempt in our third Festival only one week before the third Festival started'.

Such concerns continued for as long as Customs acted as case-by-case arbiters of exemption. There is little reason to extend the history of the exemption into wartime,[99] except for a few points which reflect back on its pre-war history.

In late 1943, to avoid disputes between Customs and Excise and CEMA, which contested Customs' competence to assess these cases, the Treasury set up an independent committee under Sir Ernest Pooley to do so.[100] Sir Archibald Carter, Chairman of Customs and Excise, accepted that this might rather be CEMA's role. He wrote privately to John Maynard Keynes, CEMA's Chairman, in January 1944:

> If we once could get C.E.M.A. recognised. . . as a permanent institution, then it would clearly be natural to use it as the sole channel through which Government assistance to the drama and the arts was given, and if part of that. . . was still to be given in the form of relief from taxation (against which a good deal could be said), to make C.E.M.A. the judge in cases of doubt.[101]

Keynes attempted to take over the system, but had to report a rare failure to CEMA's council in March 1944: '. . . the suggestion of giving CEMA control over tax exemption had been made both to the Chancellor and to the Board of Customs and had been refused.'[102] He was not a good loser, subsequently describing Pooley's committee to Carter as 'ignorant of the matters with which it is dealing to the point of illiteracy'.[103]

From 1946 it was no longer necessary for any government body to decide whether specific performances or productions were 'partly educational'. That year's Finance Act provided that if Customs and Excise were satisfied that an organization was not established for profit and had partly educational aims, then any entertainment it produced would be tax-exempt. Thereafter Entertainments Duty was far less of an issue for not-for-profit theatres, orchestras and concert halls.

Finally, as seen in the quotation above, Sir Archibald Carter acknowledged, in his January 1944 letter to Keynes, that exemption from Entertainments Duty was a form of 'Government assistance to the drama and the arts'. This view, explored further below, is questionable; it applies far more to the tax changes discussed in the next section. But it confirms the importance of Entertainments Duty in the history of government funding of the arts.

## The Campaign 1933–9: 'Why should "Crazy nights at Clacton" escape?'

While not-for-profit organizations like the Vic-Wells gained tax exemption from 1934 for events deemed partly educational, Entertainments Duty remained uniform on all other entertainments. The theatrical world reacted to the Vic-Wells decision with a mixture of approval, envy and calculation. *Drama* magazine's editorial response was typical:

> ... the result has only been effected by persistence and clever presentation of the case on the part of the Old Vic management. The question naturally arises, how far can the same result be achieved by other theatres? The precedent is a valuable one.... a step in the right direction but still only a step. What we demand is nothing less than the total abolition of the tax...[104]

Several organizations were established between 1916 and the 1930s to campaign for this. The evolution of their names indicates how those putting on live performances came to distance themselves from the film industry: the Entertainments Protection Association, the Entertainments Tax Abolition League,[105] the Entertainment Organisations Joint Committee,[106] and the Stage and Allied Arts Defence League (the 'Defence' was later dropped).

The 'Defence League', established in late 1933, campaigned almost as strongly against tax relief for cinema as in favour of tax relief for theatre. Its leaders were Walter Payne and Geoffrey Whitworth: Payne coming from commercial West

End theatre, Whitworth the founder of the British Drama League, editor of *Drama*, leader of the campaign for a National Theatre, and among Alfred Wareing's most formidable adversaries.[107] Whitworth set out the Defence League's aims in *The Spectator* in February 1934,[108] focusing on the industry's economics. The marginal cost of live performance was far higher than that of cinema, and the duty caused theatres to close. The League sought to redress the balance:

> ... to establish the right to fiscal preference for the play and the concert, the variety show and the circus, over all mechanical forms of entertainment. In short, wherever the human element predominates in an artistic performance... the present entertainments tax of approximately one-sixth of gross receipts... should be remitted if not totally abolished.

Writing before the Vic-Wells' tax exemption, Whitworth did not emphasize the arts' educational value; this 'would be a case for special pleading and would surely be unnecessary in view of the theatre's manifest claims on the solid ground of orthodox finance and common equity'. There were strong tactical reasons for this approach. The 'partly educational' exemption would benefit only not-for-profit organizations, while Payne's and Whitworth's League was a far broader coalition: '... almost without exception every organisation and Trade Union concerned in the presentation of Musical (including Orchestral Concerts and Opera), Dramatic and Variety entertainments throughout Great Britain',[109] ranging from the Musicians' Union to the League of British Dramatists to the Association of Circus Proprietors.[110]

The League's President was Lord Lytton, a role which, as already noted, may have conflicted with that of chairing the Vic-Wells. The League corresponded frequently with Neville Chamberlain and Sir John Simon, successive Chancellors of the Exchequer, offering new examples to bolster old arguments about the economic plight of live theatre and music. In 1934 Walter Payne pointed out to Chamberlain:

> ... the enormous increase in the number of Wireless Licences from which the Government derives a substantial revenue... and... the Dog Tracks with the mechanical hare combined with the great attraction of betting.... [which] have attracted millions of persons who formerly patronised the more popular places of entertainment. Attendances at Dog Races... increased from 5 millions to 17 millions in 3 years.[111]

Throughout 1934 such arguments continued to meet with refusal by the government, but behind the scenes the view was softening. As early as February 1934 Chamberlain requested that Customs and Excise consider:

The question of some relief from the Entertainments Tax charged for the cheapest seats. (With special reference to the burden of the change as it falls on sideshows and the like).

The question of some relief from the tax as it affects theatres. (Vide the recent agitation...

And what would the cost be? [*sic*][112]

His civil servants acknowledged the growing agitation in and beyond Parliament for a tax cut for live performances, but advised that 'first consideration should be given to a restoration of the duty to the pre-1931 level [that is, removing the tax imposed then on the cheapest seats; this would benefit mainly cinema-goers]'.[113] When a Backbench amendment to this effect was tabled to the 1934 Finance Bill, Payne wrote to Chamberlain that this 'could only... [cause] further and most serious injury to the interests which our League represents'.[114] The amendment was withdrawn, and the government maintained its public position into 1935. Meanwhile Customs continued to analyse changes to the duty, including (for no obvious purpose or benefit) mapping its yield against average figures for unemployment, rainfall and hours of sunshine.[115]

The Vic-Wells' tax exemption provided a further argument for campaigners before the 1935 Budget. Payne wrote to Chamberlain that it served 'to increase the grave anomaly and injustice' suffered by commercial providers of theatre and live music. They not only had to pay the tax, but now also faced unfair competition from the newly tax-exempt not-for-profit sector.[116] Customs dismissed this. All that had happened 'was that a legal opinion had somewhat modified, in favour of the taxpayer, the previous interpretation of a provision... in force since the entertainments duty was imposed....'[117] But Chamberlain was sympathetic, asking Customs for 'a draft of the kind of Clause that would be necessary to give effect to the League's requests'.[118]

Submitting the draft clause, Sir Evelyn Murray of Customs and Excise made his views clear: '...once any breach is made in the fundamental principle... that it is a tax on the patrons of all entertainments, without regard to the particular type of entertainment... it is difficult to find a satisfactory dividing line.'[119] He elaborated the point to Chamberlain's Private Secretary:[120] it would favour middle-class theatre-goers over working-class cinema-goers, and 'will exempt many entertainments... of the lowest calibre while maintaining the tax on much more wholesome amusements in the region of sport. Why should "Crazy nights in Clacton" escape while cricket matches are taxed?' He wondered whether a tax reduction for stage plays alone might be preferable; but this would not meet the League's aims, and 'could only be defended as a specific measure to meet the plea ad misericordium of a deserving and hard hit industry'.

In the 1935 Budget Chamberlain tried to please everyone. He removed the tax on cheap seats for all performances, including cinema, and reduced it on higher-priced theatre and live music performances. In his Budget speech he explained the changes with a rather confusing combined reference to Snowden re-imposing the duty on cheap seats in 1931 and the problems of those putting on live performances:

> [Snowden had] desired to give an opportunity to all sections of the community to contribute towards the nation's needs... [but] the intentions of the author have not been altogether fulfilled. Particularly the duty on the cheaper seats in the cinema houses and that on those entertainments in which living performers have been putting up a very gallant struggle for survival against the forces of mechanical performances, seems to have fallen largely on the proprietors rather than on the public.[121]

Removing the duty on tickets costing up to 6d would lose the government £2,300,000 a year in tax revenue; reducing the duty on tickets for live performances, but not sports events, costing more than 6d would lose the government £400,000 a year. Chamberlain was confident that those who put on live music and drama 'will not fail to appreciate the importance of a change which, for the first time, differentiates between this kind of performance and another, and differentiates in their favour'.

They did appreciate it, but their supporters in Parliament attempted immediately to extend the concession. An amendment to the 1935 Finance Bill would have removed the tax on tickets for live performances costing up to a shilling. Chamberlain supported the principle, congratulated himself on the concession already made to assist live music and theatre, and opposed the amendment; it was heavily defeated.[122] Another amendment, to provide additional tax relief where musicians and actors were involved together in stage performances, was withdrawn before it could suffer a similar fate, though Chamberlain again expressed sympathy with the principle.[123] The previous pattern was resumed: lobbying by the Stage and Allied Arts League (now without the 'Defence') and member organizations; sympathy from the Chancellor; no consequent action in the Budget speech; and clauses to reduce or end the tax tabled by sympathetic MPs during the passage of the Finance Bill, and withdrawn or voted down.

Geoffrey Whitworth's role as (among many other things) editor of *Drama* magazine allowed him to use the magazine as a mouthpiece for the Stage and

Allied Arts League. Chapters 4 and 5 discussed how *Drama* promoted the abolition of Entertainments Duty above gaining subsidy. In the late 1930s *Drama* repeatedly returned to the subject. Its November 1936 editorial[124] made Wycherley's Restoration comedy *The Country Wife* a focus of discontent. Performances of the play at the Old Vic were tax-exempt on 'partly educational' grounds, despite *Drama*'s view that it 'is not a suitable play for schoolchildren. Twenty years ago it would not have been considered a suitable play for adults either!' A case could be made that it was educational 'to the stage historian or student of manners.... Though we should not have thought that the Authorities at the Custom House were competent... to make this somewhat subtle distinction.' The League, and *Drama* magazine, repeatedly identified alleged anomalies in the 'partly educational' exemption, often suggested that Customs and Excise were unqualified to operate it, and more than once cited *The Country Wife* in this context.

The League lobbied the government mainly in private, but also had a public face. By 1938 its letterhead listed forty-two distinguished Vice-Presidents, though most may have contributed nothing beyond their name. They included the actors Edith Evans and John Gielgud and MPs active in the campaign such as Alfred Denville, though not A P Herbert; also, among other parliamentarians, Clement Attlee and Winston Churchill.[125] And it did indulge, on occasion, in public campaigning. After Malcolm Sargent wrote to *The Times* in June 1937[126] proposing that central government should offer matching funds to encourage local authority subsidy for music, Walter Payne attempted to win him and others to lobby instead for tax cuts for live music: 'If... Dr. Sargent and the many thousands who think as he does will, with strings, brass and wind, accompany (*fortissimo*) the annual prayer addressed by the Stage and Allied Arts League... even the Treasury portals may fall, and assistance in the form of further relief from taxation be secured.'[127]

There was much support in Parliament for the League's position. In 1937 a body called the Parliamentary Stage Committee presented Neville Chamberlain with a 'Memorial' signed by 305 MPs, calling for the duty to be removed from live entertainment.[128] In *'No Fine on Fun'* A P Herbert recalled active pre-war lobbying led by 'a small but enthusiastic band of Members, drawn from all parties.... I made the most indignant speeches.'[129] He believed that Sir John Simon, Chancellor from 1937, 'a much better and greater man than most people ever knew, had a genuine affection for the theatre... and, I am sure, disliked this tax. But for the war, I believe he would have abolished it.'[130] As will be seen, there is evidence to support this view.

In 1937 Herbert tabled an amendment to the Finance Bill to end the duty not immediately but the following year. This would not endanger that year's revenue but would 'compel… the Treasury to take thought'.[131] In the debate on the amendment he said: '… we object to it because it is a tax on the things of the mind, because it is a tax on receipts and not upon profits, and because it is operating against the higher quality of entertainment.'[132] He flattered Simon shamelessly: '… in point of culture and appreciation of the arts, the right hon. Gentleman is not the least among his colleagues. He is a great master of the language,… and with his upbringing and background I am perfectly sure that in his secret soul he cannot persuade himself that this is a good tax.' Concerning tactics, 'Our intention is that he shall be the first Chancellor of the Exchequer to have the great opportunity and honour of saying that this barbarous tax, which has endured for 21 years, shall be by him remodelled and reshaped and made into something better.'

Simon – while flattering Herbert in return – was not swayed. He agreed that Entertainments Duty was a bad tax. But 'Is there a good tax? All taxes, in my view, are evil.'[133] As to where the tax fell: 'I agree that it is a misfortune that you should have an instrument of taxation which hits… the finest and most beautiful examples of art and culture in exactly the same way as it hits very much more vulgar, less elaborate or less well contrived forms of entertainment. But how are you going to do otherwise?'[134] The amendment failed.

Campaigning was still more intense in 1938. Customs' view was that those putting on live entertainment needed no further concessions.[135] Their situation was better than in 1935 due to a general economic upturn and to the 1935 tax cut, 'tantamount to a transfer of £400,000 a year or more from the Exchequer to the pockets of the proprietors, since prices were not reduced in consequence'. Walter Payne accepted that takings had increased, but argued that costs had risen faster and profits were down; more productions were showing a loss caused or made worse by the duty.[136] Customs responded to the Chancellor that such arguments applied equally to any industry subject to indirect taxes.[137] As for Payne's repeated point that the tax had been a wartime emergency measure: 'So also were other taxes… which remain in force. Financial burdens resulting from the war have still to be borne – not to mention the new re-armament programme.' One League argument did apply to Entertainments Duty alone, that the 'partly educational' exemption meant 'the Grand Opera is exempt from duty, while other musical entertainments [promoted by commercial companies], such as concerts, are taxed'. Customs were unimpressed. This was '[simply] the effect of the law as it has stood since 1916.… [The] fact that the Opera is, as the League say, largely a social function is not relevant.'

In March 1938 Sir John Simon and Sir Evelyn Murray received a delegation including Payne, Whitworth, and management and union representatives from theatre, music and variety. The Treasury's transcript of the meeting[138] reveals little new on the Entertainments Duty campaign but contains picturesque details: a digression by Simon about Sarah Siddons' career at the Theatre Royal Bath; a pencilled addition that 'At this point a note was handed to Mr Payne of the result of the Grand National – Battleship, Royal Danieli, Workman'; cultural one-upmanship when Payne used 'a play like "The Country Wife" of Congreve' to support his view that the 'partly educational' exemption was anomalous, with the pencilled comment: 'He means Wycherley, of course!' Simon professed his love for the theatre and promised to consider the delegation's arguments.

But there was no action in the 1938 Budget. During the passage of the Finance Bill A P Herbert repeated the tactic of tabling an amendment to abolish the tax the following year. This was supported by all speakers apart from Simon. The Conservative Ralph Assheton described Simon as 'a man of culture, a man of learning and intellect and devoted to the arts. . . . if such a man continues to tax the theatre and does not tax betting, I confess that I shall find it difficult to understand the workings of his mind'.[139] His colleague Walter Higgs noted that although 'Probably I attend the theatre less than any other hon. Member. . . I consider this to be a thoroughly bad tax'.[140] The Labour MP Ellen Wilkinson linked – as so many did – the subjects of tax relief and subsidy, despite the Stage and Allied Arts League's hostility towards the League of Audiences:

> . . . the British Government is the only Government in Europe that taxes the theatre instead of subsidising it. . . . In Norway, Sweden, Denmark, Iceland and Poland, and of course in Russia, enormous subsidies are given. . . . Here, in. . . one of the richest countries in the world. . . we have this vexatious tax. . . . we do not want the Americanisation of the artistic life of our country. It is not only a question of the theatres; where is the reservoir of talent to come from if the living theatre is closed down? It means that the reservoir of talent for our films will be dried up.[141]

Simon's response was partly the mixture as before, sympathy mingled with regretful inaction. But a further pattern was becoming apparent: lobbying on behalf of theatre and live music, continued resistance by Treasury and Customs officials, but a gradual softening of view by the Chancellor of the day. This had been the case with Neville Chamberlain before the 1935 Budget. It was now the case with Sir John Simon in the even more difficult circumstances of 1938 and 1939. In addition to the usual platitudes Simon gave this undertaking:

> I do share a great deal of the feeling against this particular form of tax.... I offer... this assurance: I am willing to make it my business... to examine the working of these taxes, and... I will during the year have them studied from every point of view, recognising, as I do, that there is great force in this argument, especially as applied to the living theatre.[142]

(It is notable that, despite the concessions being about live performances of music as well as drama, all leaders of the campaign were from the theatre world and discussion invariably focused on 'the living theatre'.)

Customs officials met League representatives before the 1939 Budget. The officials' main conclusion was that 'only complete repeal [of the tax] would satisfy the theatre industry'.[143] This was indeed the theme of pre-Budget lobbying. The Parliamentary Stage Committee called for abolition.[144] Separately a delegation to Simon of MPs and theatre impresarios led by the National Liberal MP William Mabane, a parliamentary ally of A P Herbert,[145] was organized, indeed stage-managed. Writing to Simon's office, Mabane set out the deputation's plan: following his opening statement, speeches of two minutes from each of his seven colleagues ('Mr. Alan Herbert from the point of view of the Author.... Mr. Poole on employment in the theatre. Colonel Sandeman Allen on the building of theatres...').[146] He attached a memorandum[147] intended 'to show that... abolition of the Tax will materially improve the position of the living theatre and all those connected with it'. The memorandum was an unusually rigorous examination of the economy of the theatre. It made a quantified case that without the tax, some failed theatres would have survived, some plays would have had longer runs, theatre wages would have been higher and ticket prices lower. It concluded with an argument which may have been generally xenophobic, specifically prejudiced or simply anti-Hollywood: 'In these days when a National culture can easily be lost, a revived theatre would provide resistance to other cultures essentially alien.'

Advising Sir John Simon,[148] Sir Evelyn Murray first wrote about the impossibility of giving tax advantages to sport: '... football, cricket, horse and dog racing, etc.... excite no sympathy – except perhaps cricket. But as you informed the President of the M.C.C. (Major Astor, M.P.) last year, it would be extremely difficult to differentiate in favour of cricket.' The tax on live performance posed greater presentational problems: 'The "living" entertainments... are responsible for most of the opposition to the tax.... the theatres have secured a great deal of sympathy and support in attacking the duty, and it is natural that they should push their attack to the utmost limit.' Ending the tax, however, would not solve live theatre's financial problems, while another tax cut would assist it even less and 'certainly could not be expected to extinguish the annual campaign which the theatre interests conduct for total abolition'. But Murray seemed to accept that he had lost the argument and that Simon intended to reduce the tax on theatre and live music. He advised Simon that 'a scale can be constructed to cost approximately whatever Revenue you are prepared to surrender'.

This was what Simon intended: 'I feel I must make some further concession to the living theatre. Could a scale be constructed to give up about £250,000?'[149] Murray responded that the duty on live performance currently yielded £1.25 million, so such a cut would be substantial.[150] He produced several possible scales, costing between £160,000 and £340,000 a year in lost tax revenue. He made clear his distaste for the exercise: the concession 'is frankly intended to go into the pockets of the proprietors and will not therefore involve any alteration of prices'. If West End theatres were intended to gain the most benefit, the tax cut could be concentrated on the higher priced seats; but then the scale 'would be less symmetrical and more vulnerable to attack from those who would get less of the loot'. As to timing, given the need to print and distribute tax stamps for tickets at the new rate, no change could take effect before July 1939. This would reduce the lost tax revenue in the first year. Delaying the change beyond this would further reduce the short-term loss.

Simon agreed to a delay, but chose one of Murray's more generous options. In his 1939 Budget speech[151] Simon reminded the House that theatre and live music had received tax relief in 1935 and continued:

> The chief difficulty under which the living theatre labours is the rival attraction of the cinema... [but] the Duty does aggravate the disability from which the living theatre suffers.... I propose therefore to give the entertainments in question a further reduction of duty of one penny per admission.... It will cost £190,000 this year and £290,000 in a full year.[152]

The timing was remarkably unpropitious. The following day, Neville Chamberlain announced the introduction of conscription, stating that 'the circumstances in which we are living... cannot possibly be described as peace-time';[153] and the reduction in duty would take effect on 3 September 1939.[154]

A P Herbert was partly grateful: 'I should like, on behalf of many Members in all quarters... who have for many years pressed the case of the living theatre for relief from the Entertainments Duty, to thank the Chancellor for what he has done.'[155] But he was also partly disappointed:

> What the Chancellor has done is to give us one-quarter of what we asked for. The total abolition of the tax would mean a loss of revenue of £1,250,000, and he is

> losing £300,000 in a full year. . . . It would have been a fine thing. . . if at this grave time, when we are compelled to spend these incredible and unprecedented sums on weapons of destruction, he had been able to say, 'We are not pressed so far by that barbarous necessity that we cannot afford to take away altogether what is generally regarded as an undesirable tax upon the things of the mind.'[156]

Herbert was not alone. He recorded in *'No Fine on Fun'* that 'undeterred by this concession, or the talk of war, Mr George Hall (Labour) proposed to abolish the tax on the living theatre. (Note the date, 22 June, 1939.)'[157] Hall's Labour colleague George Benson was particularly grudging: 'It is true that. . . the Chancellor of the Exchequer is proposing to give a concession to the living theatre, but, while we are moderately grateful for that, it must be stressed that the concession is not a very generous one.'[158] Benson's view was that even with this concession the cards were stacked in favour of cinema:

> A 6d. seat. . . on which there is no taxation may be occupied four, five, six, or even more, times during the day. . . . but because the revenue is composed of sixpences not a single penny is paid in taxation. You do not get that sort of thing in the living theatre. . . . it is not true to state that. . . the incidence of taxation upon the seats in the living theatre is lower than in the cinema. It is not. On the contrary, it is very much higher.[159]

In reply, the Financial Secretary to the Treasury, Harry Crookshank, noted that 'This is. . . what almost inevitably occurs on these occasions. When the Chancellor of the Exchequer makes a concession, at once everybody concerned asks why it is not a much bigger one.'[160] The amendment was defeated.

Thus on the day the war broke out, a second reduction came into effect in tax rates on admission to theatre and live music performances, further differentiating them from tax rates for cinema and sports events. Together with the 1935 reduction the total amount of tax foregone in a full year would have been around £700,000.

As a postscript, it should be noted that this use of the conditional is necessary: in the 1940 Budget tax rates rose again, and live theatre and music lost most of their 1939 gains. Alfred Denville claimed that 400 MPs opposed to this rise had been ignored and 'It. . . lowers one's pride when one feels that a large body of Members of this House are treated like school children and are not consulted at all. One realises that there is a war on and that certain taxation must be put on to win that war, but why put it on something that will do more harm than good to the war effort?'[161] In a less than full-hearted endorsement, Herbert noted that Denville 'spluttered valiantly'.[162] Denville's was a lone voice. The new Chancellor,

Sir Kingsley Wood, was able to tell the House of Commons that 'we did consult, confidentially, with a very representative body of the living theatre, the Stage and Allied Arts League.... They... have said, after careful examination, that... the industry would accept the scale and they raised no objection at present in view of national needs.'[163]

## Conclusion: 'Bringing an aesthetic principle into politics'?

During the 1930s theatre and live music enjoyed three substantial relaxations from the full rigour of Entertainments Duty: from 1934, exemption for 'partly educational' performances and productions, widely defined, put on by not-for-profit organizations; and in 1935 and 1939, tax cuts for all theatre and live music performances, treating them more favourably than cinema performances and sports events. The first of these, while strongly campaigned for, resulted from the law's interpretation by the government's own lawyers. The second and third were granted by Neville Chamberlain and Sir John Simon due partly to campaigning and partly to their explicit wish, against officials' advice, to assist the 'living theatre'.

Despite its being in effect forced on the government, many saw the first concession as a decision by government to support the arts. As noted in Chapter 3, *The Sunday Times* argued[164] that when the government exempted the Old Vic and Sadler's Wells from the duty, 'for the first time it brought an aesthetic principle into politics', and that the remission of the tax was 'a form of subsidy'. At the time the government did not see it this way – it was simply bowing to legal necessity. But in his January 1944 letter to Keynes, Sir Archibald Carter, Chairman of Customs and Excise, seemed to accept *The Sunday Times*' view: 'It was more or less by accident, and not of set policy, that section 1(5)(d) of the 1916 Act came to be used to give assistance to music and the drama by means of relief from taxation.'[165] As noted above, he also suggested that CEMA was the appropriate channel for both allocating subsidy and deciding tax exemption cases.

If the 'partly educational' exemption amounted to government financial help for music and drama, as Carter suggested, this help was not only largely involuntary but also of unknown extent. Once the exemption was granted, Customs had no knowledge of or interest in a production's takings, so the amount of tax foregone could not and cannot be assessed. The tax reductions of 1935 and 1939, by contrast, resulted from positive decisions by the Chancellors of the day, who knowingly accepted a loss of tax revenue calculated in advance. As early as 1933 Customs suggested to Neville Chamberlain that 'special relief from the entertainments duty in respect of theatres and music halls would be tantamount to giving them a State subsidy in a disguised form'.[166] This 'subsidy in a disguised form' was substantial: £400,000 a year from 1935 and a further £290,000 a year from 1939 (though the latter turned out to be short-lived). The 1939 concession alone was worth more than the grant to the Arts Council in either of its first two years,[167] while except for special allocations for the Festival of Britain the annual grant to the Arts Council did not exceed £690,000 – the annual combined value of the 1935 and 1939 tax cuts – until 1953.[168]

Thus twice in the 1930s, the second time in the final budget before the outbreak of war, the government used the tax system specifically to help theatre and live music, a policy move more expensive in terms of lost revenue than the allocation it was to make to the Arts Council in any year before the 1950s. The point was not lost on *The Musical Times*. In May 1939 it urged its readers to support the League of Audiences' Music and Drama Bill, pointing out to those who doubted that the government could find money for the arts that it had just found £300,000 a year in the form of tax cuts.[169]

Alfred Wareing's League and John Christie's 'Council of Power' demonstrated that the quest for government financial support of the arts was active and widespread in the 1930s. Their history also undermines the view that government financial support for theatre and live music was almost inconceivable before the war. The 1930s campaign against Entertainments Duty provides even stronger, indeed conclusive, evidence to this effect. Its successes, Chamberlain's and Simon's tax cuts, are proof that the government was not only sympathetic to live music and theatre, but was ready to provide them, and did provide them, with substantial financial support in this period of rearmament and approaching war.

## Notes

1 *Sunday Times*, 7/4/35.

2 National Archives file CUST153/1: Entertainments Duty Volume 1: Historical Memoranda 1916–1938 (hereafter 'CUST153/1'), p64; first page of undated (late 1930s) Customs and Excise (hereafter 'C&E') note on the history of the tax.

3 London: Methuen, 1957; hereafter 'Herbert'.

4 Quoted in Herbert, p12.

5 Ibid., p13.
6 Herbert, pp15–16.
7 National Archives file CUST153/2: 'Entertainments Duty Volume 2: Questions of Policy 1915 to 1943' (hereafter 'CUST153/2'), pp1, 1A and 2, C&E paper 7/12/15, 'Suggested Taxation of Amusements'.
8 *The Times*, 13/4/16, p10: report of first day of the Bill's Committee stage.
9 CUST153/1, p226, undated (but 1939) C&E briefing note to the Chancellor of the Exchequer.
10 CUST153/2, p11, C&E briefing note, 20/3/16.
11 CUST153/1, p5, 'Mr Reade's History of the Entertainments Duty 1916–1925' (hereafter 'Reade'); Reade's history runs to 63 pages.
12 Ibid.
13 National Archives file ED10/210, for instance, deals solely with applications for tax exemption for celebrations connected with the 1937 coronation.
14 Finance (New Duties) Act 1916, s1(5).
15 Ibid.
16 *The Times*, 20/4/16, p7.
17 Ibid., 18/4/16, p10.
18 Ibid., 6/4/16, p9.
19 HC Deb 30/6/38, vol 337, col 2242.
20 HC Deb 2/7/17, vol 95, col 796.
21 Ibid., cols 794–818.
22 Ibid., col 810.
23 CUST153/2, p20, Carson-Bonar Law, 17/12/17.
24 Ibid., p21.
25 Ibid., p117, (unsigned) C&E briefing for the 1923 Budget, 9/6/23.
26 Ibid., p138.
27 Ibid., p225, 1925 pre-Budget briefing by Chairman of C&E to Winston Churchill.
28 CUST153/1, p41, Reade.
29 Ibid.
30 Ibid.
31 HC Deb 16/6/25, vol 185, cols 376–7.
32 London: HMSO, 1926.
33 Ibid., pp36–41.
34 London: Michael Joseph, 1936; see also Chapter 4, p44.
35 Ibid., p244.
36 CUST153/1, p312, minute from 'A.J.D.' (not otherwise identified) to 'Mr Grylls' and Sir Francis Floud, 25/6/29.
37 Ibid., p313.
38 13/12/30, p13.

39 National Archives file CUST153/5: Entertainments Duty Volume 5: The Living Theatre 1932 to 1940 (hereafter 'CUST153/5'), p8, C&E briefing to Financial Secretary to the Treasury, 21/3/32.
40 HC Deb 2/12/30, vol 245, col 1980.
41 HC Deb 28/7/31, vol 255, col 2107, question by Charles Williams MP.
42 CUST153/5, pp3–4, Payne-Chamberlain, 2/3/32.
43 Ibid., p6, Payne-Chamberlain, 15/3/32.
44 See Chapters 3 and 5. The League of Audiences was formed two years later.
45 CUST153/5, p10, C&E briefing to Walter Elliot, 21/3/32.
46 Ibid., p13, Denville-Chamberlain, 10/12/32.
47 Ibid., p15, Chamberlain-Denville, 20/12/32.
48 Ibid., p14.
49 11/3/33.
50 CUST153/5, p16, Chantrey, Button and Co-Chamberlain, 21/3/33.
51 Ibid., p27, C&E briefing for Chamberlain, 25/3/33.
52 Ibid., pp30–1, C&E briefing 29/3/33.
53 Ibid.
54 Ibid., pp41–4, Payne etc-Chamberlain, 8/7/33.
55 CUST153/5, pp47–50, briefing 'ADO'-Ferguson, July 1933.
56 The memorandum is quoted in National Archives file CUST49/1749: 'Entertainments Duty: Historical Survey of the Partly Educational Exception' (hereafter 'CUST49/1749'), briefing paper of 9/5/34: 'Entertainments provided for partly educational purposes'.
57 HC Deb 14/7/37, vol 326, cols 1339–40.
58 CUST49/1749, Law Officers' opinion, 18/5/17.
59 CUST153/1, pp46–7, Reade.
60 17/4/26, p13.
61 *The Drama in Adult Education*, p9.
62 nationaltheatre.org.uk/about-the-national-theatre/history, eno.org/about/history-of-eno/, and roh.org.uk/about/the-royal-ballet/history, respectively; all accessed 12 March 2017.
63 *The Drama in Adult Education*, para 81.
64 CUST49/1749, pp11–13.
65 National Archives file CUST49/1510: 'The Earl of Lytton KG. The Old Vic and Sadler's Wells Theatres Application for Exemption from Entertainments Duty' (hereafter 'CUST49/1510'), Lytton-The Secretary, C&E, 15/5/33.
66 Ibid., illegibly initialled manuscript minute, 18/5/33.
67 Ibid., undated.
68 Ibid., Rowe-Chamberlain, 31/5/33.
69 Ibid., [illegible]-D Fergusson (Chamberlain's private secretary), 19/6/33.

70 Ibid., manuscript note by Fergusson on briefing.
71 Ibid., Flynn (C&E)-Lytton, 13/7/33.
72 Ibid., Lytton-Chamberlain, 18/7/33.
73 Ibid., [illegible]-Wilson Smith, 25/7/33, and Chamberlain-Lytton, 28/7/33.
74 Ibid., Lytton-Chamberlain, 13/3/34.
75 Ibid., Chamberlain-Lytton, 23/4/34.
76 CUST49/1749, 9/5/34, p6.
77 Ibid., p3.
78 Ibid., p6.
79 Ibid., pp6–10.
80 CUST49/1510, note of meeting of 24/5/34, for all quotations in this and the following paragraph.
81 Ibid., Colville-C&E Solicitor, 1/6/34.
82 Ibid., Murray-Chamberlain, 12/6/34.
83 Ibid., 'Royal Victoria Hall and Sadler's Wells Foundations. The Finance (New Duties) Act 1916. Opinion of the Law Officers of the Crown', 20/7/34.
84 Ibid., Murray-Fergusson, 27/7/34.
85 Ibid., Lytton-Murray, 13/8/34.
86 National Archives file CUST49/1728: 'Entertainments Duty: Tests to determine whether entertainments are partly educational in view of Law Officers opinion'. This has two sub-files: 'Entertainments Duty, Finance (New Duties) Act 1916 sec 1(5)(d), "Partly educational" exemption. Board's decisions on various cases' (hereafter 'CUST49/1728/1'); and 'Entertainments Duty, Finance (New Duties) Act 1916 sec 1(5)(d), Opinion of Law Officers' (hereafter 'CUST49/1728/2'). Memo of 1/8/34, signed EWL, in CUST49/1728/2, reporting C&E Board discussion of 27/7/34.
87 Ibid.
88 CUST49/1728/1, ESB, 19/9/34.
89 Ibid., FitzRoy, 20/9/34.
90 For instance *The Observer*, 26/8/34, and *Manchester Guardian*, 25/ and 27/8/34.
91 CUST49/1728/1, ESB 28/9/34, and for the following examples.
92 Ibid., conclusions of C&E Board meeting of 3/10/34, for this and the following quotation.
93 National Archives file ED10/210, Backway-Board of Education, 2/6/37 and Board of Education-Backway, 8/6/37.
94 CUST49/2373, 'Covent Garden English Opera', Treasury (unsigned)-Customs and Excise, 23/2/39.
95 Ibid.
96 CUST49/2790, London Philharmonic Orchestra. The certificate quoted dates from August 1939.
97 *Drama* Vol 15, No 2, p24.

98 Glyndebourne Box 1, Christie-Turner (Treasury), 14/12/36.
99 This is covered in Weingärtner, pp122–7.
100 Ibid., pp121–2.
101 Carter-Keynes, 12/1/44, quoted in Weingärtner, p125.
102 V&A/EL1/7: Minutes of CEMA's 26th meeting, 14/3/44.
103 V&A/EL2/9, Keynes-Carter 12/5/44.
104 *Drama*, Vol 13, No 1, October 1934, p23.
105 CUST153/1, pp15 and 40 respectively, Reade.
106 CUST153/5, p6, Payne-Chamberlain, 15/3/32.
107 See, generally, Chapters 4 and 5.
108 'The Claims of the Living Actor', 16/2/34.
109 CUST153/5, p83, Payne-Chamberlain, 26/2/34.
110 Ibid., p64, the League's draft rules.
111 Ibid., p84, Payne-Chamberlain, 26/2/34.
112 CUST153/2, p403, manuscript note headed 'Note by Chancellor of the Exchequer (sent to Chairman by Sir R. Hopkins) – February 1934'.
113 Ibid., p413, briefing note by E R Forbes, 26/2/34.
114 CUST153/5, p94, Payne-Chamberlain, 1/6/34.
115 CUST153/2, p420, unsigned annex to note dated 10/3/34.
116 CUST153/5, pp96–7, Payne-Chamberlain, 13/11/34.
117 Ibid., p104, C&E briefing for Chamberlain, 4/3/35.
118 Ibid., p110, Murray-Chamberlain, 20/3/35.
119 Ibid., pp113–14.
120 Ibid., pp108–9, Murray-Ferguson, 20/3/35.
121 HC Deb 15/4/35, vol 300, cols 1631–2, and for the following quotation.
122 HC Deb 18/6/35, vol 303, cols 187–95.
123 Ibid., cols 212–20.
124 Vol 5, No 2, p24.
125 National Archives Treasury file T172/1883, 'Deputation Stage and Allied Arts League, 25/3/1938' (hereafter, 'T172/1883'), letterhead on letter Payne-Simon, 28/2/38.
126 23/6/37, p12; see also Chapter 6, p105.
127 *The Times*, 26/6/37, p10.
128 CUST153/5, pp200–1.
129 Herbert, p28.
130 Ibid., p29.
131 Ibid., p30.
132 HC Deb 14/7/37, vol 326, col 1342.
133 Ibid., col 1344.
134 Ibid., cols 1344–5.

135 CUST153/5, pp168–9, C&E briefing for Simon, 31/1/38.
136 Ibid., pp174–6, Payne-Simon, 14/2/38.
137 Ibid., pp183–6, 'WWS'-A J D Winnifrith, 16/2/38.
138 T172/1883, 'Notes of a Delegation to the Chancellor of the Exchequer from the Stage and Allied Arts League'.
139 HC Deb 30/6/38, vol 337, col 2253.
140 Ibid., col 2255.
141 Ibid., cols 2253–4.
142 Ibid., cols 2262–3.
143 CUST153/5, p193, note of meeting with deputation from the Stage and Allied Arts League, 22/2/39.
144 Ibid., pp200–1, Sandeman Allen, Denville and Groves-Simon, 6/3/39.
145 Herbert, p35.
146 CUST153/5, pp203–4, Mabane-Chancellor's Private Secretary.
147 Ibid., pp205–11, memorandum attached to Mabane's letter, for all quotations in this paragraph.
148 Ibid., pp212–14, Murray-Simon, 14/3/39.
149 Ibid., p235, note by Sir John Simon, 31/3/39.
150 Ibid., pp240–2, Murray-Simon, 4/4/39, and for all later quotations in this paragraph.
151 HC Deb 25/4/39, vol 346, cols 975–96.
152 Ibid., col 991.
153 HC Deb 26/4/39, vol 346, col 1155.
154 HC Deb 25/4/39, vol 346, col 991.
155 Ibid., col 1022.
156 Ibid., col 1023.
157 Herbert, p38.
158 HC Deb 22/6/39, vol 348, col 2550.
159 Ibid., cols 2251–2.
160 Ibid., col 2260.
161 HC Deb 8/8/40, vol 364, col 470.
162 Herbert, p40.
163 HC Deb 8/8/40, vol 364, col 473.
164 7/4/35.
165 Carter-Keynes, 12/1/44, quoted in Weingärtner, p125.
166 CUST153/5, pp30–1, C&E briefing, 29/3/33.
167 See ACGB First and Second Annual Reports (London: 1946 and 1947, respectively).
168 ACGB Ninth Annual Report 1953–1954 (London: 1954), p59.
169 May 1939, pp374; see also Chapter 5, p79.

10

# Restoring the Picture

## The Picture Revealed

In October 1934 the *Birmingham Mail* asserted: '. . . the "League of Audiences" is the latest alias and device of that active group of persons who are anxious to put music and the drama on the rates or taxes.'[1] This claim guides us into the lost story revealed in earlier chapters of this book. These are some of the main elements of that story.

Contrary to assertions at the time and since, theatre and live classical music in the 1930s were in a healthy condition. The evidence suggests that cinema had not damaged the appeal of live theatre, while live classical music was buoyant, largely due to the gramophone and the BBC. Recording and broadcasting meant that, for the first time in history, classical music was widely available. But the impact went beyond this – the new availability also increased the public's appetite for live music. The BBC, largely responsible for creating this demand, also helped satisfy it. It established several orchestras during the 1930s and, through paying for the broadcast of live events, subsidized live performances by other musicians. It is unlikely, for example, that Sir Thomas Beecham's London Philharmonic Orchestra, founded in 1932, could have survived without fees from the BBC and royalties from gramophone records.

Nevertheless, Beecham was among many writers, composers, performers, politicians and senior clerics who were deeply suspicious of the effects on audiences of the 'mechanized arts' of film, recording and broadcasting. The campaign for state subsidy by the League of Audiences was driven largely by this 'fear of the machine'.

The fear took several forms: Beecham ranting against the BBC's 'monstrous monopoly of the air';[2] the reactionary extremism of the playwright and critic St John Ervine: '. . . we are in grave danger of rearing up a machine-maddened people who have lost their sight and their hearing and the use of their hands, and have no taste. . .';[3] the anti-authoritarianism of the actor-manager Lena Ashwell:

'It is an age of Producer-Directors: Stalin at Moscow, Mussolini in Rome, Hitler in Berlin, conducting a mass-mind and using such instruments as death or ruin as penalties for independent thought or independent action';[4] and the moral crusade of William Temple, Archbishop of York, against the 'Peril to Whole Spiritual Life'[5] posed by the mechanized arts. For all of them, state subsidy of live music and theatre was an essential weapon against the 'devouring onrush of mechanical amusement'.[6]

The influence of the campaign waged by the League of Audiences is confirmed not only by its distinguished supporters and the weight of positive press coverage it received, but also by its opponents. T S Eliot's attack on the League, in his magazine *The Criterion* in 1938,[7] illustrates its significance – 'an organization from which in the past I have received leaflets which I fear I have treated with inadequate attention'. For if the League prevailed, according to Eliot, 'Such confusion will ensue that in time there will be a call for a 'dictator of the arts'. . . to put things to rights. . . . The more the State takes over, the less will be the private initiative.'

For many reasons – lack of finance, internecine squabbles within the arts community, the feeling that, as war approached, government money could not be diverted in this way – the League did not, by 1939, achieve subsidy for live music and theatre. But alongside its significance in the 1930s, it had two major legacies. Many future leading figures of CEMA and the Arts Council, senior staff and council members, learnt their trade as League activists in the 1930s. And the structure proposed by the League – a body at arm's length from the state, independently allocating funds provided by the Treasury – was that adopted by the government for both CEMA and the Arts Council. The League's supporters saw this as no coincidence. The playwright James Bridie, who became Chairman of the Scottish Committees of both CEMA and the Arts Council, wrote of Alfred Wareing, the League's founder, that 'there is no doubt that he is its [the Arts Council's] "onlie begetter". The Arts Council rests on his dreams, on his hard work, and on his martyrdom.'[8] And the ex-Cabinet Minister Walter Elliot wrote that Wareing, who died in 1942, 'battered away at these enormous barriers. All the barriers broke up. . . others walked through to enter into the kingdom. Wareing did not go through. . . . Such is the reward of prophets. . . .'[9]

But Wareing has been wholly forgotten.

Once CEMA and then the Arts Council were founded, they faced a dilemma both unresolved and, for decades, imperfectly concealed behind the often-repeated phrase 'the best for the most': how to choose, with limited resources, between 'the best' and 'the most'. This dilemma, too, was not new. It was discussed at length during John Christie's 1938 Glyndebourne conferences, which launched his 'Council of Power'/National Council of Music. So also were other issues which have persisted for much of the Arts Council's history, such as the balance between support for professional and amateur arts and artists. Christie was clear where he stood, as was John Maynard Keynes when Chairman of CEMA and of the Arts Council: both were emphatically on the side of (as Christie put it) the 'good stuff' rather than 'the rubbish', raising standards rather than increasing availability, supporting professionals rather than amateurs.

By 1939 Christie too had failed to persuade the government to fund his cause. Nonetheless, the government not only showed that it was sympathetic to the principle of supporting live music and theatre financially, but it had put the principle into practice. Chancellors of the Exchequer Neville Chamberlain and Sir John Simon, in 1935 and 1939 respectively, cut Entertainments Duty on live performances in order to help theatre in particular respond to the challenge of cinema. The government came to see these tax cuts, and exemption from Entertainments Duty for 'partly educational' performances of theatre and music, as equivalent to subsidy. The reductions were substantial: the consequent annual budgeted loss of revenue was greater than the annual grant given to CEMA or the Arts Council in any year before the 1950s.

Meanwhile, John Christie continued into wartime his campaign for subsidy to be channelled via his proposed National Council of Music. The campaign was wholly separate from CEMA – indeed, it disregarded it entirely. The many distinguished supporters Christie gathered during the war, including CEMA's Deputy Chairman Sir Kenneth Clark, saw no overlap or conflict between CEMA and Christie's council. For them, CEMA was a wartime expedient of no long-term significance.

Then, when Rab Butler, as President of the Board of Education, his civil servants and Keynes began to plan what became the Arts Council, one of their spurs to action was the desire to pre-empt Christie. As Sir Robert Wood of the Board of Education wrote to Tom Jones, one of the guiding forces behind CEMA, as early as September 1941: '. . . there are various stirrings of the waters, e.g. John Christie with his proposed National Council of Music, but I am not at all sure that these stirrings will always produce waters of healing, and it behoves us, perhaps, to be thinking ahead a bit.'[10] This combination of wary respect for and suspicion of Christie soon evolved into outright opposition and ridicule, to the point where Mary Glasgow, Secretary of CEMA and later Secretary-General of the Arts Council, could write to Wood in 1942, with no apparent need to explain or expand the reference, that 'The Christie persecution has extended to Sir Stafford Cripps'.[11] Christie became all too aware of their attitude: 'Chairman Keynes... refuses to see me. Jacques [CEMA's head of music] a second class musician & Miss Glasgow a civil servant and school inspector. All they do is spread mediocrity.... It is depressing.'[12] Thus Christie's initiative became as forgotten as Alfred Wareing's League of Audiences and the campaign against Entertainments Duty – three important movements quite overlooked in histories of the state and the arts in Britain.

## Completing the Picture

Earlier chapters have explored these three movements in detail. But there are other aspects of the relationship between arts and government in 1930s Britain which have only been touched upon. Three in particular reinforce the point that this relationship was richer and more complex than generally depicted.

The first is the role of the BBC as a funder of the arts. Historians of arts subsidy have rarely considered the link between subsidy and the 'the greatest music making machine... that has ever existed', as Arthur Bliss described the BBC in 1932.[13] In his 1945 radio talk marking the foundation of the Arts Council, Keynes acknowledged one of the BBC's roles:

> Our war-time experience has led us already to one clear discovery: the unsatisfied demand and the enormous public for serious and fine entertainment. This certainly did not exist a few years ago. I do not believe that it is merely a wartime phenomenon. I fancy that the B.B.C. has played a big part, the predominant part, in creating this public demand....[14]

This was a reasonably generous tribute. But it missed the point that from the 1920s, the BBC not only created demand for live classical music but was largely responsible for supplying it – for maintaining the health of the classical music industry.[15] Writing in 1936 for the BBC magazine *The Listener*, Keynes ignored what the BBC had achieved in this respect. Indeed, he suggested that the government's lack of vision had prevented the corporation from becoming a major patron of the arts:

> ...instead of its [the BBC's] receiving large subsidies from the state as one would expect, an important proportion of the ten shillingses that the public contribute is withheld from it as a contribution to general taxes. This was a new and difficult business... capable of revolutionising the relation of the state to the

> arts of public entertainment. . . . Yet, even in its earliest and most precarious days, we considered it a proper object of taxation.[16]

Keynes saw this as 'only the extreme example of the general principle that we penalise music, opera, all the arts of the theatre with a heavy, indeed a crushing, tax'.[17] Given his view of the BBC and his failure to acknowledge the 1930s campaigns for subsidy, it is not surprising that Keynes presented the arrival of CEMA and then the Arts Council as a break with the past rather than continuity: 'I do not believe it is yet realised what an important thing has happened. State patronage of the arts has crept in. It has happened in a very English, informal, unostentatious way – half baked if you like.'[18]

Other commentators recognized that the BBC was potentially or actually a state institution, and that by the 1930s it was a major and well-established 'state patron of the arts'. In the *Daily Sketch* in 1938 'Candidus' supported the League of Audiences' campaign for subsidy partly on the grounds that 'the grievance of music and drama would not be so grievous but for the rise of wireless entertainment, [which]... enables the Government to say that its patronage of the arts is not confined to pictures'.[19] And some commentators went beyond this, seeing the BBC as the harbinger, and weapon, of an authoritarian state. Thus 'Scrutator' wrote in the *Sunday Times* in 1935: 'For the first time, the State set up in the business of entertainment. . . . It made a monopoly of arts and pleasures. . . . it risked creating a tyranny all the more monstrous and dangerous because it was exercised over men's minds'[20] – echoing Beecham's 'monstrous monopoly of the air'. But historians of arts funding have followed Keynes in treating the BBC as largely irrelevant to their subject.

Funding of the arts by local government also deserves attention; research into this has been patchy at best. Concerning music, while a number of local councils supported local orchestras or concert seasons financially in the 1930s,[21] there is no account of its scale across the country, the forms it took or what motivated the councils involved. Similarly, concerning theatre, little attention has been paid to the extent of support by London boroughs, to cite just one example. In *Myself A Player* Lena Ashwell, who had provided touring theatre for troops in World War I, described how collaboration with London boroughs enabled her to carry on similar work in peacetime:

> Major [Clement] Attlee, Mayor of Stepney and Chairman of the Labour Mayors, saw our work. A meeting was held to discuss the project of performances at the Town Halls or the Baths of the boroughs of Greater London. It was agreed that the letting should be at a nominal fee,. . . [and] that our advertisements should go out with the rates demands. . . .[22]

Without a clearer picture of local government's relationship with live music and theatre before the war, an important strand is missing from the history of the state and the arts in Britain.

The same can be said of a third area, the 1930s campaign for a National Theatre. This claim may be surprising – much has been written about the history of the National Theatre. What is missing, however, is the story from the government's point of view. The assumption, implicit or explicit, has been that, in Jörn Weingärtner's words, 'the government only supported the National Theatre so long as no claim for money from the Treasury was staked'.[23] The record of a Cabinet discussion in 1937 suggests that this may not have been the case.

In a Cabinet memo of March that year[24] Earl Stanhope, First Commissioner of Works, raised the issue of a vacant plot in South Kensington bought by the Office of Works in 1912 as a new site for the Royal College of Art but no longer needed for that purpose. Stanhope planned to sell the plot to the highest bidder, but then 'I was approached – and I understand that the Prime Minister and others of my colleagues have also been approached – by parties interested in the scheme for the provision of a National Theatre'. They sought to buy the site by private negotiation with the Office of Works rather than through open tender.

Stanhope recommended refusal: '. . . I am primarily concerned to obtain the best possible return for the Exchequer for a site which is no longer required for Government purposes. . . .' But he added that not only did he have 'I must confess, every sympathy with the desire to establish a National Theatre', but that he supported the principle of subsidizing the project. If the National Theatre committee had shown that government assistance would make their plan feasible, 'I should, even at a time like this, have suggested that a subsidy was justifiable. But I should still have felt that a direct cash subsidy was the proper method', rather than the uncommercial purchase arrangement proposed. In the subsequent Cabinet discussion[25] Stanhope's approach was agreed. On the more general issue, 'No decision was asked for or taken on the principle of a National Theatre... [and] the comment was made that this was not a time for suggesting a subsidy of this kind. . . . [but] There was general agreement that if a subsidy was ever to be given towards the establishment of a National Theatre, it should be a direct subsidy. . . .'[26]

Thus the usual presentation of government attitudes in the 1930s to theatre and live music – indifference in general and hostility on the specific issue of subsidy – may be as misleading in relation to the National Theatre project as to the matters discussed in detail in this book; certainly, the subject deserves fuller research.

Turning to wartime, despite the attention CEMA has received, substantial gaps remain. Most writing about CEMA has an institutional bias. There has been exhaustive coverage of CEMA's policies and practice, and of its relations with the Board of Education and the Treasury. What is lacking are broader perspectives on CEMA. This book's exploration of John Christie's wartime work has shown how he and his associates viewed CEMA – as temporary, short on strategic vision and generally inadequate. But Christie's views on CEMA were clearly not typical, even if they seem to have been shared by his colleagues on the NCM project. Little has been published about how CEMA was regarded at the time not just within government or by its own staff and council, but by theatre and concert-goers, those working in these industries and the general public. Was it seen as marking a new relationship between the state and the arts or as fulfilling only a limited wartime role? Writers about CEMA have mainly taken the former view. More work is needed to assess this.

A related question is how much CEMA contributed to the growing public appetite for live classical music and theatre, an issue touched on in the context of the BBC's role. Keynes' uncharacteristically modest view, quoted above, was that the BBC was more important in this respect. Writing after the war, Mary Glasgow, by then Arts Council Secretary-General, agreed:

> The effect of radio on literature and drama has been considerable, but the most important success has been in the influence of broadcasting on music. When, during the war, concerts were taken by C.E.M.A. to unlikely audiences in remote districts and by E.N.S.A. to the armed forces, it was discovered that a large and genuine audience for music existed.[27]

Some later commentators, however, have suggested that CEMA had a more important role in increasing public demand for the arts. Janet Minihan wrote that CEMA 'helped to create an environment in which the arts figured regularly, sometimes even prominently, in community life'.[28] Jörn Weingärtner went further. The subtitle of his history of CEMA is a model of overstatement: *Britain and the Shaping of National Morale in World War II*. But one notable contemporary observer, at least, demonstrated by omission that he was less impressed. In two of his BBC 'Postscripts' talks in 1940, J B Priestley made the case for state support for the arts. But CEMA formed no part of his vision. In August he argued that live music and theatre of all types should be widely available in wartime:

> Let us by all means have four young women in green silk playing 'Oh Johnny, Oh Johnny', but at the same time let's have the great symphony orchestras pealing out the noblest music, night after night, not for a fortunate and privileged few, but for

> all the people who long for such music. Let's have comedians in the canteens, but at the same time let's have productions of great plays in our theatres. . . .[29]

He returned to the theme in October: 'This winter, here in Lancashire, everything from the Halle Orchestra pealing out the finale of Brahms's Fourth Symphony, to a bit of clog dancing should be in full swing.'[30] Both talks argued that culture should be more democratic and less haphazard. Thus, in October: '. . . some official assistance will soon be urgently needed to make certain that. . . gaiety has some communal outlet; in other words, recreation and entertainment should be planned and organised. . . .' For Priestley, wartime dangers made this need more urgent: 'The gayer and richer the life we have to defend, the more anxious we shall be to defend it. Noble words finely spoken, great music, all the treasures of art, laughter and lights, and song, these mustn't be banished but should be given a greater place than ever in our lives.'

If CEMA had been the force that Minihan and Weingärtner suggest, it would surely have had a central role, or at least some role, in Priestley's thinking. It received not a single mention in either talk. By contrast, Priestley expressed his support for 'Mr. Basil Dean. . . and his Ensa organisation.'[31] Clearly a single commentator, even one as influential as Priestley in 1940, may not have reflected public opinion. Perhaps public perceptions changed once Keynes became Chairman of CEMA. But as noted above, those who have written about CEMA have generally relied on official sources. It would be rash to assume that CEMA was regarded similarly in the country at large. Research is lacking into the question whether, and if so when and how, CEMA came to be seen outside official circles as an important vehicle for making 'high culture' widely available.

Despite its date Priestley's polemic does not support those who believe that public funding of the arts became salient only on the outbreak of war. Priestley himself was a strong pre-war campaigner for subsidy.[32] And his argument in 1940 was not that the war had created a new obligation on the government to support music and drama, but that it had made it more difficult for the government to ignore a pre-existing obligation: 'It may be possible yet, even while we struggle and endure. . . to achieve what's *long been overdue* in this Island. . . . No burden, it seems, is too great for the people. Then there can't be too rich and great a reward for the people.'[33]

* * *

The focus of this book has been three forgotten stories: Alfred Wareing's League of Audiences, John Christie's 'Council of Power'/National Council of Music, and the theatre industry's campaign against Entertainments Duty. Among the pleasures of the research has been exploring and getting to know such personalities as Wareing and Christie. This book has aimed to deepen understanding of some aspects of British cultural, social and political history in the 1930s and early 1940s. It has uncovered a picture of cultural policy before and during the Second World War which has been long neglected, then forgotten and even denied. The brief consideration this chapter has given to several other areas suggests that the picture is still by no means complete. There is more to learn about this fascinating and crucial period in the history of the relationship between the state and the arts in Britain.

## Notes

1 *Birmingham Mail*, 12/10/34.
2 Quoted in W R Anderson: 'Wireless Notes', *Musical Times*, November 1934, pp990–1.
3 *The Observer*, 22/9/35.
4 Lena Ashwell: *Myself a Player* (London: Michael Joseph, 1936), p260.
5 *Daily Telegraph*, 3/2/38.
6 *Daily Telegraph*, 5/12/36.
7 'A Commentary', *The Criterion*, March 1938, pp478–85, for the following two quotations.
8 Isaac, px.
9 Ibid., pxiii.
10 V&A/EL2/4, Wood-Jones, 27/9/41.
11 NA ED136/188B, Glasgow-Wood, 20/6/42.
12 Glyndebourne 5/2, John Christie-Audrey Christie, 1/6/42.
13 'What Broadcasting has done for Music', *The Listener*, 16/11/32; reprinted in Gregory Roscow (ed): *Bliss on Music: Selected Writings of Arthur Bliss 1920–1975* (Oxford: OUP, 1991), p62.
14 'The Arts Council: Its Policy and Hopes', reprinted in *The Listener*, 12/7/45.
15 See above and Chapter 2.
16 'Art and the State', *The Listener*, 26/8/36, reprinted in Moggridge, Donald (ed): *The Collected Writings of John Maynard Keynes Volume XXVIII: Social, Political and Literary Writings* (London: Macmillan/Cambridge University Press/Royal Economic Society, 1982), p345.
17 Ibid.
18 'The Arts Council: Its Policy and Hopes'.
19 14/2/38.

20 7/4/35.
21 See, for instance, Simon Frith, Matt Brennan. Martin Cloonan and Emma Webster: *The History of Live Music in Britain, Volume 1: 1950–67* (Abingdon and New York: Routledge, 2016 [originally published 2013]), pp41–4.
22 Ashwell, pp238–9.
23 Weingärtner, p49.
24 NA CAB/24/268, 'Proposed Site for National Theatre', memo dated 5/3/37, and for the four following quotations.
25 CAB/23/67 – minutes of Cabinet meeting of 10/3/37.
26 Ibid., p22. Historians of the National Theatre have not cited this episode. See for instance John Elsom and Nicholas Tomalin: *The History of the National Theatre* (London: Jonathan Cape, 1978) and Daniel Rosenthal: *The National Theatre Story* (London: Oberon Books, 2013).
27 B Ifor Evans and Mary Glasgow: *The Arts in England* (London: The Falcon Press, 1949), p16.
28 *The Nationalization of Culture* (London: Hamish Hamilton, 1977), p225.
29 J B Priestley: *Postscripts* (London: William Heinemann, 1940), p53 (broadcast 11/8/40).
30 Ibid., p93 (broadcast 13/10/40), and for the following two quotations.
31 Ibid., p51.
32 See Chapter 3, pp30–1.
33 *Postscripts*, p53; emphasis added.

# Bibliography

## Primary Sources

### (a) Archives

Individual files and documents are specified in the text. The following list sets out the archive and collection in which each is located.

**Victoria and Albert Museum Theatre and Performance Archive**
League of Audiences papers
Council for the Encouragement of Music and the Arts papers
Arts Council papers

**Glyndebourne Archive**
John Christie papers, primarily those files relating to the 'Council of Power'/National Council of Music and those containing Christie's wartime correspondence with his wife

**BBC Archives**

Papers relating to the League of Audiences

**Lambeth Palace Library**
The papers of Cosmo Lang when Archbishop of Canterbury

**National Archives**
HM Treasury files
HM Customs and Excise files
Board of Education files

**East Sussex Record Office (The Keep)/University of Sussex Library Special Collections**
Benn Wolfe Levy papers

**Senate House Library Special Collection**
Annotated copy of Winifred Isaac's biography of Alfred Wareing

**Online archives**
bbc.co.uk
hansard.parliament.uk
nationalarchives.gov.uk

## (b) Newspapers and Periodicals

Individual references are specified in the text. The following list is of the newspapers and periodicals where the news reports and articles cited are to be found.

### *(i) English/British National Newspapers*

*Daily Herald*
*Daily Sketch*
*Daily Telegraph*
*Evening News*
*Manchester Guardian*
*Morning Post*
*News Chronicle*
*The Observer*
*The Sunday Times*
*The Times*

### *(ii) British Regional/Local Newspapers*

*Birmingham Mail*
*Birmingham Post*
*Evesham Journal*
*Glasgow Bulletin*
*Glasgow Herald*
*Lancashire Daily Post*
*Leicester Mercury*
*Liverpool Post*
*Malvern Gazette*
*Northern Echo*
*Sheffield Independent*
*Staffordshire Sentinel*
*Stratford-upon-Avon Herald*
*Wolverhampton Express*
*Yorkshire Observer*
*Yorkshire Post*

### *(iii) Non-United Kingdom Newspapers*

Australia

*Adelaide Daily Mail*

Canada

*Montreal Daily Star*

India

*The Hindu*

New Zealand

*The Dominion*

South Africa

*Cape Argus*

*Natal Advertiser*

### *(iv) Magazines and Periodicals*

*The Author*

*Catholic Herald*

*The Children's Newspaper*

*Christian World*

*The Criterion*

*The Church Times*

*Drama*

*The Era*

*The Listener*

*The Musical Times*

*Music & Letters*

*The Quiver*

*The Radio Times*

*The Spectator*

*Theatre Managers' Journal*

## (c) Official Publications

Arts Council of Great Britain: *1st Annual Report 1945* [1945–46 annual report] (London: ACGB, 1946).

Arts Council of Great Britain: *The First Ten Years: The Eleventh Annual Report of the Arts Council of Great Britain 1955–1956* (London: ACGB, 1956).

Board of Education: *The Drama in Adult Education – A Report by the Adult Education Committee of the Board of Education, being Paper No. 6 of the Committee* (London: HMSO, 1926).

British Information Services, Information Division: *Entertainment and the Arts in Wartime Britain* (New York, NY: BIS, 1944).

## (d) Books, Articles and Other Publications

This list includes books, articles etc cited in the text which are (i) broadly contemporary with the subject of this book, and/or (ii) written by individuals discussed in it, including memoirs, and/or (iii) written by individuals directly involved with the issues discussed in it.

Agate, James: *First Nights* (London: Ivor Nicholson and Watson, 1934).

Agate, James: *Ego 3: Being still more of the autobiography of James Agate* (London: Harrap, 1938).

Ashwell, Lena: *Myself a Player* (London: Michael Joseph, 1936).

Bliss, Arthur, edited by Roscow, Gregory: *Bliss on Music: Selected Writings of Arthur Bliss 1920–1975* (Oxford: OUP, 1991).

Bliss, Arthur: *As I Remember* (London: Faber and Faber, 1970).

British Drama League: *Twenty-Five Years of the British Drama League* (London: BDL, 1944).

Britten, Benjamin, edited by Evans, John: *Journeying Boy: The Diaries of the Young Benjamin Britten, 1928–1938* (London: Faber and Faber, 2010).

Browne, E Martin: 'The British Drama League', *Educational Theatre Journal*, Vol 5, No 3 (October 1953), pp203–6.

Chisholm, Cecil: *Repertory: An Outline of the Modern Theatre Movement* (London: Peter Davies, 1934).

Dean, Basil: *The Theatre at War* (London: George G Harrap, 1956).

Eliot, T S: 'A Commentary', *The Criterion*, March 1938, pp478–85.

Eliot, T S: *Notes Towards the Definition of Culture* (London: Faber and Faber, 1948).

Ervine, St John: *The Theatre in my Time* (London: Rich & Cowan, 1933).

Evans, B Ifor and Glasgow, Mary: *The Arts in England* (London: The Falcon Press, 1949).

*The Film in National Life – Being the Report of an Enquiry Conducted by the Commission on Educational and Cultural Films into the Service which the Cinematograph may Render to Education and Social Progress* (London: George Allen and Unwin, 1932).

Geissmar, Berta: *The Baton and the Jackboot: Recollections of a Musical Life* (London: Hamish Hamilton, 1944).

Glasgow, Mary: 'The Concept of the Arts Council', in Keynes, Milo (ed): *Essays on John Maynard Keynes* (London: Cambridge University Press, 1975), pp260–71.

Greene, Graham, edited by Parkinson, David: *The Graham Greene Film Reader: Reviews, Essays, Interviews & Film Stories* (New York: Applause Books, 1995).

Herbert, A P: *'No Fine on Fun': The Comical History of the Entertainments Duty* (London: Methuen, 1957).

Isaac, Winifred F E C: *Alfred Wareing: a biography* (London: Green Bank Press [privately published by the author], 1951).

Jones, Thomas: *A Diary with Letters 1931–1950* (London: Oxford University Press, 1954).

Keynes, John Maynard, edited by Moggridge, Donald: *The Collected Writings of John Maynard Keynes Volume XXVIII: Social, Political and Literary Writings* (London: Macmillan/Cambridge University Press/Royal Economic Society, 1982).

Lambert, Constant: *Music Ho!: A Study of Music in Decline* (London: Faber and Faber, 1934).

Levy, Benn: 'A Free Theatre', *The Author*, Summer 1936.

Marshall, Norman: *The Other Theatre* (London: John Lehmann, 1947).

Orwell, George: *The Collected Essays, Journalism and Letters of George Orwell – Volume I: An Age Like This, 1920–1940* (Harmondsworth, Middlesex: Penguin Books, 1970).

Orwell, George: *The Collected Essays, Journalism and Letters of George Orwell – Volume II: My Country Right or Left, 1940–1943* (Harmondsworth, Middlesex: Penguin Books, 1970).

Orwell, George: *The Collected Essays, Journalism and Letters of George Orwell – Volume III: As I Please, 1943–1945* (Harmondsworth, Middlesex: Penguin Books, 1970).

Orwell, George: *The Collected Essays, Journalism and Letters of George Orwell – Volume IV: In Front of your Nose, 1945–1950* (Harmondsworth, Middlesex: Penguin Books, 1970).

Priestley, J B: *English Journey* (London: William Heinemann/Victor Gollancz, 1934 [1937 cheap edition]).

Priestley, J B: *Midnight on the Desert – A Chapter of Autobiography* (London: William Heinemann, 1937).

Priestley, J B: *Postscripts* (London: William Heinemann, 1940).

Priestley, J B: *Out of the People* (London: Collins/Heinemann, 1941).

Priestley, J B: *The arts under socialism: being a lecture given to the Fabian Society, with a postscript on What the government should do for the arts here and now* (London: Turnstile Press, 1947).

Priestley, J B: *Theatre Outlook* (London: Nicholson and Watson, 1947).

Russell, Thomas: *Philharmonic* (London: Hutchinson & Co, 1942).

Vaughan Williams, Ralph: *National Music and Other Essays* (London: Oxford University Press, 1963).

Vaughan Williams, Ralph, and Holst, Gustav, edited by Vaughan Williams, Ursula and Holst, Imogen: *Heirs and Rebels: Letters written to each other and occasional writings on music by Ralph Vaughan Williams and Gustav Holst* (London: Oxford University Press, 1959).

White, Eric W: *The Arts Council of Great Britain* (London: Davis Poynter, 1975).

Whitworth, Geoffrey: 'The Claims of the Living Actor', *The Spectator*, 16 February 1934.

Whitworth, Geoffrey: *The Making of a National Theatre* (London: Faber and Faber, 1951).

## Secondary Sources

Addison, Paul: *The Road to 1945* (London: Jonathan Cape, 1975).

Anthony, Scott: *Public Relations and the Making of Modern Britain: Stephen Tallents and the birth of a progressive media profession* (Manchester: Manchester University Press, 2012).

Barker, Clive and Gale, Maggie B (ed): *British Theatre between the Wars* (Cambridge: Cambridge University Press, 2000).

Blunt, Wilfrid: *John Christie of Glyndebourne* (London: Geoffrey Bles, 1968).

Briggs, Asa: *The History of Broadcasting in the United Kingdom: Volume I – The Birth of Broadcasting* (Oxford: Oxford University Press, 1961).

Briggs, Asa: *The History of Broadcasting in the United Kingdom: Volume II –The Golden Age of Wireless* (Oxford: Oxford University Press, 1965).

Briggs, Asa: *The History of Broadcasting in the United Kingdom: Volume III – The War of Words* (Oxford: Oxford University Press, 1970).

Briggs, Asa and Macartney, Anne: *Toynbee Hall: The First Hundred Years* (Abingdon, Oxon: Routledge, 2011 [reprint of 1984 edition]).

Carpenter, Humphrey: *Benjamin Britten – A Biography* (London: Faber and Faber, 1992).

Cockett, R B: 'Ball, Chamberlain and *Truth*', *The Historical Journal*, Vol 33, No 1 (March 1990), pp131–42.

Cox, David: *The Henry Wood Proms* (London: British Broadcasting Corporation, 1980).

Davies, Andrew: *Other Theatres: The Development of Alternative and Experimental Theatre in Britain* (Basingstoke: Macmillan Education, 1987).

Day, James: *Vaughan Williams* (London: J M Dent and Sons, 1961).

Dent, Edward J: *A Theatre for Everybody: The Story of the Old Vic and Sadler's Wells* (London: Boardman, 1945).

Diaper, Jeremy: '*The Criterion*: an inter-war platform for agricultural discussion', *Agricultural History Review*, 61.2 (2013), pp282–300.

Doctor, Jenny: *The BBC and Ultra-Modern Music, 1922–1936* (Cambridge: Cambridge University Press, 1999).

Doctor, Jenny: 'A New Dimension – the BBC takes on the Proms, 1920–44', in *The Proms: a New History*, ed. Doctor, Jenny and Wright, David, consulting ed. Kenyon, Nicholas (London: Thames & Hudson, 2007), pp74–129.

Donohue, Joseph: Review of *The London Stage 1890–99: A Calendar of Plays and Players* by J P Wearing, *Educational Theatre Journal*, Vol 29, No 2 (May 1977), pp268–71.

Dorris, George: Review of *The London Stage: A Calendar of Plays and Players* by J P Wearing, *Dance Chronicle*, Vol 18, No 3 (1995), pp505–10.

Dyment, Christopher: *Toscanini in Britain* (Woodbridge, Suffolk: Boydell Press, 2012).

Elsom, John and Tomalin, Nicholas: *The History of the National Theatre* (London: Jonathan Cape, 1978).

Foss, Brian: *War Paint: Art, War, State and Identity in Britain, 1939–1945* (New Haven: Yale University Press, 2007).

Frith, Simon, Brennan, Matt, Cloonan, Martin and Webster, Emma: *The History of Live Music in Britain, Volume 1: 1950–67* (Abingdon and New York: Routledge, 2016 [originally published 2013]).

Gilbert, Susie: *Opera for Everybody: The Story of English National Opera* (London: Faber and Faber, 2009).

Gray, Clive: *The Politics of the Arts in Britain* (Basingstoke: Macmillan, 2000).

Halsey, A H, and Webb, Josephine (ed): *Twentieth Century British Social Trends* (London: Macmillan, 2000).

Harrington, William, and Young, Peter (ed): *The 1945 Revolution* (London: Davis-Poynter, 1978).

Harris, John S: *Government Patronage of the Arts in Great Britain* (Chicago: University of Chicago Press, 1970).

Harris, Jose: 'War and Social History: Britain and the Home Front During the Second World War', *Contemporary European History*, Vol 1, No 1 (March 1992), pp17–35.

Harris, Jose: 'Political Thought and the Welfare State 1870–1940: An Intellectual Framework for British Social Policy', *Past and Present*, No135 (May 1992), pp116–41.

Hayes, Nick and Hill, Jeff (ed): *'Millions Like Us'?: British Culture in the Second World War* (Liverpool: Liverpool University Press, 1999).

Heinrich, Anselm: 'Theatre in Britain during the Second World War', *New Theatre Quarterly*, 26 (1) (February 2010), pp61–70.

Hewison, Robert: *Culture and Consensus: England, Art and Politics since 1940* (London: Methuen, 1995).

Higgins, John (ed): *Glyndebourne – A Celebration* (London: Jonathan Cape, 1984).

Hughes, Spike: *Glyndebourne: A History of the Festival Opera* (Newton Abbot: David and Charles, 1965).

Hutchison, Robert: *The Politics of the Arts Council* (London: Sinclair Browne, 1982).

Jones, Stephen G: *Workers at Play: A Social and Economic History of Leisure 1918–1939* (London: Routledge & Kegan Paul, 1986).

Kenyon, Nicholas: *The BBC Symphony Orchestra – The first fifty years 1930–1980* (London: British Broadcasting Corporation, 1981).

Kershaw, Baz (ed): *The Cambridge History of British Theatre, Volume 3: Since 1895* (Cambridge: Cambridge University Press, 2004).

Kildea, Paul: *Selling Britten: Music and the Marketplace* (Oxford: Oxford University Press, 2002).

Kildea, Paul: *Benjamin Britten: A Life in the Twentieth Century* (London: Allen Lane, 2013).

Lebrecht, Norman: *Covent Garden – the Untold Story: Despatches from the English Culture War 1945–2000* (London: Simon & Schuster UK, 2000).

Leventhal, F M: '"The Best for the Most": CEMA and State Sponsorship of the Arts in Wartime 1939–45', *Twentieth Century British History*, Vol 1, No 3 (1990), pp289–317.

Lloyd, Stephen: *Constant Lambert: Beyond the Rio Grande* (Woodbridge, Suffolk: The Boydell Press, 2014).

Longmate, Norman: *How We Lived Then – A History of Everyday Life during the Second World War* (London: Pimlico, 2002 [originally published 1971]).

McArthur, Euan C: *The Council for the Encouragement of Music and Arts (CEMA) and the Development of the Arts Council in Scotland: Background, Politics and Visual Arts Policy 1919–47* (PhD thesis submitted to the University of Dundee, 2005).

McArthur, Euan: *Scotland, CEMA and the Arts Council, 1919–1967: Background, Politics and Visual Art Policy* (Abingdon: Routledge, 2016).

Mackerness, E D: *A Social History of English Music* (Abingdon: Routledge, 2013 [originally published 1964]).

Miller, Toby: 'Who Are These People?', *Cinema Journal*, Vol47, No4 (Summer 2008), pp121–6.

Minihan, Janet: *The Nationalization of Culture – The Development of State Subsidies to the Arts in Great Britain* (London: Hamish Hamilton, 1977).

Mitchell, Donald: *Britten & Auden in the Thirties: The Year 1936* (Woodbridge, Suffolk: The Boydell Press, 2000 [originally published 1981]).

Morris, John: *Culture and Propaganda in World War II: Music, Film and the Battle for National Identity* (London and New York: I B Tauris, 2014).

Norris, Pippa: *A Virtuous Circle: Political Communications in Postindustrial Societies* (Cambridge: Cambridge University Press, 2000).

Pick, John (ed): *The State and The Arts* (London: City University Centre for the Arts, 1980).

Pick, John: *Managing the Arts? – The British Experience* (London: Rhinegold Publishing, 1986).

Pick, John: *Vile Jelly – The Birth, Life and Lingering Death of the Arts Council of Great Britain* (Doncaster: The Brynmill Press, 1991).

Pugh, Martin: *We Danced All Night: A Social History of Britain Between the Wars* (London: Bodley Head, 2008).

De Quetteville, Harry (ed): *Thinker, Failure, Soldier, Jailer: An Anthology of Great Lives in 365 Days* (London: Aurum Press, 2012).

Rebellato, Dan: *1956 And All That: The Making of Modern British Drama* (London: Routledge, 1999).

Rosenthal, Daniel: *The National Theatre Story* (London: Oberon Books, 2013).

Rowell, George, and Jackson, Anthony: *The Repertory Movement: A History of Regional Theatre in Britain* (Cambridge: Cambridge University Press, 1984).

Samuel, Raphael, MacColl, Ewan and Cosgrove, Stuart: *Theatres of the Left 1880–1935: Workers' Theatre Movements in Britain and America* (London: Routledge & Kegan Paul, 1985).

Sheridan, David Allen: *'Give Us More Music': Women, Musical Culture, and Work in Wartime Britain, 1939–1946* (PhD dissertation submitted to the University of Southern California, 2007).

Sinclair, Andrew: *Arts and Cultures: The History of the 50 Years of the Arts Council of Great Britain* (London: Sinclair-Stevenson, 1995).

Skidelsky, Robert: *John Maynard Keynes, Volume Three – Fighting for Britain 1937–46* (London: Macmillan, 2000).

Snowman, Daniel: *The Hitler Emigres: The Cultural Impact on Britain of Refugees from Nazism* (London: Chatto and Windus, 2002 [Pimlico edition, 2003]).

Taylor, A J P: *English History 1914–1945* (Harmondsworth: Penguin Books, 1970 [originally published 1965]).

Thomas, David, Carlton, David, and Etienne, Anne: *Theatre Censorship: From Walpole to Wilson* (Oxford: Oxford University Press, 2007).

Thurlow, Richard C: *Fascism in Britain: From Oswald Moseley's Blackshirts to the National Front* (London: I B Tauris, 1998).

Upchurch, Anna: 'John Maynard Keynes, the Bloomsbury Group and the Origins of the Arts Council Movement', *International Journal of Cultural Policy*, Vol 10 Issue 2 (July 2004), pp203–17.

Upchurch, Anna: 'Keynes's Legacy: An Intellectual's Influence Reflected in Arts Policy', *International Journal of Cultural Policy*, Vol 17 Issue 1 (January 2011), pp69–80.

Wallis, Mick: 'Pageantry and the Popular Front: Ideological Production in the 'Thirties', *New Theatre Quarterly*, Vol 10 Issue 38 (May 1994), pp132–56.

Wearing, J P: *The London Stage: A Calendar of Plays and Players 1890–1899, 1900–1909, 1910–1919, 1920–1929, 1930–1939, 1940–1949* and *1950–1959* (Metuchen, NJ, USA: The Scarecrow Press, 1976, 1981, 1982, 1984, 1990, 1991 and 1993, respectively).

Weingärtner, Jörn: *The Arts as a Weapon of War: Britain and the Shaping of National Morale in the Second World War* (London and New York: I B Tauris 2012 [revised paperback edition; originally published 2005]).

Willatt, Hugh: *The Arts Council of Great Britain – The First Twenty-five Years* (ACGB, undated but ?1971).

Williamson, Audrey: *Old Vic Drama* (London: Rockcliff, 1948).

Witts, Richard: *Artist Unknown: An Alternative History of the Arts Council* (London: Warner Books, 1998).

## Other Online Resources Cited in the Text

api.parliament.uk/historic-hansard/people/mr-harold-baker/index.html
archive.org/stream/in.ernet.dli.2015.173789/2015.173789.E-G-O-3_djvu.txt
archiveshub.jisc.ac.uk/search/archives/47d32228-2700-3c79-89f8-b2b615534fc9
arthurlloyd.co.uk/MossEmpiresJubilee1949.htm
artscouncil.org.uk/media/uploads/pdf/Norgrove_governance_review_2013.pdf
aspenmusicfestival.com/benjamin-britten
bbc.co.uk/events/rzhbj5/by/date/1938/09/07
britannica.com/biography/Constant-Lambert

britannica.com/biography/James-Agate
britannica.com/biography/Lena-Ashwell
britannica.com/biography/William-Temple
discovery.nationalarchives.gov.uk/details/c/F38062
eno.org/about/history-of-eno/
genome.ch.bbc.co.uk/a22abe624c714eec9a1f292c2e92e02a
gramophone.co.uk/features/focus/90th-anniversary-interviews-benjamin-britten
hansard.millbanksystems.com/people/mr-walter-elliot
history.ac.uk/reviews/review/379
imdb.com/title/tt0019702/fullcredits#writers
lpo.org.uk/about/london-philharmonic-orchestra.html
nationaltheatre.org.uk/about-the-national-theatre/history
nimaxtheatres.com/duchess-theatre
oxforddnb.com
roh.org.uk/about/the-royal-ballet/history
samuelfrench.com/author/3342/benn-w-levy
theglasgowstory.com/story.php?id=TGSEH05
wea.org.uk
wellcomelibrary.org/item/b18228732#?c=0&m=0&s=0&cv=0

# Index

Page numbers for notes are shown as 37 n.4

Printed in Great Britain
by Amazon

56176045R00145